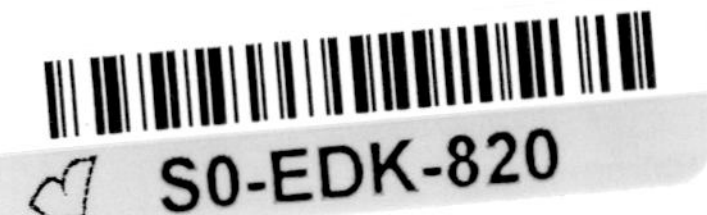

Studies and Documentation in the History of Popular Entertainment
edited by ANTHONY SLIDE

1. *Stage Dust: A Critic's Cultural Scrapbook from the 1990s,* by Charles Marowitz. 2001.
2. *The Rise of the Crooners,* by Michael Pitts and Frank Hoffmann. 2001.
3. *Thelma* Who?: *Almost 100 Years of Showbiz,* by Thelma White, with Harry Preston. 2002.

By the Same Author

Books and Collections

The Other Way (Applause Books)
Alarums & Excursions (Applause Books)
Recycling Shakespeare (Macmillan)
Directing the Action (Applause)
Burnt Bridges (Hodder & Stoughton)
Prospero's Staff (Indiana University Press)
Potboilers (Marion Boyars, Inc.)
Clever Dick (Dramatists Play Svc.)
Sex Wars (Marion Boyars, Inc.)
The Act of Being (Taplinger Press)
The Marowitz Shakespeare (Marion Boyars)
Confessions of a Counterfeit Critic (Eyre-Methuen)
The Method as Means (Barrie & Rockliffe)

Plays and Translations

Quack (Dramatists Play Svc.)
Boulevard Comedies (Smith & Kraus)
Stage Fright (Dramatists Play Svc.)
Bashville in Love (Samuel French, Ltd.)
Sherlock's Last Case (Dramatists Play Svc.)
Clever Dick (Dramatists Play Svc.)
Wilde West (Dramatists Play Svc.)
Disciples (Dramatists Play Svc.)
Hedda (Aschehoug, Nwy.)
Artaud at Rodez (Marion Boyars, Inc.)
The Shrew (Marion Boyars, Inc.)
Measure for Measure (Marion Boyars, Inc.)
An Othello (Penguin Books)
A Macbeth (Marion Boyars, Inc.)
Variations on the Merchant of Venice (Marion Boyars, Inc.)
The Critic as Artist (Hansom Books)
The Marowitz Hamlet & Dr. Faustus (Penguin Books)
Cyrano de Bergerac (Smith & Kraus)
Makbett (Grove Press)
And They Put Handcuffs on the Flowers (Grove Press)

STAGE DUST

A Critic's Cultural Scrapbook from the 1990s

Studies and Documentation in the History of Popular Entertainment, No. 1

Charles Marowitz

The Scarecrow Press, Inc.
Lanham, Maryland, and London
2001

SCARECROW PRESS, INC.

Published in the United States of America
by Scarecrow Press, Inc.
4720 Boston Way, Lanham, Maryland 20706
www.scarecrowpress.com

4 Pleydell Gardens, Folkestone
Kent CT20 2DN, England

British Library Cataloguing-in-Publication Information Available

Library of Congress Cataloging-in-Publication Data

Marowitz, Charles.
Stage dust : a critic's cultural scrapbook from the 1990s / Charles Marowitz.
p. cm.—(Studies and documentation in the history of popular entertainment ; no. 1)
Includes index.
ISBN 0-8108-4045-6 (alk. paper)
1. Theather—United States—Reviews. 2. Theater—United States—History—20th century.
I. Title. II. Series.

PN2266.5 .M374 2001
792.9'5'097309049—dc21

200102052

∞™ The paper used in this publication meets the minimum requirements of American National Standard for Information Sciences—Permanence of Paper for Printed Library Materials, ANSI/NISO Z39.48-1992.
Manufactured in the United States of America.

For Jane, the Bringer of Light,
and Kostya, the Bringer of Joy

CONTENTS

Part IV Think Pieces

EDITOR'S FOREWORD

The series, "Studies and Documentation in the History of Popular Entertainment," provides readers with biographical and autobiographical studies concerning all areas of the genre. The emphasis here is on popular entertainment in the 20th century, be it the theater, revue, musical comedy, the recording industry, or dance.

The first contributor to the series is the distinguished critic Charles Marowitz, who began his career as a stage director in New York in the late 1950s and who has been associated with Peter Brook and the Royal Shakespeare Company, directed Joe Orton's *Loot* in 1966, and founded London's Open Space Theatre (1968-1981). He is almost unique among critics in that he knows of what he writes—and he writes both very well and very knowingly with wit and vigor.

Stage Dust collects the writings of Charles Marowitz on theater, celebrities, and entertainment-oriented literature from our most recent fin de siècle. The subjects are varied, from theatrical revivals of Oscar Wilde and Rodgers and Hammerstein to Antonin Artaud and Howard Stern. The scope of the reviews are wide-ranging, from Los Angeles to New York to London, from the commercial theater to cable television. As Charles Marowitz reminds us, we are always living at the end of an era, but seldom have we had anyone more qualified to review that era.

Anthony Slide

PREFACE

Historians, in trying to recreate the shape and feel of a bygone era, invariably root around in the minutiae of the times they are exploring. Often the day-to-day realities of a period evoke a clearer picture than the compressions that make up the generalized history. Broadsheets from Elizabethan England, for instance, can more vividly recreate the character of that sixteenth-century society than a learned treatise that uses them merely as a springboard for speculation. It is the minutiae, those thousand and one incidental details scrupulously drawn out of the archives, that succeed in recreating the immediacy of the past.

To the extent that one can justify any book, that is the justification of *Stage Dust*. The following pages contain an assortment of notices, articles, columns, profiles, essays, book reviews, flotsam, and jetsam that describe the performances, plays, personalities, trends, and controversies that preoccupied the cultural scene in America in the last decade of the twentieth century: what people were seeing, reading, talking, and arguing about.

It is not a history and therefore not chronological or punctilious about dates. It is not a chronicle and therefore not overly concerned with facts or statistics. It doesn't pretend to put the period into any kind of coherent perspective and so is probably useless as sociology. It is more in the nature of those flashcard-books that are activated by one's thumb. By flicking through its pages, a series of disparate images will flash by, hopefully creating a sense of the period.

I have selected pieces that seemed to me representative of the general consciousness; things that were in the air, on people's minds and therefore on their lips. The collection extends beyond plays and theatrical events and includes reports on films, TV, and books, as more and more all these arts tend to overlap. The collection is highly personal and eschews all attempts at balance or objectivity. It unabashedly preserves all the prejudices, predilections, and idiosyncrasies peculiar to its author.

Where it seemed applicable, I have incorporated a certain amount of linking commentary that will provide a minimal amount of information about the foreground or background of the items being considered. Since they are all the work of a journalist-critic and culled from a variety of publications, including but not restricted to *Theater Week Magazine, In-Theatre Magazine, The Jewish Journal, L.A. Weekly, American Book Review,* the *New York Times, American Theatre Magazine,* the *London Times,* the *London Sunday Times,* the *Guardian,* and so forth and so on, their styles may vary, depending on the publications from which they have been extracted. I would hope, however, that the author's tone of voice remains fairly constant and recognizable throughout. A critic likes to think that he retains his literary personality no matter what publication he writes for—although there are plenty of examples where this is embarrassingly untrue.

Apart from passing observations in the pieces themselves, I have deliberately resisted sweeping generalizations about the character of the period being surveyed, as I truly believe that for such generalizations to have validity they have to be made at a much further remove than I am now from the 1990s. I know what I feel about that period now, but those feelings are so mired in subjectivity and the immediate aftermath of recorded events, they cannot possibly hold up in ten, or even five, years' time. So I have tried to be neither categorical nor Olympian.

The furthest I will venture in the direction of general commentary is to point out that in the 1890s, the theater was entering an era teeming with Naturalism. The influences of Zola, Ibsen, Andre Antoine's Theatre Libre, Konstantin Stanislavsky's Moscow Art Theatre, Tom Robertson's work in England, and Gerhart Hauptman's in Germany, all swept through Europe and, in two decades, would dominate America. Social realism in the '30s melded with psychological realism in the '40s and '50s, and throughout, art, with a few significant exceptions, was being graded on how "true to life" it was.

Looking back at all that from the vantage point of the 1990s, it is clear that although many meritorious works came out of the century's obsession with verisimilitude, as we approached the new millennium there was a strong recoil against it as a prevailing style and a profound sense of inadequacy with plays and performances that blankly threw back our own reflections from the looking-glass. The most tantalizing aspect of the immediate future is, now that realism has proved to be partial, falsifying, and insufficient in dealing with the complexities of our inner states or the world around us, with what will it be replaced?

Whatever it is, it will give our own time a certain warm nostalgic glow similar to what we now feel about the '60s, the '20s, or the turn of the century. It is either tantalizing or depressing—I don't know which—to recognize that whatever it is that stokes our enthusiasm today will be relegated and transcended by tomorrow. We are always living, thank God, at the end of an era.

Charles Marowitz

I

ON THE STAGE

Broadway in the '90s was in danger of becoming a theater entirely dominated by revivals. Musicals were very expensive propositions. They now cost millions to mount. A show with a track record and name recognition was the safest way to go. Damn Yankees; Showboat; The King and I; Chicago; Jesus Christ, Superstar; A Funny Thing Happened on the Way to the Forum; Kiss Me Kate—*the retrospectives were endless. Although a good deal of that financing should have gone into riskier new work, a case could be made for showing newer generations the blockbusters that had regaled their parents. And so, with the cost of musical productions mounting stratrospherically, Broadway felt obliged to play it safe.*

1

GOING ROUND AGAIN: *CAROUSEL*

If Lorenz Hart had lived to see it, I think he would have loathed *Carousel.* Not that he wouldn't have admired Hammerstein's skills as a lyricist and Rodgers' swelling, Rombergian melodies or the ingenuity with which a grim, Hungarian black comedy could be transformed into a weepy piece of American uplift, but his mordant, sharp, gay sense of irony would have recoiled at the show's sentimentality and submerged religiosity. "When you walk through a storm . . . , " he would have quipped, "you just get bloody soaked." And "June is bustin' out all over" is "what you get when June tries to stretch a 32" bra over a 38" bosom!"

Hart was the personification of the cynical, urban sensibility that, in the '30s and '40s, dominated Broadway. "We'll have Manhattan, the Bronx, and Staten Island, too . . . " wasn't merely a convenient internal rhyme but a proclamation of a deep-seated urban philosophy of life. "Keep it light, keep it crisp, don't get mawkish and turgid. Don't be so distracted by the sugar on the doughnut that you neglect to notice the hole in the middle. Every silver lining still delineates a great, big, dark cloud that, at any moment, can piss down on your head." It was, I suppose, the essence of the New York sensibility that could be traced back to reverberating cultural roots like the Algonquin Round Table, the stories of Damon Runyon, and the arch humor of George S. Kaufman.

Hammerstein, of course, was much better adjusted than Hart and could be relied on to meet deadlines, polish, and revise. The Rodgers & Hammerstein oeuvre became the iconography of the modern Broadway theater and works like *Carousel,* shining examples of what American composers, lyricists, and book writers could do best.

At the heart of *Carousel,* one can already begin to discern the gestating mushiness that would saturate shows like *The King and I* and *The Sound of Music.* They were all solid structures and they did precisely what they were calculated to do, and, from the standpoint of sheer craftsmanship, one has to doff one's cap to a show like *Carousel*—especially in Nicholas Hytner's perfectly modulated mise-en-scène now at the Ahmanson as part of what I'm sure will be a long and successful national tour.

Despite the inevitable overkill of songs that have been hammered into our skulls for over fifty years, the score remains positively Brahmsian in its ballads and Sullivanesque in its big, rousing chorus numbers. The author and the composer take certain freedoms with the form, which pushes Broadway musicals forward into opera and sideways into territory that Sondheim, a couple of decades later, was to stake out as his own. The mix of homespun romance and musical fantasy is, by and large, deftly handled, and although the death of Billy Bigelow ushers us into a kind of gooey metaphysic reminiscent of simplistic fantasies such as *It's a Great Life, Death Takes a Holiday,* and *On Borrowed Time,* the otherworldliness is never mawkish or implausible.

The show sets up a "star-cross't lovers" situation between a "bum" and an "angel" and with clever, narrative ingenuity effects a posthumous conversion in Billy Bigelow and a stoic acceptance of the past on the part of his battered wife. Shit happens, it seems to be saying, but with the passage of time and a firm belief in redemption, even tragedies can produce epiphanies.

This is good, reassuring stuff and the pudding out of which appetizing Broadway successes have been made for many years. It requires us to suspend not only our disbelief, but all our realistically rooted "beliefs" as well. It is the artistic equivalent of going to a cozy church service on a sun-filled Sunday morning where you'll see a lot of familiar faces and you don't mind being there as there isn't very much else to do anyway.

The Broadway production, despite a startling mise-en-scène, was handicapped by some weak singers and make-do actors. Although Sarah Uriarte's Julie Jordan is several notches above the New York Julie, Patrick Wilson's Billy lacks danger and even a certain masculinity. The result is something of a mismatch. Whatever one might have thought of John Raitt or Gordon MacRae, they were butch and their grittiness invested Jan Clayton and Shirley Jones with a certain feminine vulnerability that gave point to the relationship.

The Kenneth MacMillan choreography (resuscitated by Jane Elliott) looks and feels dancey and impedes rather than reinforces the story line, particularly in the second act where the ballet of Bigelow's daughter and her fairground-boy courtier goes on so long it feels like an *entr'acte.* Hytner is marvelous at whipping up breezy and unexpected stage imagery but neglects the subtle pieces of timing required to make us feel Julie's grief at Billy's death and Billy's outrage at being a posthumous burden to his daughter. The show's big moments are splendid, but many of the small moments are unattended. The real hero of this production is designer Bob Crowley, whose false-perspective miniatures of New England, with their spare but evocative lakes, hills, harbors, and dens, are consistently imaginative and strikingly minimalist.

Carousel, it is alleged, was Rodgers's favorite musical and, given its complexity and its sweep, one can easily see why. But there is a flair and buoyancy in works such as *A Connecticut Yankee, The Boys from Syracuse,* and *Pal Joey* that bespeaks an entirely other temperament and a much more cynical mind-set. If we could properly define precisely what Rodgers—and Broadway—lost when we bade farewell to Hart and threw out the red carpet to Hammerstein, we might put our finger on what has vanished from the modern musical theater.

2

McKELLAN'S *RICHARD III:* JUNK SHAKESPEARE

The '90s were good for Shakespeare on film. Had Will been a working screenwriter during this period, he would have found himself in the very highest tax bracket. Kenneth Branagh's Much Ado about Nothing, *Mel Gibson's* Hamlet, *Laurence Fishburne's* Othello, *Oliver Parker's* Midsummer Night's Dream, *Al Pacino's* Looking for Richard, *Derek Jarman's* Tempest, *Peter Greenaway's* Prospero's Books, *Baz Luhrman's* Romeo and Juliet—*everyone seemed to be having a go. It effectively laid the groundwork not for a knock-out motion picture treatment of one of the plays, but for John Madden's wittily ironic and period-perfect* Shakespeare in Love. *On the way there, it produced a number of clinkers like McKellan's* Richard III.

★★★

One of the most misguided productions of modern times was Richard Eyre's 1930's Mosleyite rendering of *Richard III,* starring Ian McKellan, which opened in London 1990 and toured extensively both here and abroad. Swamped in imagery redolent of the Third Reich, McKellan turned Shakespeare's scheming Machiavel into a charismatic tyrant who bore a striking resemblance to Adolf Hitler (with not a little of the absurdity that Charlie Chaplin brought to the same role in *The Great Dictator*). The parallel between Richard's ascent to the throne and the imaginary rise of a scheming fascist in a context of the British aristocracy was a banality of the kind that makes people desperately search for extenuating circumstances on the part of the perpetrators. But none could be found. Eyre, using all the massive resources of England's National Theatre, genuinely thought that by cramming *Richard III*'s richness and complexity into an oversimplified parable about British black shirts and Nazi sympathizers, Shakespeare's larger purposes would be imaginatively served.

Not content with demonstrating that simple-mindedness conjoined with an unlimited production budget could produce some of the most fatuous drivel in the annals of classic theater, McKellan and his cinematic collaborator, Richard Loncraine, have now taken the seed of that mindless production and placed it in the womb of an even more costly United Artists film. The result is as if a grainy little doodle were to be enlarged to fifty times its original size, in order to prove conclusively that the original image was as foolish as it seemed to be in miniature.

The film, to give credit where credit is due, contains a number of striking and sweeping images. Formidable British venues such as the Senate House of London University, Earl's Court, the St. Pancras Chambers, and the Brighton Pavillion are the sites of some dazzling cinematography. The prewar period in a stuffy and complacent England is beautifully captured by Director of Photography Peter Biziou and Costume Designer Shuna Harwood and used to maximal advantage by Director Loncraine. A cast of unimpeachable British stalwarts, including Nigel Hawthorne, John Wood, Maggie Smith, and Jim Broadbent, support Sir Ian with all the fastness of a steel jock strap: a beautifully embossed frame surrounding the doodle.

Of Annette Bening, the victimized Queen Elizabeth whose family is sacrificed to Richard's ambitions, one would say she was out of her depth except that her irredeemable shallowness makes the mention of "depth" sound like a non sequitur. Ms. Bening grasps the verse as if it were a liquified bar of soap and every time she opens her mouth, it slithers out of her hands. Purportedly Wallis Simpson (for whom the Duke of Windsor abdicated the throne in the 1930s), she has about as much class as a British Airways stewardess. John Wood, as the wheezing King Edward, is something right out of *Beyond the Fringe:* a winning comic portrait of a suspirating Monarch. (They obviously couldn't get Jim Carrey.) And Robert Downey, Jr., as a Yankee Lord Rivers has one of the most hilarious bedroom sequences on celluloid, where, after his strumpet (presumably Jane Shore) has gone down on him, his coitus takes the form of an erect dagger protruding from his chest as if his erection had suddenly become both de-railed and transmogrified. With elegant touches like this, we need never fear that Director Loncraine, wherever he may wander, will ever stumble into the softer verges of good taste.

Neither the classy casting nor the lurid cinematic choices are to any avail, since the film is entombed in the fallacy that British fascism and the calamities of World War II can in some way mirror the rivalries and intrigues that generated the Wars of the Roses. Before long the blackshirts, the Yorks and Lancasters, and the Nazi symbology all merge—not into the idealized timelessness intended by the filmmakers, but into a time-warp that is neither Now or Then, neither relevant historicity nor multifaceted modernity—just typical British fudge and fustian. Fifteenth-century incidents, seventeenth-century attitudes, and twentieth-century pretensions, as if jammed into a single panel of a revolving door, circulate endlessly, giving us fleeting glimpses of one image, then another, crying "Shakespeare!" "Modernism!" "Political Relevance!," but producing only a babble.

As a result of this modernizing, popularizing, and vulgarizing approach, most of Shakespeare's language has to be jettisoned and once you remove that from *Richard III,* you are left only with the bare bones of Raphael Holinshed, from whose chronicles the playwright originally fashioned his masterpiece. In short, you've got an Outline, precisely the kind of thing film-makers dote on. Now just add a flashy actor, a trashy script, and a patina of class, and you're ready to compete for the Oscars in 1996.

Among the women, Kristin Scott Thomas's Lady Anne is by far the coolest and most effective performance. The almost impossible scene in which Lady Anne, accompanying the bier of her dead husband, is intercepted by Richard is, in this film version, cleverly played out in a hospital morgue with the corpse of Henry VI spread out on a slab surrounded by other cadavers. There are no coffin-bearers to intrude upon the scene in which Richard, the murderer of Lady Anne's husband, courts the bereaved widow. The visual impact of the scene almost makes up for its lack of credibility, and Ms. Scott Thomas's underplaying goes a long way toward rendering it believable. As the film progresses, she wastes away with a combination of marital misery and drug addiction (the fatal consequence, the film seems to suggest, of marrying such a specious leading man), but her performance leaves a strong afterglow.

Among the men, Jim Broadbent is an officious and punctilious Buckingham—not so much a scheming peer of the realm as a politic statesman who knows on which side his scone is buttered. In its rootedness and lack of ostentation, it perfectly etches in the social context in which the film-makers are trying to position their duplicitous demagogue.

Lines from the play waft through the air like fugitive snatches of melody from a piece of music one vaguely recognizes but to which one cannot put a name. Trapped in a stalled jeep from which he cannot accelerate, Richard calls for "A horse, a horse, my kingdom for a horse," which is a slight improvement on the equestrian pantomime McKellan performed in the stage production but is still a rhetorical flourish steeped in silliness. Surely, "A jack, a jack, my kingdom for a jack" would have made more sense.

Mercifully, the battle scenes are short and rapidly graphic. No long-winded preparations between Richmond's forces and Richard's—just a few bomb blasts and machine-gun fire and before long, Richard, out-gunned by

Richmond, is delineating a campy, slow-motion descent both out of the world and out of the film. It's all highly colorful and rather tongue-in-cheek, but as Gloucester topples off some gridwork into hell, he takes nothing of the audience's empathy with him. The dying-swan descent, like so many preceding moments, is offered as yet another flashy cinematic touch in a movie that is so intent on winning the audience over to its strained reading, it smothers every breath of contradiction.

Clarence is always the plum cameo role in *Richard III,* and Gielgud, when he played it, almost stole the film out from under Olivier. Nigel Hawthorne's self-effacing, understated performance contrasts nicely with McKellan's garish and flamboyant Richard. We get a sudden flash of the subtlety and thoughtfulness with which, we are reminded, this play is saturated. The truncation of the text, in Hawthorne's case, is more aggravating than with others, for we know there is much more Clarence could have affected us with had his lines not been expurgated.

A passing word for Jim Carter, one of England's finest character actors, who plays Hastings with a perfect balance of resolve and vulnerability. In his troubled circumspection regarding the selection of the next monarch, you can see in a trice how the most honorable of men can become victimized when the leaders of a state spread a climate of corruption.

Maggie Smith's Duchess of York, no longer the mystical termagant of Shakespeare's play, but here a kind of smoldering dowager who is part of a crumbling older order, projects the stoicism of a long-suffering Queen Mother, very much like the present Queen Mother who, presumably, has had painfully to adjust to the dysfunctional shenanigans of Charles and Di and the immoral palace society of which they are merely the most prominent malefactors. In choices like these, both McKellan and Loncraine have cleverly found ways of transforming Shakespeare's historical characters so that they suit this modern reinterpretation. The problem is you can't really recognize them without a scorecard, and unless you know that Elizabeth equals Wally Simpson; Rivers, the Duke of Windsor; and Richard, Sir Oswald Mosley, you are only vaguely conscious of the interlocking intentions. But then, discerning the intended counterparts, your sense of history tells you they don't actually jell—so you realize you are not really being offered credible parallels, but just loose and makeshift resemblances that work only in the filmmaker's febrile imagination. It is at this juncture that the whole point of the interpretation begins to crumble, and one begins to pine for the rich, open-ended, Marlovian smash-'n'-grab of Shakespeare's original play. Promised contemporary amplitude, one is fobbed off with a flashy kind of reductionism.

At the root of the film's intellectual confusion is McKellan's desire to popularize Shakespeare. "If you put the characters in the sort of clothes we might still wear today," he has said, "it's one way of showing an audience that Shakespeare is not old-fashioned." But if you put a fifteenth-century warrior-king who believes in the Chain of Being into a modern political context charged with territorial expansionism and notions of ethnic cleansing, you are mixing history in such a way as to falsify the past and hopelessly fudge the present. Parallels that work don't need visual aids to point them up; we, the audience, draw those parallels from period narratives without the aid of pedantic actors and ostentatious directors brandishing updated Cliff Notes. And does McKellan really believe that any persons of sense consider the author of *Hamlet, Othello, Coriolanus,* and *Lear* old-fashioned?

McKellan is a meretricious actor; Loncraine, a cinematic whore; and the whole effort is mired in sophistry parading as modernism.

★★★

3

THE MAIN EVENT: *RENT*

It was inevitable that thirty or so years after *Hair,* that grandiloquent freak-out from the '60s, the show should produce an offspring. In a sense, that is what *Rent,* now at the Nederlander, is.

Both shows glom on to the subterranean youth cult that swarms beneath the facade of mainstream American society, and in both, the youths are seen to be disenfranchised, rebellious, drug-addicted, and troubled. The other thing they have in common is that the denizens of both these countercultures are self-sufficient, well-integrated in their own alternative set of values, and perfectly content with the apartheid that separates them from the outside world.

Roughly paralleled to the wastrels of *La Boheme,* from which they have been extrapolated, the denizens of this underground world are the artsy, questing, spaced-out drifters from the lowest depths of New York's Lower East Side (Avenue B and below), but despite the impecuniosity and personal hang-ups, they aren't fundamentally very different from their square neighbors uptown. It's just that, being young, they haven't yet developed the social or psychological expertise to cope with broken love affairs, cruel rejection, and the sudden demise of loved ones. In fact they are "us," in that wondrous stage of becoming that we all recognize from our own adolescence, which is why we instinctively warm to them.

The various interactions between Mimi and Roger (read *Rudolfo*), Joanne and Maureen, her performance-artist companion Tom and the transvestite drummer whom he meets shortly after being mugged, are largely lost in the general clatter of the world they all inhabit. Clearly, Jonathan Larson, who was responsible for the book, music, and lyrics, was creating a full-scale mural rather than a series of individual portraits, and it is the ambiance rather than the details of the show that stays with us after the final fade out. Although only remotely related to Puccini's masterpiece, *Rent*'s *liebestod,* using the anguished whelps of rock 'n' roll, achieves every bit as much poignancy as that visited upon Mimi in the last moments of the opera. Larsen's music, particularly in duets like "Light My Candle," ballads like "Seasons of Love," and thumping chorus numbers like "La Vie Boheme" are fresh, vital, and intrinsically theatrical. Michael Greif's staging is sometimes lax and sometimes overly orderly, with a disturbing penchant for horizontal, Rockette-like formations before the proscenium, but his real contribution has been to shape and nurture the material almost from its inception. One senses that he was mentor, architect, and editor for what could easily have been a glorious stew.

Some shows are enshrined in the annals of theater because they are events rather than outstanding specimens of any particular genre. *Rent,* like *Hernani* or *Ubu Roi,* falls into that category. *Rent* was conceived, created, marinated, and executed by an unknown cast that seemed to be pulled off the very streets that their characters inhabit. It won the Pulitzer, as well as rave reviews from almost all of the New York critics, and quickly transferred to Broadway. Its *animateur,* Jonathan Larson, died of a brain aneurysm at the age of thirty-five only days before the official opening. These stark and headline-grabbing events have created a niche for this show that no amount of criticism can ever erode. It makes us realize that life can be as histrionic, wayward, and unpredictable as anything ever mounted on a stage.

★★★

4

MARCEL MARCEAU

Marcel Marceau, on the stage of the Wiltern Theater, looking as he did ten years ago, and twenty years ago, and probably fifty years ago, plunges one irretrievably into a time-warp. The frizzly-haired man in white flowing flannels with a painted face cannot be seventy-five, but he must be. Once the frizzly-haired wig is removed and the clown-white wiped off his face, he must appear a wizened and weather-beaten senior citizen. Or is it possible the hair is real and the face totally unlined? Is there, in some Parisian attic, a painting of the real Marcel Marceau, ghoulishly corroding in the darkness while his youthful counterpart continues to walk magically against the wind?

One harps on the age of this astounding performer because he appears to be doing in 1998 precisely what he was doing in 1948 and with the same elasticity and precision. Even the repertoire is pretty much the same. He still compresses human life into three telling moments, as he immovably perambulates through *Youth, Maturity, Old Age, and Death*. He is still the desperate and agonized mask-maker trapped under the wacky smiling face of one his papier-mâché disguises. He is still, as Bip, taming lions and encountering Parisian archetypes in the *Jardin Publique*. He is still the living-breathing reincarnation of Jean Baptise Gaspard Deburau, the legendary nineteenth-century mime who, for over a quarter of a century, magically realized Pierrot on the boards of Theatre des Funambules. And he is still the Chaplinesque spin-off who also reminds us of Buster Keaton, Stan Laurel, Harry Langdon, and Harpo Marx; a superb technician who, using *"pantomime blanche,"* recreates the foibles and fatuities of everyday life.

Groups such as Mummenschantz and Pilobolus and individual mimes such as Jacques Le Coq in France and Paul Curtis in America have gone somewhat further with the art of mime; that's to say, they have transcended the traditional lyricism that Marceau inherited from Etienne Decroux in the '40s and was so superbly expressed by Decroux's other star pupil Jean Louis Barrault, in *Les Enfants du Paradis.* But essentially, mime has languished in the conventions inherited from Commedia dell' Arte, used to cadge quarters in fairgrounds, sell computers on TV commercials, or entertain at kiddies' parties.

Over the years, modern dance has nudged it into abstractionism, but it has remained stuck on weights and balances, climbing stairs, conjuring up imaginary objects, walking in place or against the wind. And yet I've always believed it had far greater potentialities than these; believed that if, instead of recreating the one-dimensional images of naturalistic behavior, it were to find ways of expressing the inner states common to us all, it could have an illimitable future.

Jacques Le Coq, the veteran French mime, first made me aware of this when he pointed out that a man turning a somersault in the air was kinetically expressing the spin-of-anger occurring inside of him. And Paul Curtis, influenced as he was by Robert Graves and other symbolist poets, also explored ways of using mime to express internalized states rather than merely mickey-mousing the minutiae of human behavior.

I can easily imagine a new kind of mime that, using techniques akin both to modern dance and modern art, would be the theatrical equivalent of postmodernist music or the literary innovations we associate with books such as *Ulysses* or *The Naked Lunch;* a mime that found a way of realizing the most subtle motions of our inner selves but still avoided the abstractionism of modern dance. Marceau's own mime-drama *The Overcoat,* based on Gogol's story, although entirely literal, made me believe that such an art-form were possible—even though I can point to no practitioners who have realized it. Grotowsky, in his early pieces such as *The Constant Prince* and *Dr. Faustus,* came very close, but those experiments led only into a stylized cul-de-sac.

If mime, instead of being thought of as the province of the New Vaudevillians, could shake off its Italian origins, its indebtedness to Pierrot and Pierette, circus clowns, and silent-screen comedians, it could become a dynamic new means of expression, one that, if realized, would totally obviate the splendid work of Marcel Marceau. I honor that work and am as astonished by the artist's technical skills today as I was when I first saw them, but I cannot shake this dogged belief that mime should be more than cupping one's thumb and fingers to simulate drinking or shuffling in place to suggest perambulation. That what should be being mimed is not our everyday habits of behavior, but the rich and endless mysteries of our inner experience. That the actor's art, using the models of dance but retaining the techniques and syntax of theater, could create a fresh new medium that, by externalizing interior feelings, would give voice to our deepest and most psychically rooted experience.

The experience of watching Marceau is this: we marvel at his ability to make visible an invisible universe, we grow frustrated at the trivial nature of his observations, and this gives way to tedium because the world depicted is too narrowly one-dimensional and its people and events too much like those already fully conveyed through language. Some part of us yearns for the silent language of mime to articulate thoughts and feelings beyond those expressed in speech, but we get only fragments of the quotidian and the tangible. Which is why *Youth, Maturity, Old Age and Death* and *The Mask Maker,* the only two philosophical items in his repertoire, are so affecting. Here, the art of mime transcends mirror-imagery and touches upon certain ineluctable universal truths: namely, that life, perfectly compressed, is nothing more than a swift journey from the womb to the grave, and that behind the most joyous social disguises, there is often an agonizing desperation. These pieces are the flagships of a fleet that could navigate the most dangerous and uncharted waters of human experience. The rest is just superb technique, which, dazzling as it is, seems to cry out for a content worthy of its high expertise.

5

"NON, MERCI": *PICASSO AT THE LAPIN AGILE*

by Steve Martin

One of the strangest anomalies in the theater is that of the successful turkey: plays that are essentially trivial, gauche, and insubstantial but still manage to achieve a certain kind of notoriety and even commercial success. *Shear Madness,* which has been playing for fifteen years in Boston, is such a play; so was *Kvetch,* which completed a seven-year run in Los Angeles, the same city in which *Bleacher Bums* ran for eleven years. *Abie's Irish Rose* racked up 2,854 performances on Broadway—although its depth could be measured with the first digit of one's pinkie finger. *No Sex Please, We're British,* which was the closest the West End theater could come to eroticism, had a phenomenal run in London. *Ten Nights in a Barroom* started in 1858 and was a staple of stock and touring companies for decades afterward, and one of Hollywood's longest recorded runs was a crude melodrama called *The Drunkard.*

Steve Martin's *Picasso at the Lapin Agile,* now revived at the Wilshire Theater, does not yet qualify for the Prime Turkey Award, but it is strongly in the running. It is a play in which mindlessness pays homage to Mind and is essentially a testament to L.A.'s slavish devotion to celebrity-hype—not only Steve Martin's but, in this case, Pablo Picasso's, Albert Einstein's, and Elvis Presley's as well. It is the kind of entertainment that persuades non-thinking people into believing they are indulging in high intellectualism.

In 1904 at the legendary Lapin Agile, an assortment of geniuses and would-be geniuses gather to celebrate the birth of Modernity and the unbounded promise of the twentieth century. (The great irony of this convocation is that we, living at the close of that century, know just how ruinously it will end.) It is a time when geniuses loom behind every glass of absinthe. Einstein is whimsically philosophical, Picasso, fervently artistic, and Schmendiman (the pseudo-genius) ebulliently effusive. Each character has his little turn and then cedes the stage to the next (belying the adage that one good turn deserves another.) In Martin's play, the quality of the turn is irrelevant; the main thing is its ability to pass the time and dispense lighthearted patter.

It is a world reminiscent of Saroyan's *The Time of Your Life,* in which a different set of bar-habitués goes through a similar round of unconnected episodes, also philosophizing about the vagaries of existence. But since Saroyan *is* something of a genius and Martin only a jumped-up gag-writer, the comparison collapses about twenty minutes into the piece. The play, without being wired into some kind of developing character structure, is simply at the mercy of its gags, and no matter how surreally cute some of them are, rootless comedy—like rootless drama—withers on the very vine from which its finest blossoms sprout.

To take seminal figures such as Einstein and Picasso and proceed to demonstrate how their influence affected the artistic and scientific character of the twentieth century is a tantalizing subject for a play—as is a dramatic exploration into the nature of genius (both the real and specious variety), but such a task assumes a philosophical grasp and intellectual edge that is wholly lacking in Mr. Martin. Failing to make any relevant connections between genius, art, science, and postmodernism, the play dwindles into high-class graffiti, a doodle around ideas that the author hasn't the skill either to develop or to focus.

As if dragged down to his natural level, Martin, at the close, introduces a time-traveling Elvis Presley and, although irrelevant to the play's premise, his appearance is very relevant to the author's inescapable, showbiz orientation. He is much more comfortable in Elvis's society than he ever was in the Left Bank world of French Bohemia. After the singer's arrival and the detonation of a few striking special effects, the play stops, rather than resolves, like a man so confused by his own circular argument that he finally opts to jump off the merry-go-round because even *he* has had enough.

Randall Arney's production is, if anything, more intolerable than the one I originally saw at the Geffen (then Westwood) Playhouse in 1995. Then the piece was chewed, aerated, and popped like the squiggly wad of bubblegum it actually was, but now, after engagements in Boston and New York, it returns to Los Angeles like a minor masterpiece, full of meaningful pauses and strained attempts at sentiment and pathos. Originally a protracted *Late Night Live* sketch about geniuses, it is now convinced that it is itself a work of art and, unfortunately, treats itself accordingly.

Mark Nelson as Einstein confers more comic nuance and subtle characterization than the piece deserves, a sterling example of how a chewed-up sow's ear can, in the hands of a talented actor, be turned into a silk purse. Paul Provenza seems to feel that the only way to express the gem-like flame of Pablo Picasso's genius is to use it to launch flares. His performance, like that of Michael Oosterom's Schmendiman and Ken Grantham's Sago, the art dealer, are monotonously exuberant throughout. Susannah Schulman, in three contrasting roles, mercifully manages to vary and refine her gusto.

Ultimately, the play is another prime example of Los Angeles' unique alchemy—the city's unfailing ability to turn crocks of shit into crocks of gold.

★★★

6

THE RETURN OF MARIVAUX: *CHANGES OF HEART*

Both Marivaux and Moliere were influenced by Commedia dell' Arte, but where Moliere depicted types, Marivaux dramatized process. That is perhaps why we feel so close to Marivaux and why he is enjoying something of a revival in the English-speaking theater. "I have spied in the human heart all the different niches where Love can hide when it is afraid to show itself," wrote Marivaux, "and each one of my comedies has for its object to make Love come out from its niche."

In Stephen Wadsworth's production of his adaptation of Marivaux's *La Double Inconstance* at the Mark Taper Forum (here sensibly rendered as *Changes of Heart*), no sooner does love come out of its niche than it dissolves entirely, only to be reborn and lured into yet another niche. Like most eighteenth-century French comedies, the plot defies quick elucidation, but here's a quick précis: Innocent country girl, madly in love with her village sweetheart, is appropriated by a prince who succeeds in capturing her heart, breaking her lover's, and generally corrupting the innocence of country life with the vanities of the Court.

Wadsworth's production is full of nimble, playful staging. Everyone runs, jumps, leaps, and squirms as if driven by an irresistible desire to relieve themselves; occasionally, characters in a low crouch insinuate slow, tentative exits, suggesting they've dumped in their pants and are taking their leave as inconspicuously as possible. (Wadsworth seems to have a horror of actors standing still. I kept hearing the admonishing voice of John Gielgud intoning: "Don't just do something, stand there!") Thomas P. Lynch's elegant open set encourages frolics and folderol and the production is choreographic, in the very best sense of the word, in that it eschews the caricatured posturing that usually deforms eighteenth-century revivals on American stages, productions in which both males and females appear to be playing in drag and sending up a lifestyle that no one can quite put his or her finger on.

When actors are constantly capering about, it sometimes blurs the fact that they aren't really very good actors; moving targets, as we know, are always harder to hit. But Mary Lou Rosato, as the court lady who appropriates Harlequin, the young girl's country lover, has the style down in spades. She combines haughtiness with eccentricity and produces a performance redolent of both Edith Evans and Bea Lillie: that's to say, grand and a little dotty. John Michael Higgins's Harlequin is endlessly playful without being very funny—but when Wadsworth draws him into a poignant finale where he becomes painfully aware of the love he has lost, both the actor and the character thoroughly exonerate themselves. It is up to Kathryne Dora Brown to convey the confused ambivalence of the young country girl committed to a peasant but irresistibly drawn to a prince, and although she, too, becomes persuasive in the last, darker half of the play, her first act suffers from a kind of vivacious monotony, as if constantly proving that her Energizer Bunny can outlast everyone else's. Paul Anthony Stewart as the besotted Prince, Maria Canals as the scheming *"mondaine,"* and Laurence O'Dwyer as the heartbroken servant have been deftly orchestrated into the director's constantly modulating score. Wadsworth's selections from Rameau's theater-music, employed to point up the mystery, pathos, and melodrama of the piece, are particularly well chosen. Every excerpt reinforces the texture of this comedy of manners, which regularly aspires to be a ballet and often achieves the grandiosity of opera.

In some quarters, Wadsworth has been taken to task for putting a dark spin on the play's conclusion, but he hasn't conveyed anything that wasn't already suggested by Marivaux himself. The marvel of this writer is that he can segue into half a dozen directions at the same time. A jaunty, capering version of this play would, by the middle of the last third, have been frothily unbearable. By finding the same kind of poignancy in Marivaux that Roger Planchon did in Moliere's *Georges Dandin* (where a farce about cuckoldry became a grim study of marital infidelity), Wadsworth has piped Marivaux directly into our modern sensibility.

While most other playwrights of the period were extolling the virtues of love, Marivaux was dissecting its schizoid nature, showing how love can be compromised by wealth or diverted by human design. One of the production's finest moments is the country girl's "change of heart" from her betrothed after being fitted into a sumptuous gown, the gift of her generous prince: as if now being attired as a court-lady, she was capable of adopting the court's shifting morality. Throughout the play, one is watching the corruption of innocence, but by people who are in no way villainous—in fact, just as confused and ambivalent as the lovers they are trying to pull. Love,

Marivaux seems to be saying, is a kind of fog, and when it descends, we all tend to lose our way. When it lifts, people find themselves on different plateaus and often with new partners.

Voltaire didn't have much time for Marivaux; he described his plays as "weighing flies' eggs in cobweb scales" and complained that the author "knew every byway of love, but missed the main highway." But then, virtually none of Voltaire's plays have come down to us, and it is quite likely that someone as blunt and macho as Voltaire could not appreciate the heightened subtlety of a Marivaux—just as the socially conscious Shaw was blind to the merits of an aesthetic Oscar Wilde. What is clear about Marivaux is that he was using the theater to go beyond the standard romantic imbroglios and, when he found human behavior contradicted, had no hesitation in expressing those contradictions. If *Change of Heart* ushers in more Marivaux and opens the doors to the riches of Corneille and Racine as well, we may have reached that happy pass where our appreciation of French theater will no longer be limited to gallumphing revivals of Molière.

7

THE NEXT BIG ONE: *RAGTIME*

It is an unwritten law on Broadway that every season there shall be at least one walloping great blockbuster that overwhelms the theatergoing public and takes its place among the titans of the past. Without such a lollapalooza, Broadway would simply not be Broadway and the scalpers, ticket agents, and columnists wouldn't know what to do with themselves. The need to have such an event becomes a self-fulfilling prophecy, and whatever reservations might silently arise, veneration for the blockbuster becomes virtually obligatory.

After a season or two, once the excitement of the coronation has subsided, it is permissible to acknowledge that the blockbuster was not everything it was cracked up to be—even to admit that because of the feeding-frenzy, serious flaws were overlooked or glossed over. But just as a newly elected head of state is entitled to a cozy "honeymoon period," so the newly proclaimed blockbuster rides the crest of its wave until, the tide gone out, it becomes a damp and soggy smudge on the beach.

Now concluding its run at the Shubert Theater in Los Angeles, it is clear that *Ragtime* is the designated "titan" for the coming New York season and will be duly crowned when it thunders into New York. The show has a faultless pedigree: an award-winning novel by E. Doctorow, a prestigious film by Milos Forman, and a sizzlingly hot producer—Garth Drabinsky—responsible for *Kiss of the Spider Woman* and the highly successful Hal Prince revival of *Showboat* and currently in tandem with corporate sponsors such as the Ford Motor Company and Canadian Airlines. In the American dominions, Mr. Drabinsky is as close to royalty as a Canuck can get.

The show, directed by Frank Galati, who deftly adapted Steinbeck's *The Grapes of Wrath* a few seasons back, is a kind of cat's-cradle strung together with several narrative strands from the novel. Its central story (as in the film) concerns Coalhouse Walker Jr.'s revenge against a bigoted fire chief who destroys his beloved motor car and insults his black manhood. Although specked with fleeting glimpses of Evelyn Nesbit, J. P. Morgan, Henry Ford, Admiral Peary, Booker T. Washington, Emma Goldman, and other iconic turn-of-the-century figures, the thrust of the musical is really about the revenge one resolute black man takes against the ruthless racism that dominated America at the beginning of the century and, if portents are to be believed, threatens to be just as volatile in the coming millennium.

But shows like *Ragtime* do beg the question: Must all musicals be reworkings of other material and former times? Kander and Ebb's *Chicago* is a dazzling show, but its dazzle is restricted to a recension of criminal scandals from the '20s; *A Funny Thing Happened on the Way to the Forum* is a rehash of vaudeville-shtick, using ancient Rome as a springboard; *Bring in da Noise, Bring in da Funk* celebrates the contributions of black Americans to both tap-dancing and civil rights; *Beauty and the Beast* is a crude Disneyfication of a French fairy tale deeply rooted in the American psyche; and the recently opened *The Lion King,* a vacuous cartoon-fable pumped up with spectacular costumes and settings. Only *Rent,* among the more recent musicals, reflects some contemporary social phenomenon and even there, much of its impetus is indebted to a nineteenth-century opera (*La Boheme*).

In plays, we are always looking for some spark, some emanation, some allusion to contemporary experience or current preoccupation. In musicals, when they are not unabashedly revivals, the assumption seems to be all we need do is find appropriate chunks of recent, or not-so-recent, history and cleverly reformulate them. Remakes, re-dos, sequels, prequels, and postquels are all the rage in films, TV, and on the stage. But musicals that deal with inescapable immediacies—for example, the vulgarization of public life through gossip and scandal; the flight from intimacy due to fear of disease; the techno-colonization of everyday life, which threatens to annihilate human interaction; the irreconcilable factionalism between people of different social, political, and spiritual beliefs; and so forth and so on—these seem to belong in the purlieus of the op-ed page or TV magazine shows.

When they first appeared, musicals such as *Of Thee I Sing, Pins 'n' Needles, The Threepenny Opera, Pal Joey, Lady in the Dark, The Pajama Game, Bye Bye Birdie, A Chorus Line, How to Succeed In Business without Really Trying, Hair,* et al.—whatever their respective merits—seemed to grow out of the contemporary terrain. But today we seem to need reassurances from the past and the comfort of "known quantities" and so we rehash old movies like *Sunset Boulevard; Victor, Victoria; The Red Shoes;* and *Big;* revamp novels like *Phantom of the Opera, Les Miserables, Jekyll and Hyde,* and *By Jeeves;* launch reprises of old phonograph records like *Smokey Joe's Cafe* and *Five Guys Named Moe;* and doggedly reincarnate icons such as Al Jolson, Elvis Presley, and Buddy Holly.

Even Stephen Sondheim, the most immediate of all contemporary composers, seems to feel the need to resort to fairy tales (*Into the Woods*) or nineteenth-century opera (*Passion*) in order to make his points.

Granted, the rehashing of previous material can, by parallel and implication, uncover fresh insight into our own condition. Still, one is tempted to ask: Is this obsession with the past and reliance on revivals a healthy stock-taking of our established musical heritage or an inability to come to terms with the relevencies of modern life? Must we assume that it is *only* "by indirections" that we can "find directions out"?

★★★

A curious footnote to Ragtime *is that producer Garth Drabinksy was sued by the Livent Company for securities fraud and misappropriation of funds, giving way to one of Broadway's juiciest pre-millennial scandals. Drabinsky, now in Canada fighting extradition to the States, was always a charismatic and highly effective impresario and still has many stout defenders. The finale to this one is yet to be played out.*

★★★

8

. . . AND ALL THAT JAZZ!: *CHICAGO*

Chicago, now playing at the Shubert Theater, is the kind of show Bertolt Brecht might have written had he been born in Manhattan, grown up around Times Square, and been represented by the William Morris Office. Its cynical exposé of the workings of American justice and romanticization of criminal celebrity feed right into the current ambivalence surrounding media favorites such O. J. Simpson and Amy Fisher. In a brilliant outpouring of trenchant song-and-dance, it rubs our noses in the national tendency to confuse notoriety with fame. It says that because we are sentimental and highly impressionable, we are prepared to commit shameful acts of exoneration and appalling acts of veneration and that so long as evil provides fodder for titillating gossip, we are prepared to withhold moral condemnation.

All of which doesn't begin to do justice to the exuberance and frivolity that John Kander, Fred Ebb, and Bob Fosse have pumped into *Chicago,* a show that, stylistically, was twenty years ahead of its time when it premiered in 1975 and, in its current revivals both on Broadway and at the Shubert, has somersaulted into the pantheon of Great American Musicals.

There is no point in quibbling about performance variables. Its original stars, Gwen Verdon, Chita Rivera, and Jerry Orbach, were in many ways sharper, darker, and more charismatic than the present L.A. company or their Broadway counterparts. There was a palpable tension running behind the squirmy sensuality of the original production that is somewhat lacking in Walter Bobbie's more amiable staging, but Ann Reinking's choreography, an homage to Fosse's angular, derby-hatted slinkiness, is just as inventively exotic and Charlotte d'Amboise (Roxie), Stephanie Pope (Velma), and Brent Barrett (Billy Flynn) just as lowdown and dirty as the many other performers who, over the years, have surfaced in these roles.

Based loosely on the cases of two sensational murderesses in 1924 (and breezily reconstituted in the Ginger Rogers's film *Roxie Hart*), the story is told in a series of discontinuous musical segments that clearly imply that "crime passionel" is a branch of the entertainment industry. The score is studded with acerbic songs that sound like '20s retrofits but that, on close inspection, reveal biting commentary on various forms of contemporary hypocrisy: Brent Barrett as a dapper kind of Alan Dershowitz, who is habitually "on the take," sings "All I Care about Is Love": Avery Sommers, as the jailhouse Matron who affectionately extorts lucre from her female inmates, sings, "When You're Good to Momma, Then Momma Is Good to You": and then Sommers and Stephanie Pope join forces to sing "Class," a nostalgic ballad dripping with irony that bemoans the very lack of scruples that both women flagrantly personify. At every turn, the musical is dispensing arsenic in Tupperware jars and rubbing the audience's nose in uncomfortable truths about our gullibility to media manipulation.

Chicago is our home-grown *Threepenny Opera,* and Fosse's brilliantly sardonic spirit pulsates beneath its exterior as Brecht's does behind *his* 1920s masterpiece. (And for the snobs in our midst who contend that Kander and Ebb combined do not equal one Kurt Weill, I can only say there is a rollicking ribaldry in American show music that Weill never achieved—even in the finest moments of *Lady in the Dark* or *Lost in the Stars.*) The style, spirit, sound, and story line of Fosse's show all hang together beautifully. The '20s setting, in this production, as in the original, is laced with the heartless opportunism and camouflaged guile that characterize our own pernicious age. In one sense, it is even more current now than it was when it first opened, as it seems to encapsulate all the national traumas we have recently suffered at the hands of people such as O. J. Simpson, the Menendez brothers, Lorainne Bobbit, and Amy Fisher. It is a musical bred by the luridness and perversity of our *National Inquirer* culture. A show at which Geraldo, Ricki Lake, Howard Stern, and Jerry Springer would feel completely at home.

★★★

9

A BRACE OF WILDES: *AN IDEAL HUSBAND*

All the stage plays of Oscar Wilde are a kind of crystal ball in which one can read the hang-ups and obsessions of the man. He may have, as he said, put his "genius" into his life and only his "talent" into his works, but the paradoxes and contradictions of that "genius" are traceable in almost every manifestation of his "talent"—particularly in *An Ideal Husband,* which opened in 1895, only a few months before *The Importance of Being Earnest,* in what was certainly the most exhilarating year of his life. Both were summarily closed after Wilde was found guilty in the second trial.

One of the most persistent strands in *Ideal Husband* is Wilde's depiction of Gertrude Chiltern, the upright wife of Sir Robert, the charismatic politician whose career is threatened by the revelation that early in his career he was guilty of insider-trading: passing a political secret to a speculator, which made him a rich man. Lady Chiltern's moral zeal is almost as insufferable in her role as Isabella in *Measure for Measure,* and one can easily imagine her saying along with the novitiate nun: "More than our 'husband' is our chastity." Wilde goes to great lengths to argue that a woman's duty is to forgive transgressions, not skewer them, and it is hard not to hear the homosexual paterfamilias pleading with the respectable woman who became his wife to condone rather than condemn what she, and the rest of her society, took to be unnatural practices. Although Sir Robert's guilty secret is a letter written in his youth to a nefarious nobleman, which both corrupted his innocence and gained him his fortune, the smoldering subtext of the scene is alive with innuendo about Wilde's own guilty secret and his need to live with it, both in his marriage and in his career.

The conflict is triggered by the arrival of Lady Chiltern's old schoolmate, the scheming Mrs. Chevely, and her attempt to get Sir Robert to back an Argentine Canal Company that, in the play, is likened to the Suez Canal project. A canal is a waterway that links two separate bodies of land. Wilde had himself built a canal that would enable him to negotiate the straight world of upper-class British society and what was then thought of as the lower world of sexual perversion. Chiltern, although guilty of the moral crime of which Mrs. Chevely accuses him, refuses to support what he takes to be "a commonplace Stock Exchange swindle." But whereas he can face down Mrs. Chevely, he shrinks from the censure of the overly virtuous Lady Chiltern. No matter how moral he may appear in the House of Commons, he acknowledges his guilt and shame before the withering gaze of his judgmental wife. His defense? That loved ones should condone weaknesses of character and lapses of good conduct. "It is not the perfect, but the imperfect who have need of love."

Without the turmoil that raged within Wilde, particularly in 1895 when he was at the height of his success and, paradoxically, at his most vulnerable, *An Ideal Husband* would have been nothing more than a Gilbertian comedy of manners. But given the intensity of his inner life, the opposition between his aesthetic pretensions and his already-budding Christian instincts, it became the richly-textured play now on view on Broadway in Peter Hall's translucent production.

Comparisons are invidious, and comparisons between a first-class British company and a regional American theater are worse than invidious, they are positively unjust. But Martin Benson's production at South Coast Rep, where the play has just opened, virtually compels such comparisons. In the first place, Benson has, almost beat by beat, reproduced Peter Hall's mise-en-scène. The decor is almost identical: pillars, palm leaves, even items of furniture placed in exactly the same relation to one another. The staging mirrors Hall's so closely one almost feels that Benson must have worked from the same prompt copy. Music, stage business, and light cues happen in almost exactly the same places.

Although the externals are eerily reminiscent of the production now on Broadway, there is a vast difference in performance style. Benson's Lord Goring, happily, does not try to reproduce the look and flavor of Wilde himself, as Martin Shaw mawkishly did in London and New York. Hall went for the complicated inner texture of events that made the play feel brand new, and Benson's company merely bounces along its surface—now broad, now straight, mixing superciliousness with low camp. At South Coast Rep, the epigrammatic attack on the text is unrelenting; it is as if every line is a Bartlett's quotation and, in consequence, much of the comedy is trumpeted where it ought to be fluted. In Hall's production because Wildean persiflage was the actors' natural tongue, speeches are played casually and witty lines seemingly thrown away, which is what garners the laughs. At South Coast, everyone seems to be in a Wildean straitjacket, dispensing language as if they were propelling jumbo jets instead of piloting Piper Cubs, helicopters, or hang-gliders.

Hall's production also had its problems. Anna Carteret was far too Danvers-like as Mrs. Chevely; once she got into the Patton tank of her characterization, the woman behind the stratagems was barely visible through the turret. But that show was blessed by David Yelland's highly modulated and endlessly subtle Robert Chiltern, a tortured innocent with whom we could all powerfully identify, and Madeline Potter's Lady Chiltern skillfully kept her character from dwindling into a prig or becoming a kind of up-market Carrie Nation. It was further enhanced by Michael Denison and Dulcie Gray, two dyed-in-the-wool West End troupers, who made the Earl of Caversham and Lady Markby deliciously simmering minor characters. At South Coast Rep, a kind of Denison-look-alike essays Caversham with almost no comic variety (and what there is in Jack Sydow's characterization seems filched from Denison's performance), and Lady Markby is grossly caricatured by a chortling porpoise who was, in fact, SCR's casting director for eleven years: a statistic that ominously throws a pall over the entire past decade.

At South Coast, Mark Capri, who has exactly the right look for Chiltern, suppurates his suffering and blusters his desperation like a man who deserves the worst that will befall him—which makes nonsense of the upright and noble politician we are told he is. Debbie Grattan flutters through Lady Chiltern like Nora in *The Doll's House* and never seems to achieve that greater wisdom that both Nora and her own character acquire in the play's final scenes. When, in that slightly maudlin final tableau where the chastened wife and the reborn husband turn front and assume a Royal Family posture and Lady Chiltern says, "For both of us, a new life is beginning," something deep within us anticipates that she will turn to her husband and yet again compel him to write out the conditions on which that "new life" will be predicated—just as she did the Chevely letter and the note to the prime minister, refusing the offer of a cabinet post. Which is just another way of saying that neither character reaches the new threshold of consciousness indicated by Wilde and the upward surge of the play's resolution.

Philip Anglim's Lord Goring at South Coast slightly has the edge on Martin Shaw's. It is based on a kind of aesthetic lassitude that suggests that nothing in the world is worth getting up for at 8:00 A.M., although almost anything is worth staying up for till four in the morning. Anglim clearly establishes Goring's deep attachment to the Chiltern family and thereby makes plausible all his efforts to extricate his friends from their imbroglios. Shaw's Goring, so preoccupied with imitating Wilde, often functioned on the play's periphery rather than at its epicenter. Hope Alexander-Willis, like Anna Carteret, plunges wholly into Mrs. Chevely's sliminess and, like her British counterpart, finds herself imprisoned in one-dimensionality. The key to Mrs. Chevely is that she would like to be restored to the British social scene from which she has been cut off—not simply that she is a ruthless speculator in a heliotrope gown spangled with diamonds. Played that way, that mawkish and implausible scene with Goring in which she proposes marriage begins to make sense.

You can take the low road with *An Ideal Husband* and play it as a somewhat refined comedy-melodrama. Benson's production does just that and utterly delights his Orange County subscribers. No play is actor-proof, but with competent professionals who deliver the text and wear the costumes smartly, you cannot injure or really violate this play. But what Hall did was to touch a hidden spring beneath the surface glitter and force us to see the anguish and paradox that occasionally raise a social comedy of manners to the level of tragi-comedy. I can't speak authoritatively about the timing of these two shows, but Hall's production, both in England and on Broadway, certainly antedated Benson's, and, given its caste and complexion, it is lunacy to ape its topography and try to duplicate its effects. There are dozens of ways of approaching *An Ideal Husband,* and given Hall's recent and widely publicized achievement, it seems bizarre not to set off in a completely different direction. Imitation may be the sincerest form of flattery, but it is also the secret bride of plagiary.

★★★

10

PINTER GOES HOME: *THE HOMECOMING*

In Harold Pinter's play *The Homecoming,* a university lecturer returns to his north London home after an absence of six years with his new wife in tow. She is immediately denounced as a whore by his father and is successively seduced by her husband's brothers, which she accepts with equanimity. Toward the end, on the suggestion of one brother who appears to be something of a pimp, Ruth, the wife, is easily persuaded to forsake her husband and three children and stay on with her in-laws as a kind of combination house-mum and part-time prostitute. Teddy, her husband, eerily reconciled to his loss, leaves Ruth to her new life and departs alone.

I've always held the theory that Pinter was actually writing about his own escalation from humble beginnings in Hackney, a poor working-class suburb of London, to the life of a fashionable celebrity and affluent British playwright. The play seems to imply that Ruth actually "belongs" more in the sordid environs of her husband's family circle (inhabited as it is by a would-be pugilist, a ponce, and a chauffeur) than she does in the more elegant surroundings Teddy has provided for her in the States. She was once, as she puts it "a body model," the inference being she led an active life of open sensuality before she ever married Teddy. It is as if Teddy knows he doesn't deserve the middle-class affluence whose most prominent symbol is the totemic wife and that he has arranged this "homecoming" in order to confront the inescapable truth about himself—namely, that he is a more craven and primitive creature than his respectable manner and appearance would suggest.

There are dozens of other interpretations of this ambiguous play, which almost seems to exist in order to be variously interpreted. For some, the real "homecoming" is not Teddy's but Ruth's, whose arrival in the home restores a mother-wife figure to the all-male menage. Teddy's punishment for having plucked up his roots is to remain rootless, barred forever from the bosom of the "new" family and relegated to alien-status in America. The play seems to be constantly picking at a scab: the guilt incurred in turning one's back on one's origins, exchanging a lowly milieu for a higher and more glittering one, constructing a posh persona to conceal the grottier truths of one's actual identity—an inversion of the preoccupation with class that has pervaded the British drama for over two hundred years.

Pinter is now married to Lady Antonia Fraser and inhabits a hierarchical niche both in English letters and English society. When *The Homecoming* was first written, it starred his first wife, Vivien Merchant, in a performance that was palpably moist with sexual heat. By then, Pinter had already scrambled out of the depths of Hackney, established an association with the National Theatre, and made the list of the Ten Best Dressed Men in England. As time went on, he wrote about his new social stratum with the same disturbing penetration that he had brought to the ramshackle world grubbily evoked in *The Caretaker.* In a sense, Pinter never had a "homecoming." His talent and his accomplishments secured a place for him in a world very different from the one into which he was born and raised. And yet, despite the social elevation, the core of Pinter is still in Hackney rather than in Mayfair—the twilight world of the disheveled bedsit, where alienated drifters and gamy hustlers try to scratch out a living for themselves.

The Homecoming is fairly early Pinter and betrays the lurches and stumbles of a playwright still trying to reconcile his means with his ends. The sudden death of Sam the chauffeur, the prissiest member of the family, has no real impact on the play's larger design, and the brothers' concupiscent relationship with Ruth is as much dispersive as it is ambiguous. But the fable itself is riveting and plunges the spectator into dark musings about the potential incestuousness that runs beneath family ties.

It is hard for me to be objective about the Matrix Theater Company's revival. I remember too vividly and too well what Paul Rogers, Vivien Merchant, and the others did in Peter Hall's 1965 production. I am sure that a complex play can be done in any number of different ways, but I suspect that the broadness of Andrew J. Robertson's production goes against the grain of what the author intended. Pinter's talent was always poised between the influences of Ionesco and Beckett, his best work always veering toward the latter. This production is an Ionesconization of *The Homecoming,* where the sexual transfer at the heart of the play registers more as an absurdity than a mysterious transformation. The laughs it gets are born out of the incongruity of the situation—a man delivering his wife to a family that rapidly proceeds to sexually devour her—but if you believe the play is about territorial struggle between people who have made it and people who haven't, a surface piece of naturalism with a profound metaphysical undertow, it is hard to accept a production that settles for oddity. It *"can"* be played as an absurdist comedy (anything can be played *any* way, I suppose), but the loss of resonance far outweighs the small gains in comedy.

★★★

Pinter's longevity is quite remarkable. From the late '50s, when The Birthday Party *first appeared and was brutally savaged by the British press, through a long, dry, "blocked" period in which he produced virtually nothing, his oeuvre has remained consistently alive. Nothing in the later period can compare with the underground reverberations found in early works such as* The Caretaker, Old Times, *and* No Man's Land, *and there was a period in the '80s when he seemed to be parodying himself. As I write, audiences are discovering hidden treasures in previously neglected works such as* Betrayal *and* The Lover, *and* The Caretaker *is enjoying a stupendous revival at the Royal National Theatre. As one looks back on the British New Wave, there are very few of its standard-bearers (John Arden, Arnold Wesker, John Osborne, David Mercer, James Saunders, N. F. Simpson) who have flourished right through to the end of the century. The outstanding hold-outs appear to be Pinter, Osborne (to some extent), Joe Orton, and, paradoxically, Alan Ayckbourn.*

11

HE WHO PLAYS THE PRINCE: BRANAGH'S *HAMLET*

The most astonishing fact about Kenneth Branagh's four-hour, uncut version of *Hamlet* is how intrinsically cinematic Shakespeare's play is. Although the screenplay is interlarded with flashbacks, flash-forwards, and subliminal imagery illustrating situations alluded to in the text, this is essentially Shakespeare's structure as he conceived it and it fits together like a piece of tongue-and-groove jointure.

There is a certain archival satisfaction in having every word of the text down on celluloid and played, in the main, by a highly competent group of English actors who perform it with clarity and understanding. This film would be a perfect artifact to include in that buried time capsule intended to show future generations where we, on the cusp of the millennium, stood in relation to this treasured classic. It would also preserve most of the received wisdom about this play that has been accumulating over the past half-century for, apart from a few innovations that I shall shortly mention, this is Shakespeare-straight: an interpretation blended together from the ideas most current about this play. For those who instinctively recoil from postmodernist freakouts, this *Hamlet* provides aid and comfort.

The new wrinkles are mainly these: Polonius (an earnest Richard Briers) has been shorn of all the dottiness we tend to associate with Felix Aylmer's frail councilor in Olivier's *Hamlet.* This is a protective father and a politic statesman with a weakness for voyeurism. He eavesdrops on his daughter from behind palace doors, sics spies onto his potentially licentious and wandering son, and is not averse to having a bit-on-the-side himself. Briers, a popular light comedian in Britain, is apparently delighted at being reborn "a serious actor" and, truth to tell, he plays Polonius well—but in a play so leavened with seriousness, one regrets the loss of comedy where it could legitimately surface.

Fortinbras (Rufus Sewell) is established early on as having colonial ambitions in regard to Denmark and, in the final moments of the play, the invading armies of Old Norway occupy Elsinore just as the plot's final combustion litters the stage with the corpses of Laertes, the King, the Queen, and the Prince. This gives the play the kind of spectacular conclusion that film epics are supposed to have and tries thereby to resolve both the personal and political conflicts. In a nod to topicality, the final image of the film is the icon of King Hamlet, like the battered statue of Lenin, being pulled down and smashed to bits by the invading army.

Having said how, from an academic viewpoint, it is useful to have the full brunt of *Hamlet* on screen, one must immediately add that it convincingly makes the case for compression. Excess verbiage has always been one of Shakespeare's pitfalls; that and prolixity of expression, which blurs the spectators' immediate perception, remain good reasons for streamlining much of the canon. It is because what is essential in Shakespeare is the centrifugal imagery and the sweep of character that the words need not be treated as if they were the Elgin Marbles. Although I welcomed the sound of speeches and scenes that are usually deleted in stage revivals, no sooner was my literal sense satisfied than my critical sense questioned their relevance.

In the '30s and '40s, film studios used to enjoy putting out films chock full of star cameos, mainly to utilize underemployed contract-players hanging around the lot (e.g., *Paramount on Parade, The Show of Shows, Thank Your Lucky Stars, Stage Door Canteen,* etc.). The stars, mustered into service for these promotional appearances, usually looked awkward and hard-done-by, as if resenting the exploitative motives of their studio bosses. Occasionally, Branagh's *Hamlet* resembles such pictures, in that "stars" cast in supporting roles appear to be strangely out of place. Jack Lemmon is a makeshift Marcellus. He mouths the text in his bland transatlantic diction and seems to be waiting for Walter Matthau to come along to effect a rescue. Billy Crystal is snide and stand-up as the First Gravedigger—transforming a rustic comic character into a kind of officious funeral-parlor director who, in order to keep his payroll costs down, is doing the grave-digging himself. Robin Williams's Osric wears a shit-eating grin throughout and displays none of the flounce and flutter attributed to this character by Shakespeare, and Richard Attenborough, looking like a Whitehall politician from the series *Yes, Minister* who has wandered onto the wrong set, delivers his upper-class peroration as the English Ambassador and vanishes from sight. All of these star performers working for scale are apparently there to bask in the glow of Branagh's high art, which, if it were truly high art, would have taken more pains to cast these roles appropriately. But this is an internationally tooled Castle Rock Entertainment vehicle and, as everyone knows, the presence of

American star-names provides a certain commercial fillip—although encountering them in this context is a little like finding members of the Brat Pack manning gas pumps.

In the somewhat meatier small roles, Charlton Heston, playing the Player King like a man for whom celebrity has become a shroud, judiciously filters all the schmaltz out of the Hecuba speeches. Unlike Williams, Crystal, and Lemmon, this is a perfect piece of casting—and beautifully partnered by Rosemary Harris who, if there was any justice in the world, would have been playing Gertrude, a role diminished by a vapid and ingratiating Julie Christie who gives no intimation of any guilt for her incest or awkwardness for her delicate public situation. Derek Jacobi, being a founder-member of the Branagh Stock Company, is awarded Claudius, a role for which he is neither physically nor temperamentally suited, and so the "bloat King" is turned into a kind of Metternich-figure that pouts more than he pounces and seems always to be on the brink of being unmasked.

Nicholas Farrell's Horatio, dressed like a troubadour and suggesting that he and Hamlet were the hippie-outcasts of Wittenberg University, perfectly combines staunch camaraderie and level-headedness—a kind of older brother who makes sure his younger sibling will not flunk out or get summarily expelled. Brian Blessed, with laser-like blue contact lenses, performs the Ghost's narrative speeches without ponderous elaboration, thereby rendering them both comprehensible and compelling. (He could have played the be-Jesus out of Claudius—nor would it have been too far-fetched to think of Derek Jacobi as a tenderer, somewhat wistful Ghost.) John Gielgud, in a wraithlike, subliminal flashback, mimes Priam to Judi Dench's noiselessly wailing Hecuba, an image powerfully reminiscent of Helene Weigel's "silent scream" in *Mother Courage,* and even the much-beloved music-hall comic Ken Dodd makes an appearance for all the mums 'n' dads as a mugging Yorick, rough-housing with a prepubescent Hamlet.

As for Branagh-the-actor, he has three colors in his palate—snarling aggression, whispering sensitivity, and playful bitchery—and he manages to alternate these throughout the length of four hours. His finest moments are with Ophelia (Kate Winslet) in the Play Scene, where he becomes an ebullient emcee for the staging of "The Murder of Gonzago," converting his filial pain into a kind of tortured sarcasm. Throughout, as if consciously haunted by Olivier's achievement, Branagh makes choices as far removed from the earlier film as possible. Instead of gloomy castle corridors, the setting is bold and colorful: a nonparticularized nineteenth-century Scandinavian society where the darkest deeds are played out in the brightest surroundings. The sumptuous interiors provide a strong counterpoint to the mad, treacherous, and guilty creatures that inhabit them. (But this was first done by Olivier in his storybook *Richard III.*) The opening Court scene, which introduces us to the main characters and is attended by scores of Danish dignitaries, feels far too public for the personal imbroglios played out there. It's as if the whole of Denmark was witnessing the newly ensconced monarch arbitrating private family affairs, an instance where the setting, though cinematically effective, works against the logic of what is taking place.

Branagh's personal chutzpah—both as an actor and a director—perfectly fertilizes his approach to the character. This is a Hamlet who burns with ambition; is shattered by acts of disloyalty, whether from Ophelia or Rosencrantz and Guildenstern; and only seems implausible when he rails against his own personal inadequacies. Somehow it is hard to believe that the forthright activist who challenges ghosts, mounts plays, confounds royal trickery, and outpoints his fencing adversaries cannot get his act together in regard to a vulnerable king. Although the prince constantly alludes to his weakness, it is always played out with the most robust strength.

"How all occasions do inform against me," in many ways one of the most subtle and ego-driven speeches in the play, is used by Branagh as a landscape design to end the first part of the film. Instead of the smoldering soul searching indicated by Shakespeare, it is employed as a rhetorical set-piece to allow us to see the formation of Fortinbras's troops as they mass behind the exiled prince. I suppose Branagh-the-director needed a big finish to the first half, and although, cinematically, it might make sense to fill up the full canvas of the 70mm screen and make the audience gulp at the vast panorama, the fact remains, it is achieved at the expense of the soliloquy.

For Branagh, *Hamlet* is in the weave of the verse and the spiral of the soliloquies. His way of expressing the character's inner state is to pump meaning into the language and so, to know what the character is feeling, we merely have to interpret the vocal nuances of his delivery. The permutations of his inner self don't really come into it. Olivier, with those hooded, baleful eyes and that irrepressible world-weariness, caught our sympathy because of his emanations: the woefulness that oozed from his silences and clustered behind his throwaway phrases. With Branagh, it's all out there—spread-eagled in the language and immediately decipherable. It is just possible that a play that for over four hundred years has been a triumph of ambiguity doesn't need so forthright a degree of explicitness.

For Branagh, *Hamlet* is the excitement, the violence, the danger, and the melancholy of what happens to the character. From the moment he first saw it at the age of fifteen performed by Derek Jacobi, he knew he "wanted to play the role." It was the actor's obsession to experience the gamut of the character's emotions, the trajectory of his rise from despair, his surge toward vengeance, and his philosophically accepted downfall that stirred his blood. But *Hamlet* is much more than a sequence of exciting scenes and eloquent speeches. It is also a magnificent microphone through which the voice of a distinctive artist can convey his conception of longing and loss, identity and dissolution, moral imperatives and rationalizing evasions. Highly wrought as the play is, it is also a tabula rasa on which a director or an actor can inscribe a new message, a new way of doping out the contradictions of life. In short, it is an artifact that, because it is both porous and dense, can provide a new dimension of meaning to a public already familiar with its plot and incidents. But for Branagh, it is only "a great role" and a compelling story—which is perhaps another way of saying that he finds in *Hamlet* everything that has always been there, but he brings nothing to it that can increase its meaning or illuminate its mystery.

Ultimately, we come out of the film feeling the magnitude of all the great actors who have ever played it and silently rue the lack of character of the young man who now brandishes the text in our face. For Hamlet is, of course, Branagh—just as he once was Booth or Barrymore, Gielgud or Olivier. It is not so much a role as a frame in which the character of the actor fills out the shapes limned by the playwright. But Branagh's character is as Hollywoodized as his star casting or his sumptuous sets. It is a Hamlet for the Now generation—that's to say, that teeming horde of indiscriminate bozos who prefer the custom-made comfort of a sleek masterwork to the ambiguities and contradictions of a classic that forces them to undergo the pain and complexity of art. If it were a book, it would be one of those highly burnished leather-bound jobs that stood on the shelf proclaiming the owner's cultural status, rather than a dog-eared volume that had stirred his heart and exercised his brain.

★★★

12

SADEAN SEX FANTASY: *QUILLS*

Based on the fact that when the Marquis de Sade was at the asylum in Charenton the authorities confiscated his quills and writing paper to prevent his pornographic imagination from running amok, Doug Wright has fashioned an extravagant fantasy almost as lurid and cruel as the novels created by de Sade himself. *Quills,* at the Geffen Playhouse, is what might have happened to the phallocentric Marquis had his real life been as demented as his dream life.

Not that his actual life didn't already have all the elements of a baroque nightmare. He was incarcerated through most of it and hounded by a cruel harpy of a wife who ultimately became his most remorseless tormentor. Spurned by the French aristocracy, which viewed him as a sexual psychopath, he was temporarily lauded as a hero by the French revolutionaries but quickly earned their condemnation as well and, having roused Robespierre's antagonism, was almost guillotined. After his death, his works were proscribed virtually everywhere until late in this century. As a literary figure, he remains wildly controversial, with critics simultaneously defending and defaming him. Although Guillaume Apollinaire, Antonin Artaud, and Simone de Beauvoir tried to rehabilitate him, to the majority of Western readers he remains abominable—which, of course, gives him a certain caché among intellectuals.

So long as human beings are plagued by bestial impulses and prone to unnatural acts of self-gratification, de Sade will remain a pertinent cultural force and this despite the fact that his works push pornography to the screaming edge of monotony and his obsessiveness is as predictable as his style is stodgy. Some artists triumph through treatment and some through subject matter. De Sade's uniqueness lies in the fact that no one has ever plumbed the depths of sexual depravity quite as conscientiously. Those (like Camille Paglia) who believe he is an arch satirist writing with tongue-in-cheek totally misread him. De Sade, like Genet, writes to masturbate to his own fantasies, and the commitment he reveals to his warped imagination is what makes him unique. If he is funny at all, it is in the way that certain writers who cannot shake off their obsessions are sometimes unintentionally funny to readers who do not share those obsessions. But de Sade's immorality and atheism are the blades of his double-edged sword, and he flays the reader with them as assiduously as he does the flesh of his virginal heroines. He is a writer (again like Genet) who has deliberately aggrandized evil and celebrates it unconscionably. It is, in fact, the absence of conscience that makes de Sade appear to be the "monster" so many critics have found him to be. A more humane author, it is supposed, would somewhere, at some point, have revealed a glimmer of moral reflection. In de Sade's universe, all moral laws have been wiped from the books, and since, in the twisted labyrinth of our own psyche, those moral laws never existed in the first place, de Sade will always manage to speak to that primitive part of ourselves that more civilized authors do not reach. His curious appeal is that for the length of a novel, he can make inhuman behavior appear more fetching than civility. Anyone who can consistently achieve that kind of moral topsy-turveydom, it seems to me is an artist worthy of note—no matter what his subject matter may be.

Playwright Doug Wright hounds his demonized protagonist through the agency of an ostensibly sympathetic clergyman who, once he has been corrupted by Sadean sadism, divests himself of all Christian feeling to the point where he actually vivisects the diabolical nobleman. During the course of a Nathaniel West–like dismemberment, de Sade loses his tongue, his limbs, his penis, and ultimately his head—but his influence lives on, corrupting the very avenger who tried to rid the world of his evil.

Howard Hesseman, who plays de Sade, is a middle-aged actor with a strong rhetorical delivery. He spends a lot of his time in the nude (another institutional punishment) but, to his credit, conveys the impression that he is as unashamed of his naked anatomy as de Sade was of his immorality. It is a slightly hectoring performance, with more surface than soul, but it makes all of Wright's points firmly and lucidly. Martin Rayner as the Abbey de Coulmier, who loses his own soul in the vain attempt to save the prisoner's, neatly graduates from moral indignation to moralizing malevolence, demonstrating, in a classical Sadean manner, the hypocrisy of the Church. Adrian Hall's production is bold and gritty, with a strong emphasis on presentational acting (i.e., downstage, out-front delivery), sometimes to the detriment of the play's plausibility but always to the benefit of its argument. It is not his fault that Peters, Brook, and Weiss got there first and that often *Quills* looks and feels like *Son of Marat/Sade.* But whereas Weiss's approach was philosophical, Wright's is journalistic. For him, Sade is the victim of a vindictive literary suppression and so a martyr to censorship. This seems to me something of a loaded argument, as the most invidious censorship is political rather than sexual, and whatever virtues de Sade may have as an author, he wasn't exactly Tom Paine.

Whatever quibbles one might have about either the production or the acting, the overriding fact is that Wright has written a highly literate and bubblingly intelligent tirade against official expurgators and given it enough plot twists and character transformations to keep it airborne from beginning to end. It was courageous of Gil Cates to begin his season with such a hot and horny play and to give Los Angeles a whiff of the kind of theater that sustains, and often electrifies, the best European repertoires. *Quills* is a play that has something to say and says it with raucous intelligence—straight into your face.

★★★

To the astonishment of many who were familiar with Doug Wright's original play, Philip Kaufman transformed Quills *into an award-winning film that appeared in 2001. From that standpoint, it fared very much better than* Marat/Sade, *to which it was distantly related, and maintained the illustrious tradition of the theater nourishing its younger and more affluent media-relation.*

13

CORPORATE FOLLIES: *HOW TO SUCCEED IN BUSINESS WITHOUT REALLY TRYING*

When *How to Succeed in Business without Really Trying* opened in 1961, the specter over America was conformity: men in charcoal gray suits sopping up individuality and replacing it with three-button-down orthodoxy. The repulsion with an America sanitized by the Eisenhower years and regulated by Madison Avenue mavens who dictated our tastes and wormed their way into our psyches is what brought the Beat Generation into being and ultimately unleashed the bitterest confrontations of the '60s. The Business Ethic, what Harding had personified and Hoover had glorified, was revealed to be the seamy underbelly of the American Dream.

If anything, corporate morality has gotten worse in the intervening years—hitting its nadir in the '80s with the Savings and Loan scandals and the insider-trading of Messrs. Miliken, Bosky, et al., and so there should be something rueful and squirm-making about *How to Succeed.* But since most American musicals are merely pretexts for production numbers and pizzazz, whatever social implications they may contain are flattened by steamrollers of song and dance. Somehow, on Broadway, "mindless" is the adjective that invariably precedes "musicals"—and that seems to be the way everyone prefers it.

The moral of this Frank Loesser/Abe Burrows musical now at the Pantages and touring southern California is that studied deception wrapped in personal geniality is the most effective route to professional success, a lesson so ingrained in the American psyche that it could be taught in the schools as "Ingratiation 101." Whether taught or not, everyone learns it and its efficacy is constantly demonstrated in all walks of life. J. Pierpont Finch, a name that subtly combines the great Wall Street tycoon and a genus of bird whose "short, stout conical bill is adapted for crushing seeds," rapidly climbs up the corporate ladder with the help of one of those conniving "get-rich-quick" books that, next to steamy sex novels, slimming guides, and political romans à clef, make up the bulk of the country's reading matter.

After demonstrating the guile and trickery that corporate ambition fosters in ambitious young men and reaching the point where a failed advertising campaign is about to trigger a brutal shake-up between the chairman of the board and the company's officers, our Machiavellian hero incongruously segues into the number "The Brotherhood of Man." This gospel-like hymn tries to persuade us that, despite the vicious pecking order that sustains American business and keeps its rank-and-file fearful and wretched, there is in fact a glorious equality that unites all the dogsbodies, the virtues of which should be happily extolled. It makes perfect musical-comedy sense, even though it violates the implied logic of all that has gone before. But then, one cannot expect to have a Broadway show that actually demolishes the ethic upon which the country's wealth and stability are founded. In Germany, perhaps, with subversive writers such as Bertolt Brecht, it may be possible to equate capitalism with theft and depict captains of industry as the scheming and avaricious vultures they actually are, but in America, we must settle for good-natured spoofs and warm-hearted satires and, so long as no one examines the larvae eating away the weave behind the splendid upholstery, musicals like *How to Succeed* will prosper.

Ralph Macchio has taken over the part that Matthew Broderick made his own on Broadway, and he displays exactly the right kind of nerdish charm. It is a perfect "impersonation" without the added dimension of personal impishness that Robert Morse first brought to it. Shauna Hicks is his predatory love interest, and her voice is perfectly suited to the broad, sweeping romanticism of Loesser's score. As the nepotistic nemesis that threatens Finch's ascendancy, Roger Bart is consistently crafty, narky, perky, and needlingly comic.

Des McAnuff's production, and particularly Wayne Cilento's Rube Goldberg–like dance numbers, full of elaborate and seemingly disconnected kinetic outbursts, drives the evening with galvanic force. The production is backed by a giant screen that alternates imagery of the corporate Mecca with subliminal flashes inspired by passing phrases in the lyrics. As certain critics have already pointed out, it resembles nothing more than a giant CD-ROM of the show, bleeping obligatory visual commentary, and curiously dwarfs and diminishes the performers. A lot of people go to the theater to avoid the mesmerizing computer monitor that dominates their working lives. To find it accompanying the refreshing purity of live action is more a technological incursion than it is proof of theatrical modernity.

Loesser's score has two towering numbers ("I Believe in You" and "The Brotherhood of Man") and a lot of attractive functional songs such as "Coffee Break" that Cilento has staged with real élan. In terms of sheer entertainment, one has to acknowledge the peerless professionalism of the evening. The only thing that niggles is the festering moral foundation upon which this splendid panoply has been erected.

The question that a show like this leaves behind is: Why should anyone with any sensitivity *want* to succeed in business at such a price? In the final scene, Finch, having maneuvered his way into the position of chairman of the board, contemplates the U.S. presidency, and there is a certain logic to the ambition. A background in capitalist chicanery, sharp practices, and corporate deceit, the show seems to suggest, provides a rich training ground for a career in politics. There are a whole caboodle of J. Pierpont Finchs running for electoral office at the moment.

★★★

One of them became president in the bitterly disputed election of 2000, which gave this show a curious kind of irony. The Burrows-Loesser musical and its accidental hero became something of a self-fulfilling prophecy.

14

ANNETTE BENING'S *HEDDA*: ONCE OVER LIGHTLY

It takes a certain amount of courage for a film celebrity to expose herself to the vagaries of stage performance. Films are washed away in a rolling sea of national reviews and ultimately judged by box office takings rather than criticism. But a theatrical performance is defined in a very particular place and by a small contingent of writers who often have a strong loyalty to one particular community. So it was a ballsy decision on Annette Bening's part to tackle one of the major roles in the modern repertoire at the Geffen Playhouse in Los Angeles.

And "ballsy" is the adjective that most readily comes to mind in her rendition of Ibsen's *Hedda Gabler.* She starts strong and self-assured and, with occasional bursts of ennui at being trapped in an airless marriage of her own making, stays that way throughout. This is a Hedda that both appropriates and wields the power that the Male World would deny her. A control-freak. Which seems an entirely appropriate tack for an actress who succeeded in roping and branding the hitherto untamable Warren Beatty.

The problem is that Hedda, apart from being dominating and manipulative, is also vulnerable, lyrical, desperate, and manic-depressive—qualities that rarely if ever intrude in Ms. Bening's performance. When this Hedda says she's bored, you feel she'd be perfectly diverted by a wild night at Spago's. But at the root of Ibsen's Hedda is a world-weariness that has cosmic rather than social dimensions. Bening is adept at portraying the social surface of this multifarious character, but when the play delves into its deeper layers, moving from the ego into the id and even beyond, it leaves her behind.

Daniel Sullivan's production is as cautious and conventional as the Tesman household in which it unfolds. It yields no dazzling insights into either theme or character and has only a kind of snappy continuity to recommend it. Its dramatic high points—for example, Loevborg weakening to take a drink of punch, which will eventually lead him to despair and suicide—are almost perfunctory; Hedda's heady triumph in reasserting her influence over her old lover, only barely implied; the idealized fantasy about a lover with "vine leaves in his hair," a mawkish intrusion from someone on whom lyricism sits uncomfortably. And when she falls into the trap Brack has set for her by revealing that he knows it was her pistol that fired the fatal shot that killed Loevborg, there is no sense of the net tightening around Hedda. Consequently, when she blows her brains out, the final suicide seems to be an act of inexplicable irrationality rather than tragic inevitability. Given the choice of explosive emotions and agonizing contradictions, Sullivan always opts for the low road.

Byron Jennings craftily avoids the pitfall of making George Tesman a blithering idiot, inferring a match that would have been more scandalizing to the socially sensitive Hedda than even a court appearance alongside Mme. Diana, the local brothel keeper. Jennings fine-tunes Tesman so that his ineffectuality is simply a lack of social aplomb, but his fastidiousness and academic integrity confer a credible respectability and make him a reasonable catch for Hedda. It is a perfectly contoured performance that redresses the imbalance of innumerable translations, from William Archer through Michael Meyer and into the present.

Paul Guilfoyle's Brack strikes a note of smarmy casualness and pipes it relentlessly throughout the evening. One looks in vain for some other dimension of the man when he is alone with Hedda. Patrick O'Connell's Loevborg, a character originally modeled on Byron, Goethe's Werther, and other nineteenth-century romantics, comes across as a journalistic hack who does a little serious writing on the side. Being almost as mundane and respectable as Tesman, one loses the contrast between the wild bohemian and the fastidious bourgeois. Carolyn McCormick plays Thea Elvstead as a wily, naturally emancipated foil to Hedda's cowardly, captive bride. It is Thea, of course, and not Hedda, who is the New Woman in *Hedda Gabler* and she should really give her bourgeois counterpart a run for her money. But although McCormick is centered and intelligent throughout, one never feels that she poses a temperamental alternative to the cautious and closeted Hedda. It is a performance, like the others, etched in monochrome, with technicolored emotions crying to get out. Everything in Sullivan's production—including Jon Robin Baitz's cautious adaptation, which opens no new ground on the play—is staid, predictable, and bloodlessly efficient.

If the Geffen were a regional rep in the hinterlands and Bening merely its local leading actress, this would be a perfectly satisfactory revival. But in a landscape already dotted with Maggie Smith's tempestuous diva, Glenda Jackson's tremulous neurotic, and dozens of outstanding European reinterpretations, one looks for more than a once-over-lightly of a richly ambiguous masterpiece.

Breaking a long-standing taboo, several film celebrities ventured on to the stage in the '90s. Stars such as Nicole Kidman, Kevin Spacey, Al Pacino, Woody Harrelson, Holly Hunter, Matthew Broderick, Glenn Close, and so forth. Sometimes the impulse was simply to return to their theatrical roots, but a lot of the time it was the magical notion that if they were ever to be considered "real actors," they had to be validated on the stage. In the past, such reversions often generated disasters, and Broadway critics, using wicked invective, liked to show motion picture celebrities that the legitimate theater was unimpressed by their star status. This changed considerably in the '90s, when a troubled theater desperately sought the economic transfusions that sometimes only stars could bring.

15

RODGERS, HAMMERSTEIN & HART: *THE KING AND I*

When Lorenz Hart died in 1943, Richard Rodgers transformed from a sharp, urban composer of sophisticated musical comedies into a formidable American monument. It was a little like the creased and rounded lines of the Taj Mahal turning into the Eiffel Tower. Although his collaboration with Oscar Hammerstein II produced some outstanding early works, such as *Oklahoma!* and *Carousel,* the slide toward nauseous sentimentality had begun and would soon chuck up maudlin mementos such as *South Pacific, The Flower Drum Song,* and *The Sound of Music.*

The King and I, the current revival at the Pantages, is a monument in blancmange commemorating cuteness. Cute little Siamese wives and cute little Siamese children and cute little Siamese settings that evoke all the tinselly glamour of an Oriental whorehouse.

The story itself, based mainly on Anna Leonowen's book *The English Governess at the Siamese Court,* could be perversely condensed as follows: An upper-middle-class English teacher, summoned to tutor the children of a Siamese emperor in Western language and customs, pollutes the rich traditions of an ancient culture with superficial notions of Christianity and democracy, subverting the king's authority, destabilizing the state, and, after humiliating him before his royal entourage and straining his weak heart with excessive dancing of the polka, ultimately brings about his death. It being a musical soap opera, it is implied, of course, that the king has secret hankerings for the British tutor, which, tacitly, are reciprocated.

The most curious aspect of the culture clash is that what most seems to get Anna's goat is the fact that the ancient hierarchical customs impose a rigid caste-system that demands slavish obsequiousness from all the king's subjects. An odd objection in the late nineteenth-century, when England itself was one of the most class-ridden societies in the world and the deference due to British royalty, although less flamboyant, was every bit as severe as that accorded the king of Siam.

In the role of the English governess (originally created by Gertrude Lawrence, who was very much closer to the right age) is Ms. Marie Osmond, who has a limpid voice that is almost entirely devoid of character. Someone ought to inform the actress that only parodic Music Hall comedians pronounce the word *know* as "ni'yoh" and that in England *romance* doesn't rhyme with *ponce* but with *pants.* Ms. Osmond wears her English accent as lightly as if it were the anchor of the *Titanic.* She looks like a piece of Dresden china and, unfortunately, acts like one as well.

As the Siamese potentate, Victor Talmadge is tough, terse, and authoritative but constantly operating under the cloud of Yul Brynner's definitive performance. A radically different approach, one that played up the king's insecurities rather than his pomposity, might have reaped greater rewards. The rest of the cast is dramatically negligible and musically undernourished, the strongest and most delineated performance coming from Helen Yu as Lady Thiang, the king's sympathetic stalwart at the palace.

As in previous revivals, the Siamese version of *Uncle Tom's Cabin,* tastefully choreographed by Jerome Robbins, is the highpoint of the evening, a hard-edged little gem amidst the soft-centered bon-bons that surround it.

The show's most durable virtue is, of course, the music and numbers like "I Whistle a Happy Tune," "Hello, Young Lovers," "Getting to Know You," and "Shall We Dance," which are unexpungeable show tunes. The problem is that these are slotted into Hammerstein's book according to the formulaic requirements of the Broadway stage: a light-hearted comedy number followed by a love song, followed by a large production number, leading to a reprise and a big finale. The building blocks of the musical are more apparent than the dry-walling, plaster, and decoration intended to cover them. And throughout, we can feel our emotions being directed from one place to another as if by a bumptious tour guide who refuses to allow his sightseers to have any sensations other than those prescribed by the itinerary.

The Rodgers and Hart collaborations were far more primitive, far less polished, and cruder in every respect, but I'd sooner rollick through *Pal Joey, A Connecticut Yankee,* or *The Boys from Syracuse* any day—just for the sheer pleasure of their buoyancy and spontaneity. Shows like *The King and I* inhabit that portentous realm that is adjacent to operetta and a long bus ride away from Song-and-Dance shows. Although they are more stately and have more dignity than the genre from which they evolved, I mourn the absence of the boisterousness, frivolity, and high spirits that informed many of their predecessors.

★★★

16

PEARLS, PIGS, AND PLATITUDES: FOREMAN ON THE CUTTING EDGE

by Richard Foreman

The arrival of Richard Foreman's *Pearls for Pigs* for a one-night stand at UCLA's Freud Playhouse in Los Angeles was a kind of summons to West Coast trendoids to come out en masse in order to drink at the fountain of East Coast postmodernism. Californians tend to have a somewhat inflated image of up-market, performance-art pieces that emanate from New York. Reverse traffic, from West to East, is usually marked by a kind of wary anticipation that California airheads have, once again, mistaken the Emperor's new clothes for the cat's pajamas, but artifacts originating in the East invariably engender a wide-eyed idolatry. Traced down to its deepest roots, this stems from a long-standing (and perhaps justified) inferiority complex in regard to the performing arts.

Mr. Foreman's latest exercise in studied avant-gardism concerns the agonies of a desperate actor, the "Maestro" who, "disillusioned with the artifice of the theater" launches a number of assaults against a variety of collaborators—including his therapist, his fellow actors, and his public. During the course of his peregrinations, he impugns the egotism of artists, appeals for aid from his audience, and finally offers himself for a beheading, which, like everything else that occurs on stage, is simply another theatrical sleight of hand. Trying to reconcile the irreconcilabilities of reality and illusion, the Maestro tries to destroy the theatrical context in which he feels himself imprisoned. In a final sacrificial act, he glimpses a heroic vision, but it comes too late to reconcile him to his odious profession and he hurls himself into the chaos that has tormented him from the very outset.

In the program note, Foreman concedes that "there is no story in the normal sense" and then devotes twelve paragraphs to a synopsis of the play's events. No, it isn't a "normal" story—that's to say, linear, naturalistic, conventionally structured, or containing the classical ingredients of suspense, development, and revelation, but it isn't all that far removed from the nonlinear works of Pablo Picasso, e. e. cummings, Oskar Kokoschka, or the work of Mabou Mines, the early Grotowsky, or the Living Theater.

Although it projects no conventional narrative, Foreman insists "there is definitely a SITUATION [his caps]." This is unquestionably true and the "situation" in question is the turn-of-the-century modernist movement, which concerned itself with old saws such as reality versus illusion and forays into surrealism and expressionism rather than mickey-mousing naturalism and well-made plays. Conscious of his illustrious antecedents, Foreman realizes that his play "echoes themes of Pirandello and or Artaud." He could just as readily have added Alfred Jarry, Kurt Schwitters, F. T. Marinetti, Samuel Beckett, Eugene Ionesco, Jean Genet, the early Edward Albee, and other artists fired in the crucible of twentieth-century modernism.

What Foreman doesn't seem to realize is that this is moribund if not defunct subject matter, more applicable to theater-historians than to the immediate concerns of contemporary audiences. Almost all of Foreman's works are nostalgia-jags back to the bohemian '20s or the swinging '60s. So impressed is he with the avant-garde masters of old that it is sufficient for him merely to refloat their issues and recycle their styles. Even the costumes, with their whorled headdresses, are reminiscently Jarryesque—just as the informing spirit of *Pearls for Pigs* owes an obvious debt to the structured anarchy of *Ubu Roi* and other works in Jarry's Ubu Cycle.

In defining his shortcomings, let us not belittle his talents. Foreman has rich visual gifts—especially in his scenic frameworks—but in *Pearls for Pigs,* even these begin to look studied and archival. Though his staging has a certain impish playfulness, his language is the prolix abstractionism one associates with academia in its driest and dustiest state. Not "dialogue" in any fresh, spirited, or theatrical sense but the kind of hollow concepts and portentous epigrams one gets from professors who have spent too long in the library and not long enough at the proms.

In work of this kind, conventional assessments of "performances" mean very little, as virtually everyone on stage operates as a Foremanesque chess piece, leaping, bounding, and cavorting according to the director's calculated strategy. But Tom Nellis, who plays the Doctor, dressed in a snorkel and fully rigged-out wet-suit, exudes the strongest stage presence. David Patrick Kelly, as the Maestro, shuttles between casualness and mania but, unfortunately, is weighed down with the bulk of Foreman's ponderous text. The visual context, as always with Foreman, is mesmerizingly idiosyncratic. Would that the actions were likewise.

The disillusionment with theatrical artifice that informs the piece may well be a gesture of Foreman's own dawning realization that he has been spending a lot of time elaborately decorating a cul-de-sac; the exasperation of the Maestro with actor egotism and audience complacency, a burgeoning awareness that certain kinds of performance art, fetching as they may be to the cognoscenti, cut no ice with Mr. Joe Average, who remains hooked on identification, verisimilitude, and up-market soap opera.

The virtue of nonlinear, discontinuous performance art lies in the creative juxtaposition of its component parts. When startling contrasts bombard the mind with fresh and provocative combinations, the work theatrically justifies itself no matter how inexplicit its content. But Foreman's style has become uniform. It consists of clusters of developing situations punctuated by sudden stings of light and sound, the whole enveloped in a kind of kinetic whimsy and embossed with unreverberant philosophical commentary. Its oddity gives it a certain fascination compared to many of the contemporary plays on and off Broadway, but it lacks the aesthetic resonance that makes people feel they are being treated to the insights of a first-class mind exploring pertinent subject matter.

What I suppose I am saying, prolixly and with too pronounced a disdain, is that Foreman is simply reassembling the building blocks of the twentieth-century avant garde, and the best way of defining the difference between "resonant" and "unvibratory" art is to compare his work with the homogeneous constructs of Robert Wilson, Tadeus Kantor, Martha Stewart, and Meredith Monk.

"Linear narrative development in the theater," says Foreman, "always ends with a denouement, which delivers a 'meaning'—i.e., moral. This kind of narrative, this kind of logically arrived at 'moral' conclusion is in fact a way of reinforcing the spectators' behavioral conditioning." Unless of course, it does the opposite—that is, reveals the nature of that conditioning and causes them to "see through" the mists of banality and consoling layers of moral reassurance. Unless, that is, one is dealing with the best of Brecht, of Wedekind, of Beckett, of—dare I say it—Miller and Williams, Albee and Mamet. It is not linear development per se that is the villain, but circular thought, which is so often at the root of deadly theater.

It is not, as Foreman implies, that the world is in the grip of meaninglessness but that social, cultural, and political forces have blurred the issues by imposing their own meanings on states and conditions that intrinsically contradict them. The real job of forward-looking theater is to "un-brainwash" the audience; to scrub away the accumulation of gook that has coagulated on institutions, values, and human conduct. Rather than insist that nothing can prevent the involuntary copulation of reality and illusion, theater should pull apart the sweating "beast with two backs" and insist on distinguishing one from the other. Rather than bellyache about the meaninglessness of life, it should be trying to make things "mean" again.

17

"HYDE" AND CHIC: *JEKYLL & HYDE*

Several years ago, in an off-Broadway theater in New York, I saw a musical version of the Rod Steiger film *No Way to Treat a Lady.* Its awfulness was rooted in the fact that the material, the exploits of a schizoid serial killer given to elaborate disguises, simply did not lend itself to musical treatment.

It struck me then that there was a kind of musical susceptibility in certain kinds of material that either lent itself to the form or not; stories that, in a sense, "allowed" themselves to be sung, and others that did not. *Phantom of the Opera* certainly did, and curiously enough, because of its larger-than-life dimensions, so did *Sunset Boulevard* and so, I believe, will *Trilby,* which is now in preparation. *Les Miserables,* for my money, never did—nor did obvious miscalculations such as *Nick and Nora* and *The Red Shoes.* There has to be a natural tendency in narrative material that enables it to convert into a musical form and thereby realize some hidden potential it always possessed. I don't believe Robert Louis Stevenson's novella *The Strange Case of Dr. Jekyll and Mr. Hyde* has that potentiality, and, for me, all its problems stem from that belief.

Stevenson's thriller about the indigenous components of good and evil that paradoxically co-exist in the same human being (but wouldn't it be interesting if they could be separated?) was one of the many specimens of doppleganger literature that came out of the late nineteenth century. The genre was brilliantly enlarged by writers as various as Oscar Wilde and Hugo Von Hofmannsthal and became a staple of Otto Rank's psychoanalytic theories in the '20s and '30s. The whole notion of schizophrenia owes much to this branch of literature, and without it, we would never have pop idols such as the Wolf Man, Superman, Batman, Captain Marvel, and Zorro—all characters that, though they don't shuttle between good and evil, still mediate between one persona and another. Character duality is one of the more deeply rooted contemporary fantasies, but is it material for the musical stage?

The character of Frank Wildhorn's score is, I suppose, what you would call middle-of-the-road pop. Three of its songs were performed at the Miss

America Pageant and others have been used in the ice skating competitions of two Winter Olympics. Somehow they seem much more suited for those kinds of outlets than the musical stage. The score is constantly trying to outdo itself. Almost every number surges to a magnificent climax that neither its musicality nor the curve of the narrative can justify. Ironically, when it's all done, no one number is particularly memorable. One remembers only the strenuous desire to impress.

Nevertheless, the show has some positive virtues and striking assets, Linda Eder, who plays Jekyll's underworld hoyden, being the "most" striking. When Ms. Eder's voice is in full flow, it could propel a three-masted schooner through the Straits of Gibraltar. It is, in many ways, a magnificent voice, and it is constantly being used "magnificently" but not always on material that justifies its magnificence. Robert Cuccioli, who played Javert in the New York company of *Les Miserables,* is likewise a formidable double-threat performer. Director Gregory Boyd has seamlessly fused together all of these elements and given the show a strong, throttling pace. Externally and in terms of its sweep and clout, *Jekyll and Hyde* fulfills its scenic, and much of its dramatic, ambitions. Stevenson's tale is roaring Grand Guignol and, as such, played with great verve and panache. The nagging question for me is: Can you musicalize Grand Guignol—and if you can, can you do it using a pop idiom that goes right against the grain of the original material? Curiously enough, this was the same question that arose in my mind when Stephen Sondheim tried to Brechtify that other penny dreadful, *Sweeny Todd.*

Jekyll and Hyde's transformation, from its first faltering steps in 1979 to the full-scale jumbo-size musical that recently played the Orange County Performing Arts Center and is scheduled to open on Broadway in April of '96, has been almost as strenuous as Jekyll's own transformation from respectable Harley Street doctor to heavy-breathing ogre. In the course of a decade or so, it acquired a new book and lyrics, several interim producers, and a variety of new directors, the most fructifying being Gregory Boyd, artistic director of Houston's Alley Theatre, where it was reinvented about five years ago. The current budget hovers around $2.1 million. Anything that has gone through so many permutations (and has had so much time and money spent on it) must intimidate the juggernaut of criticism. It is just too blithe, after all that, for reviewers to say: "Yes well, no thanks, better luck next time." Also, whatever one's reservations, it would be evasive not to recognize that this show, particularly in its latest rescension, has pleased a vast number of people in many cities throughout the country and played to record-breaking business at the Alley and elsewhere.

I mention all this because it seems to me there usually is not, but ought to be, some kind of meeting ground between public taste and critical discrimination. It is a widely held view—certainly among the general public—that there is a great disparity between critics' assessments of theatrical work and the reactions of most average spectators. We all know that, ultimately, it is the public that decides these issues and not the critics. Otherwise, there would never have been an Andrew Lloyd Webber.

But I have to confess to a nagging suspicion that something may be badly amiss when critics go one way and the public another, and although one recognizes that public approval and critical evaluation are essentially two different planets, they still belong to the same solar system and should be able to be observed through the same telescope. Of course, in the theater they almost never are.

There is one part of me that feels: No matter what aesthetic objections a critic may raise against an artifact, if it confers pleasure to others, it should run and prosper. Whereas the other, more fascist part of my nature feels that flawed artistic vessels should be torpedoed out of the water or, at the very least, run aground.

An unbridgeable gulf often separates connoisseur opinion from public taste, and in that gulf you will find as many bloated corpses of critics as you will productions. And one can never truly judge whether it was the former that killed the latter or vice versa.

★★★

Jekyll and Hyde, *re-coiffed, re-plastered, cosmetically altered, with new material and a new director, finally made it to Broadway in April 1997 and played for a respectable 1,543 performances. It never quite reconciled itself with the critics, but the tug of the Stevenson story and some eye-gouging theatrical effects mustered enough public to justify all the labor pains. It closed on January 7, 2001. It never made back its investment.*

★★★

18

COWARD'S COURAGE: *DESIGN FOR LIVING*

by Noel Coward

The year was 1933. The opening was in New York. The play followed the peregrinations of three characters—two men both enamored of the same woman. In the first act, she threw over the first man to live with the second and in the second act, she threw over the second man to return to the first. In the third act, with the woman having entered into a marriage of convenience with someone else, the three decided that the most sensible course of action was for all of them to live together.

The two men, apart from their passion for the woman, seemed to share a passion for each other as well. The woman, recognizing this, was not unduly bothered. The three-petaled daisy chain seemed to suit them all, and the clear inference was that there was no serious reason that bisexuality, heterosexuality, and homosexuality could not happily coexist within the same menage so long as the exponents of each of those sexual preferences were prepared to shut their ears to the braying strictures of conventional society.

In New York, one of the men's roles was played by Noel Coward, a homosexual; the other by Alfred Lunt, a bisexual; and the woman by his wife, Lynn Fontanne, whose precise sexual orientation was never conclusively established. The play, *Design for Living,* was written in eight days on a ten-day cruise. A Noise Within, one of the most adventurous companies in California, has just revived the play in a sprightly production by Sabin Epstein.

Given the year of its opening (it was actually written in 1932) and the society into which it was introduced (a Depression-wrack't New York, as Coward wished to avoid the Lord Chamberlain's certain censorship in London), its subversion of both British and American mores makes it a pretty remarkable little piece. Without bothering to apply any special camouflage, it broaches a number of scandalous suggestions: (1) that exclusive love between one man and one woman is a shortsighted recipe for connubial bliss; (2) that if temperaments coalesce, there is no good reason that three persons of different sexes and varying sexual persuasions cannot live happily together; and (3) that by sharing a flighty and somewhat cynical view of the world, it is possible for persons of a certain temperament to opt out of conventional relationships and pursue an entirely different lifestyle that, antithetical to the majority, is perfectly suitable for themselves.

In the 1960s or the 1990s, no eyebrows would be arched at any of these propositions, but in the early '30s, when British society was sclerotically respectable and American society still largely philistine, it represents a degree of subversion that slightly staggers the imagination. Plays like *Waiting for Lefty* and *Johnnie Johnson,* which are often thought of as socially pungent and even "revolutionary," cannot hold a Molotov cocktail to Mr. Coward's mix of steaming heterodoxy. In 1933, Coward's "design" for living was like a Picasso canvas inexplicably smuggled into a Norman Rockwell exhibition.

But, of course, it wasn't because Coward was a social reformer or a propagandizing moralist. He was simply pushing his own preferences and insinuating his own agenda. I find it significant that he wrote the play during a ten-day journey to San Francisco on a Norwegian freighter teeming with Nordic revelers and awash in booze. Being on the high seas, not chained to the culture of one country or another, and experiencing that drifting sense of limbo that sea journeys induce, Coward felt freer than he ever could either in London or New York. "Those raucous evenings," he recalled, "were sufficiently charged with maritime romanticism to remain forever in my memory. One of the crew members, a strapping bearded young Viking clad in the briefest pair of shorts I have ever seen, not only played a guitar but actually wore a single gold earring." One can easily imagine an atmosphere like that instigating radical reassessments of "the good life" and drawing Coward to the conclusion that there was a painful dichotomy between the way most people lived their lives and the way they really wanted to.

The comedy glitters with self-referential one-liners about playwrights and the press, many of them ricocheting off Coward's own relations with the critics. Leo, poring over the morning reviews of his play, which opened the night before, reads to Gilda: "*Change and Decay* is gripping throughout. The characterization falters here and there, but the dialogue is polished and sustains a high level from first to last and is frequently witty, nay even brilliant." To which Gilda, succinctly nailing the critical pretension, replies: "I love 'Nay,'" But the review concludes that the play "on the whole is decidedly thin." Which, of course, was the bone-cruncher used on most of Coward's comedies. As Robert Benchley pointed out in his *New Yorker* review: "He forgot "brittle"—the other adjective regularly employed to damp down whatever praise Coward managed to wring out of his critics. Clearly, the play was scrounged out of the guts of he who, for many, was considered the most gutless playwright of the '30s.

What gives *Design for Living* its edge, sixty-four years after it first appeared, is that subversive undercurrent that ripples beneath its "brittle" comedy, an undercurrent suggesting that social decorum is really a kind of solitary confinement that, for the sake of appearances, forces us to relinquish our most passionate urges. To view it as John Lahr did, as "Coward's comic revenge" and "the victory of the disguised gay world over the straight one," goes bluntly against the facts of the play. Otto and Leo, the lissome bohemians, do not forsake Gilda for one another; they incorporate her into their menage—just as Noel himself appropriated larky, camp women such as Gertrude Lawrence and Lynn Fontanne into his own male circle. The real moral of Coward's play is the epitome of Wilde's observation that "In marriage, three is company and two is none."

19

CHRISTOPHER PLUMMER'S *BARRYMORE*: THE GREAT PROFILE IN CARICATURE

John Barrymore's career can be divided into four parts: a reigning, matinee idol in the silent era, America's most conspicuous classical actor in the '20s, a somewhat medium-sized Hollywood star in the '30s, and, in the final days, a crapulous has-been whose main stock in trade was mocking the great artist he had once been. It is this final phase that playwright William Luce and star Christopher Plummer have taken as the basis of their One-and-a-Half-Man Show, *Barrymore,* now at the Ahmanson Theatre. (I say One-and-a-Half advisedly, as Barrymore's foil throughout the evening is his devoted off-stage prompter, played winningly by John Plumpis.)

This is the second Barrymore outing in two years. In March of 1996, Nicol Williamson tried to compress the entire biography of the great actor into Leslie Megahy's *Jack: A Night on the Town with John Barrymore.* It was presented to the audience as a slightly boozy confessional by an actor who, having just been canned, proceeded to narrate his life as if to a collection of captive bar-flies. Megahy's script touched all the bases but never made it successfully around the plate. The facts of Barrymore's checkered life and career were consistently interesting, but they were like stray leaves torn out of a scrapbook rather than episodes in a progressive biography.

In William Luce's play, the details of Barrymore's life are even less pertinent. The object here is to evoke the crumbling actor a month before his final demise, when his self-effacing humor was at its richest and the man himself in the final throes of delirium tremens. Plummer, ably abetted by Luce's gag-riddled script, is thoroughly captivating in this stand-up comedy, judiciously sprinkled with deflationary anecdotes and obscene limericks. Occasionally, he grips us with a pang of anguish or a painful reminder of a vanished glory, but most of the time he is amusing us with Barrymore's self-denigration and inability to retain lines. Then, when we least expect it, he impales us with an excerpt from *Hamlet* or *Richard III,* and we are forcibly reminded that this "clown prince" with the self-mocking laugh and weakness for booze was once a marvel and the toast of two continents, and we are duly sobered.

The play never builds to any clear-cut resolution but merely dribbles to a close. No attempt is made to sum up Barrymore—either the quirks of his personality or the vicissitudes of his life and career. It is simply an evocation of a fading actor cocking his snook at the world and regaling us with his outlandish personality.

Williamson attempted a rounded portrait, but Plummer, who covers less territory, actually achieves more. He captures the reckless exuberance that inspired some of the actor's more madcap escapades. (Irritated by obstreperous bronchial attacks from several members of his audience, Barrymore, during an intermission, once secreted a batch of sea bass into the theater and, when the coughing broke out again, flung the fish at the audience, crying: "Busy yourselves with that, you damned walruses!") In Barrymore's case, anecdotes that appear to be apocryphal are usually traced back to actual events.

In the earlier show, one tended to read Barrymore's character through the prism of Williamson's personality, but Plummer, in his bearing and vocal mannerisms, actually conjures up all the eccentricities of Mad Jack himself. It is an evening of superficial delights, which is perhaps why the show has been strewn with honors, including a Tony, a Drama Desk Award Outer Critics' Circle Award, and so on. Luce's play doesn't try to come to terms with the paradoxes and contradictions of the man who, in the '20s, was arguably America's finest classical actor, but concentrates rather on the ebullient and endearing aspects of his public persona. Given the choice of an in-depth portrait or an amusing caricature, most American audiences usually opt for the latter.

Barrymore's inconsistency was his most consistent trait. He could follow an astonishing performance, in which he appeared to be draped in the mantle of Edwin Booth, with some of the most grotesque histrionics ever perpetrated on a stage. As Luce makes clear, he, his brother Lionel, and sister Ethel simply inherited the family business—just as Booth and his brothers did from their barnstorming dad, Junius Brutus. It was all flashes and filigree until Barrymore scored a success with *Richard III*. After that, and for a very brief period of time, he worked diligently to become the classical actor most American critics believed he already was. But an innate laziness, compounded with drink and a weakness for hell-raising, wore him down and eventually out. The broken-down farceur who rolled his consonants and snorted superciliously on the Rudy Vallee radio show in the '40s was a brilliant self-parody of the great actor

Barrymore actually was for a decade or so—and could have been until his death if he hadn't been abandoned by the very gods who once counted him as one of their own.

★★★

The fascination with Barrymore, more than a half-century dead, never abated. Apart from the Nicol Williamson One Man Show *that preceded Plummer's, there were retrospectives, documentaries, films àclef, and biographies* *(see review on page 158).*

20

MAKE BELIEVE: *AH WILDERNESS*

by Eugene O'Neill

The great gaping vacuum in the American theater has always been a world-class, four-square classical ensemble, a company able to put a distinctive stamp on Shakespeare, Marlowe, Jonson, Webster, and all the tough sinewy plays tossed up between the Restoration and the start of the twentieth century.

It's not been for want of trying. Stratford, Connecticut, the Guthrie in Minneapolis, the A.C.T. in San Francisco, CSC in New York, Ashland Shakespeare in Oregon, the Old Globe in San Diego, New Jersey Shakespeare—there has never been a shortage of companies grappling with the classics, but apart from brief periods at Stratford, the Guthrie, and A.C.T., nothing has ever hit the wall and stuck.

A classical theater is the toughest row to hoe, as it depends on actor continuity, long-term commitment, and a vision that transcends academic reverence or ostentatious innovation. When it works, as it did at A.C.T. under Bill Ball, the alumni of such a company fertilize all the classics into which they eventually wander. The best actors at the dreary and feckless classical revivals that occasionally appear at the Mark Taper Forum or the Old Globe tend to be A.C.T. alumni, and it is a clutch of recent graduates from San Francisco who have recently taken over an old Masonic Hall in Glendale and now give every appearance of turning into a well-sinewed company that may break the classical curse, at least as far as California is concerned.

The scope of their repertoire may seem foolhardy: *Cyrano, Major Barbara, Dolls' House, As You Like It, Ah Wilderness, Great Expectations, Tartuffe*—but if you're going to go for it, Shakespeare, Molière, Ibsen, Shaw, O'Neill, and Dickens are certainly the way to go. The Ibsen creaked a little and was conspicuously undercast in the leads, but the *Major Barbara* sparkled and was never anything less than engrossingly intelligent. The *As You Like It* was no great shakes and suffered from being conventionally rendered by a company that prosified the verse and provided no particular insights into this overestimated and overexposed comedy. (The Duke and his exiled brother Frederick were doubled by the same actor, which was a clever idea but, within the grunge of an otherwise straightforward interpretation, read like an ostrich feather stuck into a crumpled bonnet.) But *Ah Wilderness,* the company's latest offering, is lucid, well-centered, and touching in a way that you don't expect an early '30s domestic comedy to be.

The play has always been the anomaly in the O'Neill canon, the bright alter ego of *Long Day's Journey into Night,* which we know is the true story of O'Neill's wretched childhood years. In *Ah Wilderness* the mother is "mumsy," the paterfamilias tolerant and understanding. A far cry from morphine-shooting Mary and the egocentric and alcoholic James Tyrone. As O'Neill himself admitted, the play was "a sort of wishing out loud. That's the way I would have *liked* my boyhood to have been." And as an idealized image of an adolescence he never had, the playwright, for once, was able to exercise his untrammeled imagination instead of dredging up horrors from his tortured past.

But the play's real fascination is the way it captures the small-town American sensibility at the turn of the century: that period just before the nation's innocence was lost forever. The unforced camaraderie of family and relatives, neighbors, and even social adversaries depicts American types that have become almost fabled: sweet-scented refugees from *Our Town.* It limns a picture of coming of age that is miraculously devoid of the drugs, violence, mayhem, and madness that were to characterize the same society only half a century later. And yet, to the discerning eye, the calm surface of those waters is still ruffled by disturbing bubbles: Uncle Sid's unmanageable alcoholism and the stern philistinism of Aunt Lily, which condemns her to a life of solitary lovelessness. Even the budding O'Neill figure, Richard Miller, forcing his libido into poetical straitjackets in order to better control it, sends a dark murmur into the play: a young, suppressed boy trying painfully to turn a Fourth of July celebration into an act of personal independence. But the whoring is utterly innocent and the drinking, just a collegiate caper—colored tassles that conceal the chancres that we know were really there.

Here is a play by a moody pessimist pretending to a sunny bonhomie, which is as alien to his character as true comedy was to his last, best gloomy masterworks. But an uncharacteristic pose in a great artist always inspires fascination. What we wouldn't give to see a bedroom farce by T. S. Eliot or a burlesque revue by Arthur Miller.

The cast at A Noise Within is consistently low-keyed, with solid, well-modulated performances by virtually everyone and a limpid, mercifully unfussy production by Sabin Epstein. Jeffrey Alan Condon, as a fey, self-effacing, dark-seamed Uncle Sid, is a marvel of light comedy just tilted enough into orneriness to give it an unexpected edge. Neil Vipond captures the spirit of early homespun domesticity in such a way that makes *Ah Wilderness* resemble the prototype of series such as *Ozzie and Harriet* and *Leave It to Beaver.* One can just imagine what a perfect fit that role was for the jingoistic, flag-waving George M. Cohan, who first played it. When its final elegiac moments fade away and Mr. and Mrs. Miller glowingly rekindle the spark of their own early romance, we have to pinch ourselves to remember that this is the work of the man who plunged the American theater into a frenzy of guilt, neurosis, and self-flagellation.

All of which is by way of saying that A Noise Within, within a matter of a few short seasons, has managed to do what the Mark Taper Forum with all its millions has not accomplished in over thirty years: create a viable, classical ensemble steeped in good taste and emitting a seriousness of purpose that is neither musty nor pretentious. It is more than an oasis in the desert, it is a solid watering hole in a city dominated by mirages.

21

AVIGNON THEATRE FESTIVAL: 1998

Coming as it did, hard on the heels of France's dramatic victory in the World Cup, this year's Avignon Festival seemed more exhilarating than usual. The festive spirit that coursed through the streets of the town was a cross between the intoxicated joy that marked the end of World War II and the final scene of Marcel Carnè's *Children of Paradise,* where crowds of painted merry-makers swirl around the jostled figure of Jean Louis Barrault, desperately searching for a disappearing Arletty.

The choice of *Le Cid* seemed providential, and although Don Roderigue, the play's triumphant warrior, decisively routs the invading Moors that threaten Castille, the inescapable subtext for the French audience was that, yet again, a band of local heroes had soundly thumped another horde of foreign invaders, that is, cocky Brazilians. Nationalistic fervor of that magnitude rears its head in the unlikeliest of places.

Corneille's rock-hard masterpiece is a perfect example of what one might call the classical double-bind. Roderigue is obliged to kill the man who insulted his father's honor, who just happens to be the father of his own beloved Chimène. The act of vengeance duly carried out, Chimène is obliged, by the same code of honor, to seek the death of her father's killer, who happens to be the man *she* loves and to whom she is betrothed. The concept of honor runs through everyone's arteries like a rare disease of the blood—except that in the seventeenth century it was, in fact, as common as the flu. Everyone in the play is in an impossible position, and Corneille's legalistic mind squeezes every drop of ambivalence out of every stonewalling situation.

Director Declan Donnellan elucidated the play by shuffling together scenes and characters that are rigidly set apart in the original, smashing Corneille's up-tight structure and allowing for a constant circulation of ideas and plot developments. In this production, the dead are never dead. They and the living inhabit a spatial continuum unimpeded by tangible set-pieces, which simultaneously contain both past and present. Donnellan sees clearly that if there is a villain in the piece, it is the rapacious father of Roderigue, who emits Honor as if it were mustard-gas, blocking the oxygen flow for all future generations.

It would not be too great an exaggeration to say that the play, with its sadistic love of moral contradiction, foreshadows almost the whole of the French drama of the next three centuries. Donnellan's *Le Cid* was by far the best-received item in the festival and the hottest ticket.

A cantankerous old father, forcing his son to exact the vengeance he is incapable of, is the motivating factor in both *Le Cid* and Eimontas Nekrosius's Lithuanian *Hamlet,* but there the resemblance ends. Donnellan's *Le Cid* is svelte, subtle, conventionally elegant, and minutely accounted for; Nekrosius's *Hamlet* is wild, aggressive, and willfully radical.

Nekrosius, a legendary director from Vilnius, has a vast theatrical imagination, but for every good idea (for instance, the dead Polonius doubling as the Ghost in the closet scene or the duel scene played out against a rhythmic accompaniment of swishing saber strokes), there are half a dozen bizarre choices whose idiosyncrasies are fascinating until one realizes that they have no relevance beyond themselves. Andrius Mamontovas, his stridently suffering Hamlet, is a Lithuanian rock star and the faults of both his performance and the production are precisely those of bad rock: a feverish effort to dazzle, excite, and overstimulate.

Like all theater festivals, Avignon was awash with oddities (including an exuberant production of *All's Well That Ends Well* from Theatre du Soleil, directed by Peter Brook's daughter Irina). Although prestigious productions from Russia, Taiwan, Italy, and Korea provided the caviar, the solid bread and butter came from the young, bustling French zealots that made up the so-called "Festival-Off." It was their exuberance that really ignited the town and kept it flaming.

★★★

22

THE BERLINER ENSEMBLE PACKS IT IN: *THE RESISTIBLE RISE OF ARTURO UI*

by Bertolt Brecht

In January 1949, Brecht's *Mother Courage,* directed by the author and starring his wife, Helene Weigel, received a triumphal reception at the Deutsches Theatre in East Berlin. In a sense, this was the inception of the Berliner Ensemble, although the Company with Brecht as its "artistic adviser" would not be installed in its own home, the Theatre am Schiffbauerdamm, until 1954.

On the face of it, the national subsidization of Brecht's company seemed like the most obvious thing in the world. Brecht was the leading Marxist playwright in both the Eastern and Western world. He had been cold-shouldered in America, where he was considered "politically undesirable," and at fifty-six, after success in the '20s and a martyred exile during World War II, could claim to be the "grand old man of the German theater." But retaining the cunning Augsburg peasant mentality on which he always prided himself, Brecht made sure to become a naturalized citizen of Austria to ensure freedom of travel under an Austrian passport. He also put his copyrights into the hands of Peter Suhrkamp, a highly prestigious West German publisher, which assured him of Western currency and protection against East German censorship. These "protections" in place, he agreed to become the leader of a theater that boasted 60 actors and actresses, a total personnel of over 250, rehearsal periods of between 3 and 5 months, and tours to some of the most prestigious capitals in Europe.

Just as the Comedie Francaise became the House of Molière, the Berliner Ensemble was anointed as a Temple to the thought and persona of Bertolt Brecht. There is no question that from the mid-'50s to the early '70s, it was probably the most skilled acting ensemble in the world. It was the only company that formulated and practiced a style of acting contrary to the prevailing precepts of Stanislavsky and the only one in which political ideology entirely determined aesthetic goals. But too much internecine strife and too much uncritical worship of its charismatic founder eventually weakened its fiber and drowned it in the scent of mothballs. Now, after some fifty years, it is officially abandoning its primogenitor and giving itself over to a varied repertoire, in which Brecht will be only one of several authors represented.

It is hard not to view the decline of Brecht and his company as part of the dissolution of the Soviet Union and all the communist regimes of East Europe that fell in its wake. When almost the whole of your oeuvre is predicated on the precepts of Karl Marx and that credo lies in ruins along with those toppled statues of Lenin, it is hard to believe the works themselves have not lost something essential. No doubt plays such as *Threepenny Opera, Good Woman of Setzuan, Caucasian Chalk Circle,* and *Galileo* will survive the ideological blight, but much of the openly propagandist pieces will unquestionably corrode; they began to do so, in fact, long before the advent of Gorbachov. The genius of Brecht was always intrinsically poetic and its natural style, Expressionism. But being in the hire of apparatchiks for seven years and under the sway of communist ideology for twenty years before that was not the most fertile ground for his talent.

As the "old" Berliner Ensemble's "swan song," the company has brought to the Freud Theater at UCLA one of its snazziest productions: Heiner Müller's *The Resistible Rise of Arturo Ui,* the centerpiece of which is Martin Wuttke's dazzling performance as *"Der Führer as Schauspieler."*

Arturo Ui is a great stewpot of a play that combines the myths of Al Capone, Sigfried, Richard III, Goethe's Erl-King, and Adolf Hitler. A fanged political satire, it is also an allegory on how gullible nations are conned into totalitarian subjugation. In demonstrating the conscious techniques employed by the dictator to win over the German people, it is an object lesson in how politicians, using the right mix of media-savvy and theatrical gimmicry, can manufacture charisma—precisely the way great actors do—and how charisma itself can become the mesmerizing force that leads to social oppression and dehumanizing behavior. The play depicts the rise of National Socialism, with highly accurate historical parallels, as a kind of Mafia fable, the sort of stark, violent gangster movie that Francis Ford Coppola might have made had he been working in the 1930s. And more pertinently, it dramatizes the affinity between crime, capitalism, and fascism, making the sobering point that gangsters are merely frustrated capitalists who, being barred from wealth for sociological reasons, simply break the rules in order to get their rightful share.

Heiner Müller's production is stark, bold, and effusively Expressionist, in the very best tradition of the German theater and, thankfully, innovative rather than obsequious of Brecht. Every beat is just about 25 percent too long, and the irrepressible cartoon energy released by Wuttke's Ui favors farce to the detriment of political pertinence. Eckerhard Schall's Ui in the '60s, of which Wuttke's is a more fantastical extension, was maniacal within a plausible social context. Wuttke's Ui brilliantly bursts through the play's political framework. When, in the final scene, the Barker sums the play up for the audience and draws our attention to the moral behind its facade, we have been so blinded by its brightness, we are immune to its darker implications.

But Wuttke is a brilliant comedian and Ui is a role *for* a brilliant comedian. It may well be that almost sixty years after the horrors of National Socialism have been analyzed into the ground, a riff on Brecht's political "gangster show" is the only way to keep its elements alive. But what a perverse legacy it would be if the only way we could stomach Brecht in the future is by remorselessly sending him up.

★★★

The demise of the Berliner Ensemble in 1999 as a theater devoted exclusively to Brecht was a profound shock to those of us who had been brought up idolizing the work of the Company. Politics notwithstanding, it had been an artistic triumph for some forty-five years, and the idea of dismantling its beautifully coordinated aesthetic machinery was somehow unthinkable, as was a Berliner Ensemble with Brecht relegated to being simply one of its several playwrights. The only bright spot was that now the Brechtian oeuvre, freed from its doctrinaire disciples, might branch out into new and invigorating directions.

23

DEFEND US: *MONSTERS OF GRACE*

by Philip Glass and Robert Wilson

As you entered UCLA's splendidly refurbished Royce Hall, you were handed a pair of special polarized lenses with which to view *Monsters of Grace,* the first major collaboration between Philip Glass and Robert Wilson since their groundbreaking *Einstein on the Beach* in 1976.

Within moments, the entire audience had clamped these white cardboard glasses over their ears and this highly touted, postmodernist premiere felt like a throwback to the '50s, when 3-D movies were all the rage and moviegoers sat in a myopic trance, thinking they could just reach out and touch objects that, in fact, were hundreds of feet away.

The piece is described as "a digital opera in three dimensions," and Glass and Wilson have tapped the talents of high-tech special effects specialists, a 70mm stereoscopic film format, and computer-generated characters referred to as *Synthespians*—presumably "synthetic actors" (which, given the nature of most performers, is not in itself a major innovation). Although based on the thirteenth-century poetry of Jalaluddin Rumi, the Turkish poet and mystic who is thought to have been the original whirling dervish, the piece is more a testament to art's helpless seduction by technology.

Rumi's poetry deals with both human and divine love, but there is no attempt on the part of the collaborators to illustrate the root material. Glass, using contrapuntal rhythms and pizzicato stringed instruments, plucks away beneath eerily extended woodwind chords to create a kind of tonal wash that lulls you and needles you at the same time. Wilson, using computerized imagery interspersed with live action, creates brooding images of landscapes, craggy mountains, ethereal birds, helicopters, and Magritte-like human figures that move from deep focus right up to the tip of your nose.

In traditional Wilsonian fashion, the dancers don't dance and the actors don't act. Most of the "action" of the piece (the word is very much a misnomer here) consists of funereal perambulations across a vast stage. In one of the more graphic moments, a lady in white crosses from left to right, the train of her dress extending over forty feet. There are other striking images. A six-year-old boy entering an illuminated rectangle and being hoisted into the flys; the rear view of male and female figures as if glimpsed through a stereopticon slide, blending from four into two. Simple parlor prestidigitations writ large.

The thirteen tableaus have no literal meaning but are not intrinsically meaningless. There are enough texture and resonance in each of them to seduce the senses and trigger subjective interpretations. If you're prone to dive into your own imaginative scenarios, you can use the Glass-Wilson material as a series of handy diving boards.

The Royce Hall audience dutifully, but tentatively, applauded the conclusion of each scene, not very certain as to how one should respond to a largely incomprehensible "digital opera," and the entire evening was subdued by a kind of intellectual intimidation. As if to say: I'm not too sure what all this is about, but I'll be damned if I let on in the midst of this illustrious, artistic gathering. The fact is, the Glass-Wilson performance deliberately abandons literal meaning and so throws spectators onto their own appreciation of mood, imagery, and concrete poetry. For those to whom that appears to be an abdication of the theater's role to illuminate, delight, and instruct, the Glass-Wilson collaboration will be a great basket full of plastic fruit. But for others who believe that art need not be either literal or conventionally structured, the evening will provide a certain number of *frissons.*

A lot of care, attention, and technological ingenuity has been employed to allow Wilson to use the stage to paint pictures, and, fetching as many of them are, one wishes he had resorted to canvas or drawing-boards instead. Glass's music is powerfully saturated in the thirteenth-century texts of human and divine love, but being dominated by stereoscopic imagery and mutating stage tableaus, it sometimes feels as if a serious avant-garde concert and a '60s-styled multimedia event have been accidentally booked into the same hall.

In trying to widen the parameters of theatrical expression and leap into the rosy-colored prospects of the next millennium, many artists feel that to be modern they have to incorporate the startling new inventions of the cyber age. But the much-touted Information Highway seems to me to prize facts over wisdom and data above philosophy. I've always felt the only information worth knowing is the inspirational fruits of one's own imagination and that the mysteries of man's inner space are far more tantalizing than any asteroid or meteorite detected in the astronomer's telescope. And as for Virtual Reality, I'm far too preoccupied trying to sort out the real thing to be bothered with simulated substitutes.

More an exhibit than a performance, *Monsters'* considerable and very costly effort is intended to give us a taste of what the twenty-first-century theater holds in store, and if so, I for one, tremble at the prospect. To paraphrase Lincoln Steffens after his first visit to Russia: "I have seen the future and it doesn't work."

★★★

I feel an apologia is required for this notice, for, unimpressed as I was with the Glass-Wilson MTV extravaganza, I believe the mixture of multimedia and Performance Art is very much the wave of the future and one that has already begun to crash onto our shores. It is the age-old problem: how to exercise freedom and still maintain form; how to widen the vocabulary of theatrical expression using audio-visual inventions and still relate these innovations to something verifiable in our inner selves. The Dadaists simply shattered all the forms; the Surrealists tried to weave new dissonances into the old melodies; contemporary Performance Artists, heavily influenced by all the experiments of the last century, are trying to create a new diction to address social and psychological issues that resist the pat formulae of Realism. It is, in a sense, the most important quest in contemporary theater, and I always feel narky and ungrateful when I find myself recoiling from one of its efforts as I did here.

24

"SHOWBOAT" FOR THE '90S

The age of the hands-on producer may well have ended with the death of Florenz Ziegfeld in 1932. Since then, producers have thrown their weight around, interfered with directors, complained about "problems in the second act," and asserted their casting preferences, but few have gotten down and dirty with the material they were producing. When he finally agreed to do *Showboat,* largely on the strength of Jerome Kern's score, Ziegfeld voiced strong reservations about Oscar Hammerstein's book, which he felt was too sprawling and overserious. After its trial run in Washington (which ran four hours and fifteen minutes), he personally cut it down for the New York opening. Eighteen hours before the curtain went up, Ziegfeld made additional cuts, switched scenes, and entirely recast the last act. It was he who brought the twenty-six-year-old Helen Morgan in to play the role of Julie, and he was also responsible for the casting of Charles Winninger as Cap'n Andy and Edna May Oliver as Parthy. Of course, Edna Ferber's novel and Jerome Kern's score were the backbone of the show, but almost all of its individual vertebrae were put into place by Ziegfeld.

The current revival now at the Ahmanson, despite certain upgrades, is essentially the show that opened in New York in 1927. It has been supremely streamlined by Harold Prince and masterfully designed by Eugene Lee. Its mise-en-scène is smoother than it has ever been before, and Prince's revisionism at the beginning of the second act (the celebration of Ravenal and Magnolia's child) integrates material that certainly strengthens the narrative. But his artistic pride in furthering the plot line without bringing in "irrelevancies" (which Prince believes is part of a stodgy old-fashioned Broadway tradition) is misplaced—especially in the examples he cites—viz. "Too Darn Hot" in *Kiss Me Kate* and "Steam Heat" in *The Pajama Game.* "Until the '60s," explains Prince, "you opened every second act with something trivial and irrelevant." That may well have been the reasoning behind act-two openers, but there was nothing "irrelevant" about Bob Fosse's choreography of "Steam Heat" as danced by Carol Haney or Cole Porter's "Too Darn Hot," which was one of the stand-out moments in *Kiss Me Kate.* Numbers like these are like those epigrammatic embellishments one encounters in *The Importance of Being Earnest:* wholly irrelevant but utterly captivating. Some of the best moments in musicals, from Gilbert & Sullivan onward, are those in which some "irrelevant" but captivating number diverts us from the plot and provides a delicious diversion to the remorseless grind of the narrative. It was Emerson who said, "Inconsistency is the hobgoblin of little minds." In theatrical terms, it is often in the sideturnings and detours where the real treasure is to be found.

The profound pleasure of *Showboat,* Princely improvements to one side, is the *old-fashionedness* of the America being depicted. Old-fashioned mummers essaying old-fashioned melodramas; Mississippi gamblers, tough on the outside but soft at the center; hen-pecked husbands; grumpy wives; docile "darkies" providing an obtrusive background "while the white folk play"; and a score that has become as memorialized as *HMS Pinafore* or the songs of Stephen Foster. Anyone who carps at the implied racism of a story that, historically speaking, was still bound by the legacies of slavery, is as off the beam as those pro-Semites who believe that the assumption of a Yiddish accent in a comedy sketch is in some way giving aid and comfort to the enemies of Israel. If anything, the blacks come out of *Showboat* with greater dignity than the whites. While aspiring actors, pressured producers, and devious gamblers hustle to make ends meet, old Joe and the other Mississippi laborers just stand on the sidelines and, intoning Kern's elegiac melody, philosophically accept the ebb and flow of life without getting in its way: a kind of Buddhist transcendence that neither Magnolia nor Ravenal, Julie nor Steve are capable of achieving.

Ned Beatty's Cap'n Andy is all bluff and bluster, constantly shuttling between assertiveness and intimidation, endlessly good-hearted, and funnier than I have ever seen him. Cloris Leachman, employing a subtlety one rarely finds in supporting characters, turns Parthy into a miniature comic masterpiece. Never before has an actress done so much with so little. Kevin Gray lacks body as Gaylord Ravenal, although the pipes are in perfect working order. But there is somehow less poignancy in a younger Ravenal luring away a young Magnolia. Falling for an older man would have plunged the young girl into a greater disillusionment. Teri Hansen as Magnolia subtly handles the transformation from ingenue into character-lady—that is, from starry-eyed teenager into star-cross't lover. Susan Strohman's choreography grows naturally out of the unfolding story and dazzles without ever being ostentatious. In "Kim's Charleston," just before the act two finale, she lets out the stops and pushes the evening breathlessly over the top.

Showboat and Harold Prince make a perfect fit. The material, simplistic and sentimental, is essentially undemanding. You don't have to conceptualize *Showboat,* all you have to do is stage it, and Prince, the greatest stage manager in America, always performs best when his intellect is not taxed.

But when all is said and done, it is not Ferber or Ziegfeld or Prince that one comes out adoring, but Jerome Kern. It is an almost peerless score and, in this orchestral arrangement, supplemented by snatches of other Kern melodies such as "I Might Fall Back on You" and "How'd You Like to Spoon with Me?" One is reminded that when a journalist asked Kern what was Irving Berlin's place in American music, the composer answered: "He has no place; he *'is'* American music." This was really a burst of false modesty for, taking into account shows such as *Leave It to Jane; Very Good Eddie; Oh, Boy;* and *Sunny,*—as well as a staggering number of ineluctable standards for other occasions, Kern, if anything, stands shoulder to shoulder with Berlin in musical accomplishment. (Berlin, at his most inspired, never matched the Schubertian grandeur of "All the Things You Are.") So the abiding pleasure of *Showboat* is being reminded of music that has been so popular for so long, it has transcended Broadway and become part of Americana.

25

COUNTING THE HOUSE: *ARMS AND THE MAN*

by George Bernard Shaw

More and more, I have become aware that the social milieu of a performance is as great a conditioning factor as the performance itself. Seeing a play with a staid, middle-aged audience whose emotional threshold is low and whose dramatic expectations are even lower creates an ambience in which orderliness and conventionality predominate. Very different from watching a play in a freaky venue surrounded by unorthodox spectators dressed in oddball clothes and itching for novelty and provocation.

Although the circle that supported the avant-garde theater in Paris at the turn of the century was minuscule, an aesthetic discernment in that public found a responsive vibration in the works of Alfred Jarry, Guillaume Apollinaire, Tristan Tzara, Eric Satie, and Serge Diaghilev. The cognizance of that public as to what was being turned around and why, is what created the keen intellectual appreciation that we now revere as modernism. The collective character of an audience is like a sounding-board that places a work of art into the context by which it is appreciated or disparaged, comprehended or misunderstood.

The origin of this not-very-dazzling insight is a recent visit to South Coast Rep, which, being in the heart of Orange County, tends to be populated by cozy bourgeois folk and a fair sampling of suburban yuppies whose tastes, by and large, reflect the lackadaisical spirit of the Great Southwest. It is a taste that has been fashioned for some seventeen years by South Coast Rep itself and, since 1986, by the Orange County Center for the Performing Arts, a grandiose cathedral to pop culture that, like many buildings that it resembles, caters to the greatest comfort of the greatest number.

Much of what I have seen at SCR has been immaculately professional, in meticulous good taste, culture-worthy, and polished to a high and glittering finish. But almost everything has suffered from being coddled by an undiscerning and overappreciative audience that appears to park its brains along with its Volvos.

Martin Benson, who has made Shaw revivals something of a ritual at this theater, has here produced a flat and gruelingly unimaginative revival of one of Shaw's less splendid comedies. The set and costumes by Michael C. Smith and Walter Hicklin are hideous in their predictability, with painted surfaces and three-dimensional structures jabbing at each other in a scuffle of incompatibility. The acting is either overdone (as in the case of Nike Doukas's Raina) or undercooked (as in the case of Harry Groener's Bluntschli). The play shuffles out like a well-worn pack of playing cards, and nowhere during the evening does anyone play an unexpected hand or pull off an outrageous bluff. It is Shaw by the numbers and relies almost entirely on the weave of the language and the locomotion of the plot. Comedy from the neck up.

And yet, I would be making false report if I did not declare that the audience lapped it up like seals swallowing carp at feeding time. There was a buoyant appreciation for all the routine performances and lackluster personalities, each actor dutifully dotting GBS's jovial "i"s and crossing his curlicued "t"s. But for all that, it was a performance that exuded the stale odor of British fortnightly rep or the mothball aroma of second-rate summer stock.

Shaw's attempt at debunking the false romanticism of military heroes and the dreamy, Byronic women who feed on them needs a clear, stylistic definition that clearly contrasts the Idealistic and the Pragmatic, but here, everyone and everything was being guyed and so, instead of mocked romanticism, one often got parody of parody. Bluntschli, of course, is the cool, sharp wind that is supposed to disperse the colored bubbles of sentimentality, but Groener's Bluntschli lumbers like an elephant on a highwire, a characterization full of gray broods, muffled intentions, and inverted energy. Daniel Reichert's Sergius is the only performance with a vague semblance of panache, but even he loses more laughs than he gets by settling on half a dozen stock gestures and endlessly recycling them.

When *Arms and the Man* delivers the grit as well as the comedy, it reminds us that nothing that Shaw wrote, not even this jejeune effort, is not without some measure of intellectual stamina. When it doesn't, it seems fully to explain why Oscar Straus and Stanislaus Stange thought the play a perfect libretto for conversion into a lightweight musical comedy. This production is like *The Chocolate Soldier* without the music. The worst thing about the evening was the relish with which an ebullient and undiscriminating audience lapped up pedestrian performances and flat, uninvigorating comedy-playing. "This is all jolly good fun," they seemed to be saying, "and what theater is all about," and so the obviousness, the flatness, the interpretative stodginess were magically transformed into transports of delight. As I rankled my way out into the foyer, I was consoled by my companion who wisely pointed out that since this was the sticks, one couldn't expect high-grade urban discernment. This was as good as it ever got in Orange County, and it was manna from heaven for the Orangemen and women who prefer titters to belly-laughs and mildly amusing conceits to comic gusto. It all somehow defined the fulsomeness we associate with the term *suburban taste.*

The fact is, there is a soft underbelly and integral complacency at South Coast Rep that may well be the secret of its success with its docile public but that remains a thorn in the flesh of those persons who have experienced true flair, mind-jiggling inventiveness, and bold reinterpretation. It is what makes California soggy and bozo-like and justifies the sarcasm and contempt of Easterners who occasionally find themselves sucked into those air-pockets that make cultural life in the Great Southwest so uncomfortably turbulent.

It may be widening the parameters of drama criticism to examine the aesthetic deficiencies of the public as well as the shortcomings of the artists, but when the former condones and validates the latter, it, too, must be part of the artistic assessment. The social context of a play is *part* of the play and, like latitude and longitude, has a real bearing in the scheme of things.

★★★

26

DESPERATE GAMBLES: *DEALER'S CHOICE*

by Patrick Marber

As a metaphor for life, there is nothing to beat gambling. Raising the ante, bluffing, keeping a poker face, winning, losing, staying in the game, these are all transactions that symbolize the pressures, conquests, and defeats that characterize our daily lives. Of all of them, the most important is "staying in the game," which is just another way of saying, "clinging to life."

I am convinced that the unconscious appeal of gambling is that it offers a psychic replay of the trials and quests of life in circumstances that persuade the gambler that he can outwit the arbitrary motions of fate. Symbolically, the dealer is God and although He most always wins the toss, there are enough instances of the player triumphing over Him to instill the idea that, if the right system can be devised—a propitious wind made to prevail—He can be vanquished. Outwitting God means outwitting Death, and any form of activity, whether it be religion or gambling, that holds out the prospect of such a prize is regularly going to attract converts.

Although the surface of Patrick Marber's play *Dealer's Choice* appears to be concerned with the exigencies of poker, on a subtextual level it is about surviving the punishments of cruel gods. In that sense, it is the most classical work to be seen in L.A. in many a season. All of its characters suffer from tragic flaws. All are victims of a hubris that will ultimately cause their downfall. All are trying to avoid a predestination from which none can escape.

But none of the foregoing suggests the gaiety and wit on hand at the Mark Taper Forum, where Marber's parable on poker is now playing. For although, in its bedrock, *Dealer's Choice* is a tragedy, its surface bristles with scintillating one-liners and rollicking comic banter. Sometimes more than the traffic can stand.

In the first act, the play deftly introduces us to a variety of characters in a downmarket London restaurant, all of whom suffer from the same compulsion. In the second act, we have the Grand Ceremony, the midnight poker game, in which these compulsions are dramatically played out. It soon becomes clear that their gambling mania is merely a cover for a larger malaise that, to one degree or another, has infected them all. There are several circulating conflicts in the play, but the main one centers on the relationship between Stephen, the paternal restaurateur, and Carl, his gambling-addicted son. The father dispenses a lot of time and energy trying to save the boy from the fatal weakness that has already claimed his own life and that he shows no signs of kicking. Finally, he tries and fails to rescue him from the clutches of a sinister professional player to whom he is heavily in debt, and the cycle, unbroken and unbreakable, continues to revolve.

Marber invests almost all of his characters with his own literary heft and so cooks, waiters, and small-time con men are amazingly blessed with literary frames of reference and more articulateness than would seem appropriate to their callings. Like the expert card-player Marber probably is, he somewhat stacks his deck in regard to his characters, and when the evening is over, one almost feels like asking to examine the cards to make sure they aren't marked. The author's remorseless cleverness is a little like being in the presence of a comedian who is so unflaggingly "on," he doesn't realize he is beginning to browbeat his audience. But in the second act, Marber hones into the bone marrow behind the play's soft underbelly, and we are genuinely drawn into the whirlpool of desperate people trapped in inescapable circumstances.

Director Robert Egan has done a masterful job with a play that could have easily dwindled into caricature. He has assembled a cast of both Americans and Brits and managed to produce a well-integrated ensemble with a consistent tone of voice and a perfect balance between comedy and pathos. Denis Arndt shuttles smoothly between geniality and suffering as the restaurateur; Patrick Kerr is pathetically vulnerable as a waiter who can't say no; Daragh O'Malley, calm and grounded, as the cook who forfeits the wages he should have spent entertaining his visiting daughter; and Daniel Davis, combining the evil of George Zucco with the smarminess of Lionel Atwill, is excellent as an inveterate gambler trying to climb out of the hole. David Jenkin's London restaurant setting perfectly captures the seedy, greasy-spoon atmosphere that pervades so many mid-sized English bistros that, with a pretension toward classiness, never quite manage to achieve class.

★★★

27

IBSEN FOR DUMMIES: *ENEMY OF THE PEOPLE*

The trick in Henrik Ibsen's *Enemy of the People,* now in a Royal National Theater production at the Ahmanson, is realizing that a play that is ostensibly about water contamination and environmental pollution is really about political corruption. The second trick is segueing from the particular to the general in such a way that the play's delicate balance between pretext and underlying intention is evenly maintained. The third is realizing it is as much a Comedy of the Absurd as it is a play of ideas.

To avoid the more conventional heroic mold in which Dr. Stockmann is usually cast, Ian McKellan opts for a dithery, woolly-minded intellectual reminiscent of Shaw's Henry Higgins. But once made, that choice remains unchangeable throughout the performance, and so where Ibsen dictates a good-willed idealist gradually radicalized by self-serving political interests and ultimately victimized by an easily manipulated vindictive society, McKellan's Stockmann never reflects the dynamic changes constantly transforming the man. He starts dithery and ends dithery.

The garrulous, naturalistic style of the humanistic Dr. Stockmann is indistinguishable from the garrulous, naturalistic style of his canny and bigoted brother (Stephen Moore), who is the mayor of the town threatened by the medical officer's inflexible integrity. The sibling rivalry of the two brothers is established early on, but their similarity smudges the distinction between the intellectual idealist and the pragmatic local politician. The whole of the bitter ideological conflict between these men is consistently trivialized, and it seems more important to the production that it snares a few laughs than it should push its intellectual implications to their logical conclusions.

Although costumes and make-up try to make clear-cut social distinctions, everyone in Christopher Hampton's uniform adaptation seems to share the same diction and belong to Ibsen's all-embracing dialectic. John Napier's set is grossly over-designed, creating not only the minutest details of the Stockmann household and Aslaksen's printing establishment, but the rooftops and shingles of the surrounding town as well. As if the imperative of *Enemy of the People* was creating a sea-going community in nineteenth-century Norway rather than a visual plane where the play's pressing social and political issues could be dramatized.

Director Trevor Nunn's approach to *Enemy* is unwaveringly conventional. Instead of dramatizing its contradictions, he merely shuffles out the cards of Ibsen's arguments and lets the chips fall where they may. He seems to believe that the play is so fundamentally rich in ideas, a director need not determine which ones make up the arc of his own interpretation. The Meeting Hall scene (the heart of the play) is diffuse and unfocused—conventionally orchestrated between the auditorium and the stage but, because of McKellan's nebulous Stockmann, obstreperously unconvincing. The Doctor emerges as a victim, not of the town's malice, but of the production's inability to settle on a firm viewpoint.

The fact is, despite Stockmann's advocacy of progressive ideas, Ibsen's own intellectual stance is for an elitism that, if given its head, would ultimately produce an oligarchy. He is clearly using Stockmann as a stick to beat both the bourgeoisie and the working classes, and the problem with that is it begs the question as to where he himself stands on all these issues. The answer is: Neither in one place nor the other.

The play is essentially a kind of political farce disguised as a social melodrama. To Ibsen, liberalism, moderation, conservatism, and radicalism were all equally preposterous, and this was not because he opted for some rarefied political solution of his own but because his view of humanity was so jaundiced he didn't believe any system stocked with common or garden-variety human beings could be anything but ruinous. That is why the dialectical conclusion of *Enemy* is so unconvincing. "That man is strongest," says Stockmann, who "stands alone," and that's because Ibsen himself wished to dissociate himself from any organized political faction—not because he preferred one of his own but because he had grown to detest the feckless human material that corrupted them all. But the fact is, "standing alone" is itself a political position—in other words, "isolationism," and we know very well from recent history what kind of political consequences that can produce.

The real *Enemy of the People* was, of course, Ibsen himself.

★★★

28

A CLASS ACT: STRINDBERG AND LANGELLA: *THE FATHER*

by August Strindberg, starring Frank Langella

When Henrik Ibsen was sixty-seven and living in Christiana, Norway, he hung an oversize portrait of August Strindberg on the wall above his desk. It was Strindberg who, at that time, was threatening his supremacy as Scandinavia's greatest living playwright. Ibsen explained to visitors that it helped him in his work "to have that madman staring down at me. He is my mortal enemy and shall hang there and watch while I write."

Four years before, Ibsen had seen a production of *The Father,* a revival of the same production premiered in Copenhagen in 1887. There is no record of his reaction to the play, but there was a general perception throughout Scandinavia that Strindberg was somewhat demented and that, in a sense, *The Father* was the vessel that most clearly encapsulated his delirium.

Ibsen, for all his genius, never sunk into the inferno from which Strindberg dredged up his most harrowing works, and there is nothing in the Norwegian writer's oeuvre to touch the Swede's inspired fantasies *The Dream Play* and *Road to Damascus.* Ibsen, after abandoning the fanciful verse plays of his youth, pitched his tent on the firm ground of social realism. Strindberg burrowed away beneath that ground, building the foundation of what was to become the modernist theater of the next century: the theater of Jarry and Artaud, Beckett and Ionesco.

The effect of Frank Langella's *Father,* now playing at the Geffen Playhouse, is of being thrust back in time to the age of Kemble and Booth, Kean and Macready. It is an old-fashioned performance in the very best sense of that term: broad, histrionic, full-blooded, and all-devouring. When it is over, one looks to find the remains of masticated scenery strewn upon the stage and puddles of blood drying in the wings. Which is simply a hyperbolic way of saying it is a performance predicated on passion and conveyed with palpitating power. I can think of no contemporary American actor who is prepared to go that far out on a limb and who, once there, proceeds to do loop-di-loops. After interminable seasons of bland behaviorism on L.A.

stages, it is invigorating to go from polystyrene cups of soda-pop to flagons of nectar.

From the play's very first moment, when Langella is frozen in a posture of tremulous anxiety and his expression suggests that he hears the clatter of Valkyries at his window, one senses the efforts of a man trying to contain a mania that is threatening to erupt. The Captain clings to the staccato brusqueness of his military manner as a means of warding off events that are conspiring to unhinge him. It is the perfect preamble to the deterioration that ensues.

The play, all one hundred minutes of it, unfolds like a Greek tragedy. Ostensibly, the conflict between the Captain and his wife, Laura, is about the upbringing of their daughter Bertha—each parent insisting on their own preferences in the matter. But it soon shifts to the obsessive question of paternity: whether or not the Captain truly is the father of his daughter, a doubt diabolically instilled in his mind by his vampire-wife. It then grows into the battle of wills that seems to underlie all male–female relationships, marital or otherwise, and winds up being about man's helplessness in the face of a vindictive matriarchy that begins by coddling him, proceeds to render him emotionally dependent, and ends by grinding him into the dust. The feminists in the audience must necessarily loathe the play—just as every male will experience a shiver of fear at being devoured by women's carnivorous sexuality. Strindberg, well before Freud ever postulated the theory, powerfully dramatized the enervating effects of the Castration Complex but, unlike Freud, attributed the phobia to women's remorseless domination of men.

Langella's performance is full of eerie pauses and sudden neurotic lurches, all of which convey the Captain's internal pressures—like the mechanisms inside a magnificent clock-tower gradually running down. Langella employs a recurring piece of business—his fingers involuntarily counting the brass buttons on the left side of his uniform—which punistically suggests a man in fear of "losing all his buttons." When, in the final scenes, he actually flips, the actor plunges into his dementia like an Olympian swimmer into a pool of molten lead.

Langella is the central pillar of the play; unfortunately, most of the other performances represent jerry-built flying buttresses. As the Captain's plotting wife, Laura, (Carolyn McCormick) is steely and hard and effectively holds her own against her paranoid husband. It was a miscalculation, however, to start her needling bitchery from the very first scene, as it leaves her nowhere to go and, in a play where the wife is clearly drawn as the villain, one should use every possible moment one can to render her sympathetic. Ivar Brogger's

Pastor, who is Laura's brother, is unflappably genial and never suggests that he is a member of the Christian faction in the household, ranked against the Captain's agnosticism. Michael Haney's Doctor Ostermark, confronted with Laura's revelations about her husband's insanity, blithely takes the news in his stride. There is virtually no sense of his entering into a house where deteriorated personal relations require wary and discreet handling. Director Clifford Williams's brisk opening tempo continues steadily through the play, even when circumstances dictate pauses for reflection or moments of necessary adjustment. Of all the supporting players, Anne Pitoniak as the Captain's old nurse, who out of maternal concern agrees to be the instrument of his incarceration, comes off most plausibly. Some of her best moments are easing her tortured ward into the straitjacket that will finally sever him from both his family and his consciousness.

But Langella is the fulcrum and centripetal force of this production, and it is to expose oneself to the twists and turns of his terrible descent into madness that both Strindbergians and anti-Strindbergians should beat a path to the Geffen Playhouse.

29

THE WILDE BUNCH

Gross Indecency: The Trials of Oscar Wilde

Adapted by Moises Kaufman

The recent outbreak of Wilde Mania, both on stage and in films, is not difficult to understand. Of all the nineteenth-century playwrights, Shaw included, Oscar Wilde is the most modern, even, incredibly, postmodern. His coruscating wit and "up yours" insolence hovers over the work of fashionable twentieth-century playwrights such as Joe Orton, David Hare, Tom Stoppard, Alan Bennett, Caryl Churchill, and a whole clutch of sardonic scalawags in fringe and studio theaters throughout England.

In both his life and his work, he established the self-defacing grandiosity we associate with the word *camp.* His outrageous egotism, his power to deflate the most helium-stuffed of all social windbags, his horror of practicality and disdain of respectability made him a culture hero in his own time and, unlike similar icons whose statues have been rudely toppled in our century, he has frequently had new monuments erected in his honor, both in Europe and America.

The man who on his deathbed could look up with a pained expression and say, "Either that wallpaper goes or I do" was mining a vein of humor so far away from Shaw's, Gilbert's, or Lewis Carroll's as to be in an entirely unrelated mental universe.

Wilde's homosexuality was the inescapable fact of his life. His allusions to it, always highly parodied, made it no less frightening or dangerous. Moises Kaufman's collage of the three trials of Oscar Wilde entitled *Gross Indecency,* now at the Mark Taper, is a brilliant editing job and proves again (as if it needed to be proved) that when ideas are stimulatingly arranged and dramatically expressed, the Theater of Ideas is perhaps the highest form of theater we can have.

Kaufman has cunningly grafted together telling excerpts from the biographies, Wilde's own work, and newspaper accounts of the period, and, as a result, we get a compressed version of the writer's legal crucifixion such as was never obtained in the Peter Finch or Robert Morley films allegedly covering the same ground.

Wilde, invariably caricatured as a flamboyant dandy with the tongue of a drag queen and the hauteur of a fop, emerges here as the vulnerable and pathetic figure he must have been during these judicial onslaughts. This is due mainly to Michael Emerson's understated performance, which perfectly depicts the way in which Wilde cloaked his pain with pride and his weakness with wit. This is not the coruscating and charismatic Wilde who thunders out of Ellman's biography, but then, at this juncture in his life, he was vainly trying to be upright and respectable: a hopeless guise for a man of Wilde's anarchic temperament. There was probably no more ludicrous spectacle in England than Wilde balanced on his high horse, whipping it toward the moral high ground, the very turf he so powerfully demolished both in his life and work. What *Gross Indecency* makes perfectly clear is that when a literary aesthete tries to justify himself in the hard-headed precincts of "the real world," tragedy must be the inevitable outcome.

Kaufman's only miscalculation occurs in the first scene of act two, where some critical pundit in a mock interview gauchely tries to define the intellectual nuances of Wilde's homosexuality. Since everything else in the play has been purloined from historical sources, I assume that little vignette was also spawned from some lecture or other, but its anachronism looms on the surface of the play like a wart on the face of a woman with an otherwise perfect complexion.

The play also gives a certain new definition to the weasly character of Lord Alfred Douglas, temperately played here by Mike Doyle. Given the breadth of Wilde's intellect, the brilliance of his wit, and the infallibility of his artistic taste, it is incredible to imagine him going ga-ga for such a puling, vindictive, and talentless git. Bosie was not only his downfall, but the only aspect of Wilde's life that seriously leads us to question his genius. I guess, as Auden says, we really "cannot choose what we are free to love." But how convenient it would be, if we could.

The remainder of the all-male cast, whose greatest strengths appear to be Eddie Bowz, Geraint Wyn Davies, Simon Templeman, and Hal Robinson, have been rigorously drilled and succeed in dispensing text as if it were music, even at one point by providing their own percussive accompaniments. But conceptually and directorially, this is Kaufman's achievement. He has managed to imbue an old and familiar literary scandal with the kind of freshness and élan one associates with the immediacy of today's headlines and, in so doing, has given us a new and compelling dimension to the character of Oscar Wilde.

★★★

30

BALM FOR THE MIND: *COLLECTED STORIES*

by Donald Margulies

A good play is one that resists the kind of capsule descriptions that appear regularly in *TV Guide.* If it can be condensed into two sentences, it lacks the density one normally associates with art. And what is striking about Donald Margulies *Collected Stories* is that it can be described in half a dozen ways and still reverberate in a dozen more.

It is a play about the hazards of discipleship, the boundaries of intellectual property, the agony of one generation handing over power to the next, the treacheries of friendship, the exploitation that comes with love, the seductive nature of fame, the proprietary rights of memory, and the abdications that we either make or are forced to make by the onset of death.

The basis for all these tangled issues, as most people now know who have seen this play in its many incarnations, is the changing relationship between Ruth Steiner, a middle-aged writer of short stories, and Lisa Morrison, a talented disciple whom Ruth mentors and who eventually appropriates one of the most personal experiences of Ruth's life: an abortive affair with the poet Delmore Schwartz.

The nagging question as to where the permissible bounds of authorship are to be drawn has arisen time and time again. A few years back, Kenneth Tynan castigated Truman Capote for "exploiting" the inner lives of two convicted murders in the documentary novel *In Cold Blood.* Not so long ago, Claire Bloom decimated Philip Roth in an autobiography that dealt with their married life, and Roth responded with a literary counterblast of his own. One of Margulies' main inspirations for this play was Stephen Spender's contention that novelist David Leavitt had ripped off a personal love affair that the Poet Laureate had treated in his 1951 autobiography *World within World.* What makes Ruth Steiner's complaint so poignant is that her affair with Delmore Schwartz was too traumatic for her to deal with herself. Although she rails against its appropriation by her disciple, the inference is that anything that occurs in life is fair game for the artist. That sense of having one's profoundest personal experiences turned into literary fodder has consternated writers, and their subjects, for as long as writing has existed, but in an era where the rights of privacy have effectively been banished from most people's lives, it is an issue worth revisiting.

The Geffen production, under Gilbert Cates's beautifully contoured direction, is blessed with two perfectly balanced performances by Linda Lavin and Samantha Mathis. In the play, Lavin sarcastically suggests that if her life were made into a film, it would be played by Thelma Ritter, were that acrimonious grouch still among us. Truth to tell, Lavin has the same bilious nature as Ms. Ritter, but when it deepens into rancor and betrayal, as it does in the last scene, Lavin achieves a Medea-like intensity that was never visited upon Ms. Ritter. Using exquisitely shaped run-on sentences that crunch together thoughts that are usually cleanly separated, Lavin manages to be both dryly comic and pathetically touching. Samantha Mathis's transformation from precocious schoolgirl to budding author to literary luminary is far less hyperbolic but every bit as compelling. From her jaunty first entrance to her anguished last exit, Ms. Mathis holds her own on the Geffen stage, and together these two actresses mold a relationship with as many grooves and curlicues as a Byzantine temple.

In the play's climactic scene, the issues that have been reverberating throughout the evening become explosively explicit. Here perhaps, Margulies says too much, too repetitively, and risks the danger of losing the intellectual ambiguity that has characterized the weave of the previous scenes. But that quibble notwithstanding, it is a rare pleasure to come out of a theater in Los Angeles with one's mind jingling with several antithetical viewpoints, all struggling to assert themselves. And it is equally rare for a male playwright to have captured the subtle transitions that occur in a competitive relationship between a younger and an older woman.

In a city made rancid by the junk food of predictable revivals and maudlin new work that further clogs the digestive tract, the Geffen Playhouse continues to offer balm for the mind.

★★★

31

THE WEARING DOWN OF THE GREEN: *THE CRIPPLE OF INISHMAN*

by Martin McDonough

It is hard to believe that *The Cripple of Inishman* was written only a few years ago by a contemporary Irish playwright, Martin McDonough. The play that has just opened the Geffen's new season looks, feels, and sounds like something Lennox Robinson or Lady Gregory might have dashed off for the Abbey Theatre in the early part of the century. It is not only rooted in rustic "be'gorrah" Irish culture but reveals all the makeshift qualities of play construction we associate with that earlier, more primitive period.

A downtrodden cripple boy from the Aran Isles, hearing that Robert Flaherty is filming *Man of Aran* in his vicinity, persuades a local boatman to ferry him over to the illustrious director in the hope that a Hollywood breakthrough will rescue him from the unrelieved misery of life in his stultifying hometown. Miraculously, he gets the prized opportunity and pulls up his roots. But in cruel Hollywood, the dream crumbles and, after a painful sojourn in the harsh new world, he returns to Inishman. There, he is brutally admonished for having faked the circumstances of his departure and, discovering that he was spurned even by his own parents, decides to weight himself down with cans of peas and throw himself into the brine. A pugnacious local girl, with a violent egg fetish and a predilection for fisticuffs, takes pity on the cripple and, offering to be his main squeeze, dissuades him from his watery fate. However, it is clear that, the cripple being in the final stages of tuberculosis, the union will be short-lived. If the violent girlfriend doesn't polish him off with a lethal barrage of eggs, the disease unquestionably will.—Curtain!

This is a perfect scenario for a silent film starring Clara Bow and Lon Chaney, directed by someone like D. W. Griffith or Eric von Stroheim. Chaplin, skillfully blending pathos, bathos, and high farce comedy, could have turned it into a celluloid masterpiece with Ben Turpin as the cripple and Marie Dressler as his beloved. But as a contemporary stage offering, it gives the term "Irish troubles" an entirely new connotation.

Without Irish playwrights, there would be no English theater to speak of. Subtract Sheridan, Wilde, Shaw, O'Casey, Beckett, and Behan from the mix, and the pantheon of the British theater collapses. The greatest of the Irish playwrights managed to shake the dust of "old sod" from their boots and triumph in the hated land of their masters, but there have been just as many who remained stuck in the mire of Gaelic whimsy and wistfulness.

McDonough writes comedy as if Ireland were a sitcom and its natives pasteboard characters being sweated over by a staff of TV hacks. It's not so much that the narrative is threadbare and contrived that gets one's goat, it's the fact that a modern Irishman, in the midst of one of the most historical developments in the history of their country—the attempted reconciliation of north and south—can find no more pertinent subject matter than a sentimental tale of a pixie-like cripple who finds love with a wild termagant in a Gaelic backwater. What is "old fashioned" in *The Cripple of Inishman* is not the period or the setting but the artistic objectives of the playwright: to amuse with word play, to distract with eccentricity, and to manipulate our feelings with twists and turns motivated by the crassest kind of sentimentality.

Joe Dowling's production emphasizes rather than conceals the transparency of the construction and the obviousness of the plot. Rather than "naturalizing" these characters and creating sympathy for their trumped-up dilemmas, he allows them to bound about like archetypal stage Irish men and women in a travesty of a turn-of-the-century folk-comedy.

The tearaway success of this play on Broadway only confirms the long-held suspicion that the Mecca is often as gullible as the rustic townsfolk of Inishman and that one can never assume that the alleged capitol of American theater is any more discerning than the bitterly disparaged hinterlands of Philadelphia, Seattle, Minneapolis, or, for that matter, L.A.

★★★

32

THE SHREW: RECLAIMING *THE TAMING*

If one has to do *Taming of the Shrew* at all, Mark Rucker's production at South Coast Rep is probably the best way to go.

Whatever one does with the play, it is virtually impossible to remove the moral obstacle that the twentieth century has lodged in the sixteenth-century comedy: namely, the contemptible subjugation of Kate by a cold-blooded macho-adventurer who spends all of his time fashioning the subservient spouse that was considered the ideal marital partner in Shakespeare's time. Nor do all of Petruchio's motives spring entirely from a bottomless well of male chauvinism, for the real object of his heartless brainwashing is to acquire the dowry that goes along with the marital conquest. So we are presented with the spectacle of a conniving and exploitative male protagonist who has a psychotic ego problem and is essentially trying to arrange a marriage of convenience (*his* convenience, that is) with a woman of independent mind who, from the very start, is set up to become the "goods, chattels, horse, ox, ass" that she is so ideologically opposed to from the outset. If ever a play cried out for deconstruction, *Shrew* does.

But director Rucker is clearly not vexed by the play's repugnant social doctrine. For him, as for so many, it can still be a rollicking comedy and, to his credit, he goes a long way toward making it one. The milieu is indeterminately modern, with a strong '50s flavor unfolding in what the program rightly describes as "an Italian-American world in which machismo was a given and Cool was the watchword." Everyone seems to have taken their cue in this production from Coppola's *The Godfather,* their accents from Marlon Brando, and their strategy from making people propositions they cannot refuse.

As a smeared-on dialect, the blunt Mafiosa speech works perfectly well, even as it flattens out Shakespeare's more courtly language. It also tends to point up the affinity that exists between the operatically imbued lyricism of Italian hoods and the rhetorical outbursts of characters such as Petruchio and

Lucentio. Everyone on stage acts like Chico Marx, wildly gesturing as if they were playing charades and masticating the text like conscientious immigrants just arrived from Sicily. Merely following the play's dumbshow would make it perfectly intelligible to spectators who had no English.

Marco Barricelli, whose name would lead you to believe he would be a flagrantly Italianate Petruchio is, in fact, the one actor who plays closest to Shakespeare's diction and within the orbit of the original play. I caught Barricelli at the Ashland Shakespeare Festival some seasons back, where he essayed a number of complicated Shakespearean roles with astonishing ease and effortless charm. He is a big, dark, broad-shouldered, handsome man with perfect control of the blank verse idiom and the kind of matinee-idol appeal that should soon get him onto the cover of *TV Guide.* He makes perfect sense of the verse at all times, and his Petruchio is a winning mixture of blustering geniality and macho impatience. The premeditated cruelty, in Marricelli's performance, comes across like a penchant for practical jokes and so never alienates sympathy.

Katherine is played by Cindy Katz, as the spoiled daughter of an affluent mob boss who, like Meyer Lansky, has moved into the higher reaches of suburban respectability. It is a high-spirited, devil-may-care, I-don't-give-a-shit performance in the early scenes but then has to pay the price for that libertinage by rapidly (and somewhat implausibly) knuckling under to Petruchio's domination in the final scenes. Until this point, director Rucker has cleverly negotiated all the curves and U-turns of the comedy, but when he's confronted with the impossible denouement, the play slaps him in the kisser just the way it has everybody else. Marital frolics in the pizza parlor notwithstanding, when it comes time for Katherine to bend the knee before Petruchio, virtually all the clever diversions Rucker has devised dissolve before that bloodcurdling coda in which a fiery woman thoroughly capitulates before a smirking honcho. Katz tries to step out of the way of the scene's implications but poses no viable dramatic alternative to them.

But that's only about seven minutes of the evening; for all the rest Rucker has concocted a smooth, well-paced, ingeniously staged version of the old war-horse and made it jump through hoops like a prancing circus pony. Ralph Funicello's floating set of colored panels wisely situates *The Shrew* in the world of stage-comedy rather than some place more geographically identifiable, and Shigeru Yaji's spiffy '50s costumes properly conjure up an America before the advent of Germaine Greer or Kate Millett. The cast contains no obvious clinkers, and Douglas Rowe's Baptista, Mikael Salazar's Lucentio, and Bill Mondy's Tranio are particularly well-crafted and perfectly embody the Cinzano style of the evening.

There are a few miscalculations in the production, like a burst of audience participation in which Kate's "walnut-shell" hat is tossed out to spectators and then clumsily retrieved and some arbitrary Italian dances that too crassly try to provoke a good time being had by all. All those Orange County high-jinks are unnecessary. Rucker's main achievement is that he has jammed the play into a free-wheeling contemporary context that has rendered its many twists and turns crystal clear and engendered a rampaging comic spirit that makes us understand why the fable of the ornery woman and her bronco-busting mate, in all of its former and later manifestations, has survived as long as it has.

33

SHAKESPEARE BY NUMBERS: *MEASURE FOR MEASURE* AND *MIDSUMMER NIGHT'S DREAM*

Directed by Sir Peter Hall

Peter Hall's arrival in Los Angeles had all the pomp of Cleopatra's coming down her barge on the River Cydnus. Though Hall's "barge" was not exactly a "burnish'd throne," the sense of a British deity descending upon a horde of commoners prevailed nevertheless. Gordon Davidson had persuaded him to visit culturally famished L.A. to spread the munificence of his Shakespearean scholarship and, using a largely American company of actors, mount *Measure for Measure* and *A Midsummer Night's Dream* in repertoire at the Ahmanson. Sir Peter arrived, laid on workshops, and resanctified the text. The actors duly genuflected, and everyone basked in the glory of the Bard's anointed messenger who, to make sure no one neglected the connection, was photographed wearing the same doublet as that sported by Will himself in the Martin Droeshout portrait of the Great Man.

The press performance was a marathon in which *Measure* was performed in the afternoon followed, after a dinner break, by *The Dream*. The audience for this marathon contained every cultural luminary in Los Angeles (all six of them) and, to fill up the bleachers, freebies and discounted tickets were doled out to drooling actors and assorted culture-vultures. In meticulously projecting the language and piously observing the verse structure, the productions turn what would commonly be a virtue into an ongoing irritation. There is a distinct sense of patronization in pounding every iambic and fairy-lighting every pentameter. The texts of the plays are so passionately coddled throughout that the subtext is suffocated in the embrace. We are so carried away by stress and scansion that motive and meaning fall by the wayside. Throughout, the Hallistic dictums that Language Is Supreme and that the Secret of Shakespeare Lies in the Prosody are so unwaveringly obeyed that the roughness of character and the idiosyncrasies of human behavior disappear in a mist of pedantry.

In *Measure for Measure,* Brian Murray's Duke, taking the play's title rather literally, begins with so measured a delivery it feels as if he is methodically calibrating the verse. Gradually, this overly fastidious approach to verse-speaking is taken up by the other members of the cast, which enables us to hear every single word Shakespeare (or the corrupters of this play) ever wrote, but in a way that is curiously unaffecting. Or, to be more accurate, affecting only in terms of diction. It reminds one of that snide definition of a sonnet as having three quatrains and a couplet but no poetry.

Lugubrious throughout, Murray hews away at the verse as if it were precious lumber being parceled out for sale as memorial plaques. It is all very sensible, very sonorous, but portentous as hell. After the bed trick, when the Duke decides to impose his sadistic designs upon Isabella, concealing the fact that her brother is alive and his Deputy a revealed corrupter, Murray floods the stage with ominous "indications." Angelo would have to be a fool not to realize he is being set up for a kill. Anna Gunn's Isabella, intelligent throughout and speaking with pristine clarity, lacks the emotional currents that course beneath those polished speeches, and no amount of surface glitter compensates for that absence.

The grave manner and puritanical outlook that are the fulcrum of Angelo's character are nowhere to be found in Richard Thomas's performance; instead, we have a fluttery, low-level bureaucrat elevated to a job for which he seems wholly unsuited. It is a performance violently contradicted by everything the Duke, the Provost, and Escalus tell us about the man. The comedy scenes, some of the most wretched writing ever eked out by Shakespeare (in bathos, second only to *Merry Wives*) are in fact rather well handled by Hall. The casting is adroit; David Dukes is a ponce-like Lucio, very much the town dandy; George Dzundza as Pompey, a rollickingly unreformable pimp, with a striking resemblance to an overfed Ronald MacDonald.

At the back of John Gunther's airy set of transparent doorways, a miniature model of the Capitol provides a morsel of contemporary allusion to the proceedings. Angelo, corrupt in office, seduces a novitiate nun and is caught and punished; Clinton seduces a White House intern, is disgraced and impeached, but, like Angelo, let off the hook. As political commentary, this ranks with that fifteen-minute section of dead air on one of the Nixon tapes.

In the case of *The Dream,* we could have been sitting in a theater in the middle '50s watching a traditionalist reconstruction of the '20s romanticism of Max Reinhardt. The "director" could just as easily have been a sophisticated computer downloading every received idea germane to the play, rather than a contemporary director interpreting it for a '90s audience on the cusp of a new millennium. Hall gives us a kind of *Midsummer Night's Dream* by numbers, replete with fairy-children, a horned Puck, and a behoofed Bottom. Rethinking a classic does not mean gussying it up with fancy folderol and extraneous trimming so that it no longer bears any resemblance to the original. But neither does it mean duplicating the measurements it once had and fitting it out in a set of new clothes with no reference to the passage of time or the changes it has undergone since first conceived.

The Mechanicals' scenes are as leaden as the prow of the *Queen Mary* and just as landlocked. The "Pyramus and Thisbe" burlesque, with Brian Murray's gallumphing Bottom devoid of comic ingenuity, painfully reminds us how the acting of unlettered amateurs, ferociously applied, can be like an hour inside an iron maiden. Although comparisons are odious, the same scene is the only redeemable part of Michael Hoffman's recent film version of this play. It, at least, was sprinkled with comic inventions.

Richard Thomas's tenorish exuberance is far better suited to Puck than it ever was to Angelo; Peter Francis James's Oberon is as exotically mannered as his Restoration upsweep hairdo; and a startlingly trimmed-down Kelly McGillis is oozingly horny as Titania. All in all, the players are talented and serviceable and energetically committed to lively horseplay. The problem is that none of them seem to realize they are operating in an intellectual vacuum—merely repeating the steps that generations of Lysanders, Hermias, Demetriuses, and Helenas have hoofed out before them.

It is to Gordon Davidson's credit that he wishes to raise the level of classical acting in Los Angeles, and employing Hall to tackle two major Shakespeares is a valiant move in the right direction. But he and most people in L.A. are so besotted with the illustrious theater-knight's reputation, they do not realize he is probably one of the least imaginative directors ever to have come out of England. Hall's conservative approach to the Bard (derived largely at the knee of his mentor, John Barton) puts him light-years behind people like Peter Brook, Nicholas Hytner, Deborah Warner, and Declan Donnellan, who, whatever their idiosyncrasies, operate in the here-and-now world of postmodern classical theater and not in some closeted sanctum where language is so glorified that Drama becomes incidental.

Ironically, Hall, who started his experiment with this largely American cast wanting to mine the genius of the national character of the country in which he was working, has actually "anglicized" this company—not by encouraging them into phony British accents but by immersing them in the cloying external approach that is the curse of his own homeland.

II

DRAMATIS PERSONAE

34

ARTAUD: A CENTENNIAL REASSESSMENT

September 4th, 1996, marked the centennial of Antonin Artaud's birth. There were no massed bands, fireworks displays, or dancing in the streets. In New York, the French Consulate sponsored a half-hearted gesture toward a memorial of sorts. If anything took place in Paris, no report of it made its way across the Atlantic.

My own efforts to organize a commemorative ceremony in California fell on deaf ears. None of the major universities felt the need to mark the occasion, nor did the so-called experimental theaters, the French Embassy, or its cultural attaché. One francophile organization in Hollywood suggested we combine his centennial with an homage to Maurice Chevalier, as if they were both, in some sense, part of the same double act. A potential sponsor, under the impression the poet was still alive, wondered whether we might bring him out for an appearance on one of the more popular late-night talk shows. Perhaps, I suggested, he could do a bit of surreal stand-up comedy and immolate himself on a cross in a kind of fuliginous finale. That really peaked his interest. "D'yuh think we could pull that off?"

In America, the commemoration of great artists takes place on the heads of stamps. Elvis has been so honored, as has Marilyn. Popular notoriety invariably equals fame and so the chances of a certifiably mad Frenchman achieving that kind of recognition are fairly slim.

My own burgeoning awareness of Artaud stems from 1958, when Grove Press published the English translation of *The Theater and Its Double.* The book created a small temblor in my brainpan and its aftershocks continued for the next thirty years. Around the same time, Artaud was also being discovered by Jack Kerouac, Alan Ginsberg, and Laurence Ferlinghetti and being adopted as the patron saint of the Beats. By the mid-1960s, when Peter Brook and I mounted the *Theatre of Cruelty* Season at the Royal Shakespeare Company, which was followed by the *Marat/Sade,* artists such as Jerzy Grotowsky, the Becks, John Cage, Susan Sontag, and Brook himself had already steeped themselves in his theories—theories that demanded a new relationship between the spectator and the stage, highly physicalized actions, and hierarchical stage imagery. Suddenly, Artaudian multimedia was everywhere, Performance Art was thriving, rock groups with painted faces and bold theatricalist actions were upsetting the composure of the pre-*Look Back in Anger* generations, and the theater was changed irrevocably.

Artaud's concept of Cruelty, which was really about a kind of aesthetic rigor, was mindlessly championed by sadomasochists throughout the country, and the fallacy that the *Theatre of Cruelty* was a kind of up-market Grand Guignol, characterized by whips, perforated flesh, and sundry bloodlettings, swept the cultural world as oversimplifications of theories as different as Christianity, Zen Buddhism, Brechtian *Verfremdung,* and the Method had previously done. Artaud, twenty or so years after his demise, had finally made it into the pop consciousness. He could now be distorted and bastardized along with all the other cultural icons of the '60s. Were he still alive at that time, there's no doubt he'd have found his way onto the talk-show circuit—with a jittery Charlie Rose asking him whether unanesthetized electroshock therapy was really as bad as it was cracked up to be, and was it really true that he never bathed? The Pink Floyd or Led Zeppelin would have contracted him to provide Tarahumara cries as a background to their latest rock album, probably entitled: *Artaud Gets His Rocks Off.* That done, he'd have probably wound up in some Ivy League university with a title like Eminent Professor of Theatrical Metaphysics, conducting a frantic extracurricular life seducing dreamy sophomores and shooting up with the livelier members of DramSoc.

I have never been able to reconcile the contradictions of the man whose ideas were so profound, and ultimately so efficacious, with the utter fiasco of his life and work. Everything Artaud touched turned to ashes: movies, theater, design, collaboration, and virtually all the artifacts that bear his name. In spite of all that, the power of his thought was irresistible and his vision inspired—and continues to inspire—artists of every persuasion throughout the world. The '30s were stamped by Stanislavsky, the '50s by Brecht—and the entire remainder of the century by Artaud.

His *Theatre Alfred Jarry*, founded in 1926–27 was a hodgepodge of surrealist monkeyshines. His much-touted production of *The Cenci* ran only thirteen performances. His films were botched and his one great radio-play, *Pour Finir avec le Jugement de Dieu,* never aired. Still, the Artaud influence on stagecraft, design, music, and poetry reverberates through all these arts.

Although Tristan Tzara, Filippo Marinetti, and Kurt Schwitters are clearer forerunners of Happenings (the precursors of Performance Art), it was Artaud's rhetoric that inspired most of the actual practitioners of the

'60s. His influence percolated through the bloodstreams of artists such as Arthur Brown, David Bowie, and Lindsay Kemp, not to mention Alan Kaprow, Ken Dewey, Jean-Jacques Lebel, Merce Cunningham, and John Cage. Wherever artists plunged into radical imagery and eschewed naturalism, the spirit of Artaud could be discerned—even in unlikely places such as John Barton's productions at the Royal Shakespeare Company and madcap musicals such as *Hair* and *The Dirtiest Show in Town.* His outsize totemic imagery could be found in Beckett, Ionesco, and Genet, most noticeably in works such as *Mouth, Happy Days, The Chairs, Amedee or How to Get Rid of It, Rhinoceros, The Blacks, The Balcony,* and *The Screens.*

Every deconstructionist classic over the past forty years owes something to his essay "No More Masterpieces" and the liberating aesthetic contained in the manifestos of the *Theater of Cruelty.* He is the inspirational force behind many of today's theatrical rock concerts and the unacknowledged progenitor of MTV. His spirit permeates the work of Performance Artists such as Laurie Anderson, Rachel Rosenthal, Karen Finlay, Tim Miller, and John Fleck, and his exhortations about costume and stage design can be discerned in the unlikeliest places, such as Julia Taymor's Broadway blockbuster *The Lion King* and Robert Wilson's *Monsters of Grace.*

Ultimately, what Artaud provided was a great corrective to both Stanislavsky and Brecht. In lambasting the assumptions of a falsifying naturalism and foisting a grander, more metaphysical view of experience, he literally dismantled the theater of Stanislavsky in such a way that it could never be put together again. In castigating the illusory benefits of "political theater," Artaud seriously undermined the dogma on which Brecht's epic theater was based. He made artists understand that when one spoke of "revolution," the only kind of radical transformation that really mattered was aesthetic, and that so long as the forms of artistic communication were not challenged and overturned, one was simply juggling different kinds of subject matter.

In the late '60s, while interviewing Roger Blin, the notable French director who assisted Artaud on *The Cenci,* I asked precisely what importance Artaud had in the contemporary theater. "I'm inclined to think," he answered, "that fundamentally, Artaud's importance in the theater means less than his importance on a philosophic level—defining a certain mode of thought." Which is apparent even from Artaud's first appearance in print, when Jacques Riviere published his correspondence with the twenty-seven-year-old Artaud in the *Nouvelle Revue Francaise* in 1923. Artaud described himself as being "in constant pursuit of (his) intellectual being" and the letters, the essays, and most of the poems were deliriously eloquent examples of that lifelong quest. Susan Sontag struck the same note as Blin when she wrote: "What Artaud bequeathed was not achieved works of Art but a singular presence, a poetics, an esthetics of thought, a theology of culture and phenomenology of suffering."

The Artaud whom I was initially drawn to *was* the Artaud who suffered, who saw himself as the "victim at the stake signaling through the flames." The nightmare of the Rodez asylum, his electroshock treatment, the widespread cultural indifference—all of these things endeared him to me. His friends and disciples classed him among the *poetes maudit*—people like Baudelaire, Mallarmé, Gerard de Nerval—but his damnation being so total made him in many ways more poignant.

Had his fidgety teacher Charles Dullin not feared him, more would have come out of his tuition at the Theatre du Vieux Colombier. Had the actor-director Louis Jouvet not been so wary of him, a collaboration of distinction might have resulted, instead of the angry exchange of letters that alienated both men from one another. Had he not insolently turned off Jean Louis Barrault, he could have had genuine opportunities when that early acolyte became the leader of the French theater. Had he not been pitied by Andre Gide, discarded by Andre Breton, snubbed by Jean Cocteau, spurned by his own bohemian society, less intransigent toward the bourgeois impresarios who viewed him as a maverick or a madman, he could have assembled the resources to put some of his grandiose ideas into practice. But in 1936, he was certified mad and, for ten years, incarcerated in a variety of mental asylums. By the time he was released in 1946—cancerous, toothless, and almost wholly forgotten—he could become nothing more than what he did become: a potent but obscure intellectual force destined for rediscovery a decade later; a time bomb with a stupendously long fuse that finally ignited in the '60s.

Given all that has happened since the '60s and '70s and that we are now living in a very different society, it seems reasonable to ask what is Artaud's legacy today?

In companies as different as Mabou Mines and Cirque du Soleil, in productions by directors as unlike each other as Robert Le Page and Richard Foreman, we can discern a new attitude to spectacle, a new harnessing of the actors' power—especially where combined with abstract scene design and mise-en-scène rooted in movement. Did Artaud invent metaphysical abstraction and kinetic mise-en-scène? Certainly not! Did he give both a new emphasis and a fresh stimuli? Unquestionably, he did. The many-sided aspects of Performance Art are a direct offshoot of his deconstructionist attitude to theater. His parceled-out productions at the Theatre Alfred Jarry, heavily sabotaged by the Surrealists and raided by the French police, are the clear ancestors of Happenings—although the Dadaists and earlier Surrealists were part of that progeny before Artaud ever arrived onto the scene.

The fractured and fragmented art of rock video, heavily drenched in bold, often surreal imagery, reveals the influence that Artaud exerted on rock performers forty years ago and, perhaps more significantly, the designers and stage directors who create those videos today. His influence can be discerned in the dreamlike collages that make up the work of Madonna and Michael Jackson, even if neither of these fashionable rock stars ever heard of him. (An influence doesn't require traceable derivations from a literal source. It is soaked up through the atmosphere in precisely the same way modern advertising absorbed and then exploited the influences of abstract art in the '50s. The first bastardization of any avant-garde influence invariably rears its head in the mass media.)

But as Blin suggested, perhaps the greatest legacy is the nature of what academicians call "the modern consciousness." The Beats' glorification of Artaud was because of marginal issues: his drug addiction and the higher reaches of his mental delirium. Artaud was a kind of mascot for them. His intellectual presence pulsates behind the work of poets such as Ginsberg, Ferlinghetti, Corso, and Rexroth; novelists such as Alexander Trocchi and William S. Burroughs—just as his intellectual presence can be discerned in the criticism of Michel Foucault, Roland Barthes, Susan Sontag, and others. It is part of the post-surrealist medley that plays constantly in the background of postmodernist thought.

But all that is academic berrypicking, which a talent like Artaud's inevitably inspires. Rather than exegesis, let me put this in the most personal terms I can.

After absorbing *The Theatre and Its Double* in the late '50s, that brew of passionate theory and provocative mysticism stayed with me throughout the next twenty-five years while I was directing in London, Germany, Scandinavia, and Italy. Artaud made me aware that in the theater, once text had yielded its psychological subtext, that was not the end of the matter, but only the beginning. That behind subtext lay what I came to call "ur-text," a dense, almost, unfathomable zone where our deepest and most primitive urges circulated wildly around each other like dancing amoebae in the scientist's microscope, and that to get to the core of rich and elusive works like those of the ancient Greek and Roman authors and the denser plays of the Elizabethan and Jacobean playwrights, one needed a technique that went far beyond the stilted two-step that either Stanislavsky or Brecht had provided; that tumultuous events such as the Holocaust and the Second World War, the disintegration of the Soviet Empire, and the epidemic of urban, ethnic, and domestic violence in the lives of people living in hectic modern cities needed more artistic elucidation than the formulaic theories bequeathed us at the turn of this century made possible; that the theater had changed radically but that despite that change, our performance goals and traditional dramaturgy had remained the same; that as we continued to dance the same old tired two-step of psychological realism, the intimations of the new theater were tugging us into a much more complicated choreography into which, because of our conditioning and complacency, we were loathe to go.

Artaud pointed us in that direction. He never got there himself—but then neither did Marx personally produce communism or Einstein, the hardware of nuclear technology—although neither manifestation would have been possible without their blueprints.

The ghost of Antonin Artaud haunts every unperfected moment that I encounter in rehearsal, every literary emanation that I fail to realize in a script; every methodical piece of mise-en-scène that blocks or frustrates an ineluctable idea that is clamoring to come to life. His is the voice that says: You didn't go far enough. You didn't drill deeply enough. You settled for less. You sidestepped the challenge. He is the beacon that lights the way, but often, to people like myself who are so navigationally befuddled, that new course feels like space travel without the benefit of mission control.

In a profession where habit, duplication, and lack of artistic courage are the constant pitfalls, it is important to have such a lodestar, and ultimately that may be Artaud's greatest value. He constantly raises the stakes and forces only the most resilient and reckless players to stay in the game.

On September 4th, 1996, Antoine Marie Joseph Artaud would have been a hundred years old, but, of course, even fantasizing that kind of longevity is rubbish. Artists like Artaud never peter out into old age. Invariably, they expire in early adulthood or, as in his case, at fifty-two after a life of avoidance and neglect. It is almost as if their obscurity and disregard are the prerequisites that allow later generations to excavate their bones and try to create the works that they themselves could never realize.

★★★

35

NICOL WILLIAMSON: DANGER MAN

There is a special excitement attending a show starring Nicol Williamson that doesn't apply to other actors. In normal circumstances, we may wonder if a performance will be good or bad, interesting or tedious, but in Williamson's case, the anticipation revolves around questions such as: Will he be there at all? And if so, will he walk off the stage, claiming, as he once did during a performance of *Hamlet,* that his inspiration had abandoned him? Will he punch out his producer (as he did David Merrick in Philadelphia some years ago) or assault a fellow-artist, causing the evening prematurely to terminate as it did during the run of *I Hate Hamlet?* Will an insufficient display of enthusiasm cause him to snarl and turn on his audience? Will we be berated for laughing too loudly or inappropriately or not at all? One feels that Williamson's arrival in any city should be announced by a police bulletin rather than a PR release.

Over the years, he has become that rarest of all birds: a dangerous actor. A man of volatile temperament and unpredictable mood swings. A man now labeled with the most damning adjective in the lexicon of casting: "Difficult." He has paid a price for his volatility. It is no accident that he now appears at the Geffen Playhouse in a One Man Show. There are many who allege he was giving One Man Shows even when surrounded by a large company of players.

I was living in London when the Williamson talent, like an ominous rumble from Vesuvius, first shook the complacency of the West End. He came to prominence in Peter Hall's season of new plays at the Arts Theatre Club, which was an adjunct to the main-stage work of the RSC. In plays like Henry Livings's *Nil Carborundum,* Gorky's *The Lower Depths,* and Middleton's *Women Beware Women,* his knobbly and abrasive talent rose like a node on an otherwise unblemished epidermis. His Round House *Hamlet,* directed by Tony Richardson, was a growling, savage prince with twingeing moments of private grief that clutched the muscles of the heart as if they had been fixed into a vise. In John Osborne's *Inadmissible Evidence,* he emptied out the soul of Bill Maitland's tortured character like a man bailing himself out of a sinking lifeboat. Whatever he did and wherever he did it, there was always a sense of mild cataclysm about the work. Not so much acting, but seismic activity or inexplicable cosmological disturbance.

Jack: A Night on the Town with John Barrymore is Williamson's fusion with a personality every bit as troubled and self-destructive as his own. Barrymore was a congenital alcoholic who managed to sober up just long enough to become the greatest actor on the American stage. Williamson was a tortured neurotic, who managed to curb his demons long enough to become one of the most outstanding actors of his generation. But at the core of Williamson, there is the kind of troubled solitariness we are accustomed to hearing neighbors describe when someone on their block suddenly goes on a deadly shooting spree. Barrymore, despite regular bouts of hell-raising, was much more soft-centered. There was a quality of whimsy about him that is beautifully captured in many of the '30s films. His humor was irreverent and anarchic, and he viewed everything that happened in his life through that prism. He wasn't so much a social renegade as a man who raged against himself for not being able to achieve the fulfillment of his early promise.

During the course of *Jack,* Barrymore is cannibalized by Williamson. As much as the show's pretext is the life and times of John Barrymore, we feel we are being navigated through the swirls and eddies of Williamson's psyche. He, too, reached a peak about twenty years ago and ever since has hovered between public adoration and malicious neglect. He, too, has had his emotional life dictated by the swings and roundabouts of amorous affairs and what Barrymore would have called a "bus accident marriage." He, too, has tried to follow Hamlet, Coriolanus, and Macbeth with roles worthy of his ocean-liner talent, only to be diverted into the dinghies of low-budget films and forgettable TV series.

Leslie Megahey's script has more holes than a piece of Ementhaler. Episodes that should be condensed into a few pithy anecdotes tend to be over-illustrated. The piece needs an editor more than it does a director and one who would take the writer to task for overstating the obvious and understating the essential. But Williamson makes Barrymore's downslides reverberate with pathos; his levity sparkles with Barrymore's self-effacing humor. His rages are the rages of every outsize artist mangled by media moguls who tap talent without respecting or protecting it.

Ultimately, a riveting parallel emerges between subject and object, and we come to understand that though there is little in the performance to remind us of the Barrymore we recollect from films or radio, there is a striking similarity between the components that made Barrymore a great actor and those that galvanize Williamson. Perhaps the only way to have the essence of a great actor delivered to us on stage is through the vessel of another great actor, and so long as we don't yearn for facsimiles or mimicry, we have to admit that whatever divine spark it was that lit up John Barrymore, it burns just as brightly in Nicol Williamson.

★★★

36

REMEMBERING LENNY BRUCE

On October 13, 1999, Lenny Bruce, had he not accidentally overdosed on narcotics or committed suicide (the jury is still out on that one) would be seventy-six years old. It is, of course, a thoroughly incredible notion—like an octogenarian Mozart, a superannuated Janis Joplin, or James Dean signing up for a senior citizen pension. *Poets maudits,* doomed rock stars, and self-destructive superstars are supposed to die young. Their myth demands it, and we wouldn't have it any other way.

Bruce's death at forty-one, perched on a toilet bowl with a spike in his right arm and his last typed words, "Conspiracy to interfere with the fourth amendment const . . . ," in the barrel of his still-humming electric typewriter, died characteristically. He was always associated with "toilet humor" and, throughout the last decade of his life, exhausted himself trying to demonstrate that the United States Constitution protected the free speech for which one court after another mercilessly prosecuted him. (The Fourth Amendment, incidentally, protects citizens from "unreasonable searches and seizures" and, along with the state's First Amendment violations, was as much responsible for his downfall as the cocaine or morphine.)

I met him in 1962 when he came to England for the first time to play at Peter Cook's Soho club, the Establishment. At the press conference, he spotted me among a cluster of journalists and insisted he knew me from somewhere or other—although I insisted I had never seen him before and, in fact, had been resident in England for the same eight years during which he had come to prominence in clubs in New York and San Francisco. Nevertheless, I certainly knew him by reputation and was flattered to be adopted as a crony.

The opening-night performance was, for me, cathartic. Lenny was serving up sly, coruscating insights on subjects about which I had been only half-conscious growing up on the Lower East Side of New York. He had missiled me back to my adolescence—what my adolescence would have been if it had been articulate, probing, unsuppressed, and revelatory.

The following day *The People*'s headline read: "He makes us sick," and the *Daily Sketch* wrote, "It stinks!" Bruce always seemed to inspire short, nauseous epithets—and, of course, if one is billed as a "sick comic," it goes without saying that the "healthy reaction" is to express disgust at his performance. Although these kinds of reactions were predictable, neither he nor anyone else was prepared for the tenor of the upbeat reviews. George Melly in the *New Statesman* hailed him as "the evangelist of the new morality" and compared him to Jonathan Swift. Ken Tynan, referring to the recent success of *Beyond the Fringe,* said: "If *Fringe* was a pin prick, Mr. Bruce was a bloodbath!" Others followed suit and, in most quarters, the foul-mouthed, dirty-minded Lenny Bruce was vaunted as a moral crusader and front-runner of the New Consciousness.

Lenny's opening was a walloping great success, playing as it did to a hand-picked, largely showbiz crowd. After that, the "real people" came to the club and were, on the whole, bored or outraged; occasionally, both. There were constant walk-outs—which cut Lenny to the quick, as he couldn't bear flagrant shows of rejection. As the run progressed, reactions became more vituperative. The Establishment was an intimate club and its close confines tended to encourage audience participation. Lots of people got into Lenny's act—hurling first insults, then pennies, glasses, and eventually bottles. This was no longer the idealized British public that Lenny had romanticized when he first stepped off the plane nor was it the carefully selected cognoscenti that Peter Cook and Nicholas Luard, the club's owners, had gathered for the premiere. This was the stiff-backed, toffee-nosed British public drawn from the city and the suburbs—the posh, Anglicized version of American rednecks—and they found in Lenny the personification of that same free-ranging '60s spirit that they had come to fear and loathe. Fist-fights were not uncommon. Before leaving the theater in a huff that would eventually make headlines, actress Siobhan McKenna's escort, resenting slurs on the Irish, bopped Peter Cook on the nose. "These are Irish hands," wailed Ms. McKenna, "and they are clean." "This is a British face," retorted Cook, "and it's bleeding."

Since everything was grist for Lenny's mill, he took to recording the reactions of the hostile houses and playing them back to subsequent audiences. Expecting "live entertainment," they often grew hostile at being exposed to endless reels of tape. Lenny (like Krapp, whom he came to resemble in the final days) was an obsessive recordist. On one occasion, a "nice Jewish couple" from the suburbs came backstage to compliment him on his act. Though they themselves were sympathetic, they had to point out "with all due respect" that Lenny was giving offense to certain Jewish members of the audience. Lenny was so regaled by the couple's hypocrisy that he cruelly played the conversation back to the next house, which he naively assumed would be as liberated as himself—which, of course, it wasn't.

Lenny was fascinated by the British legalization of narcotics and the fact that addicts could simply "sign on" and receive prescribed doses. He once fantasized for me a British GP's typical prescription: "Take two aspirins, a half a glass of Epsom salts, fifty grams of coke, and an acid suppository." He was forcibly ejected from two London hotels: once for stopping up the toilet with used spikes and another time for conducting a nocturnal trio of blondes in an original composition, the chorus of which ran "Please fuck me, Lenny"—in three-part harmony. In one of his temporary abodes, he threatened the chambermaids that if they reported the presence of his elaborate pharmaceutical stash, he'd get them fired and genuinely seemed to believe this "threat" would safeguard him and his larder. Often, in his private life, Lenny was not only naive and simplistic but downright imbecilic. I was always amazed at the transformation that took place when he stepped on stage. Those petty, small-scale life aggravations that seemed to occupy all his energy suddenly gave way to a soaring imagination—as if "the real world" were only a pathetic suburban airport from which Lenny's shambly little monoplane, once airborne, turned into the Concorde.

Although flattered by his more admiring critics, Lenny never allowed their eulogies to muddy the clear-cut perception he had of himself. He was a "pro"—no more and no less. Someone who had zealously worked himself up from third-rate stand-up dates in the Catskills to the point where he could command large fees and the attention of sophisticated "rooms" in San Francisco, New York, or London. "I don't read enough books," he once told me, "so I guess I'm pretty shallow. I'm a lot into the physical. With me, first attraction is never intellectual," and he proceeded to give me chapter and verse on how, on the road, he would make a beeline for the biggest jugs and roundest bum in the chorus line and not relent until he'd "shtupped it." Even in the midst of a fatal car crash, he once quipped in one of his routines, with only one male and one female survivor, horniness still rears its ugly head. Like Boccaccio or Rabelais, Bruce was always reminding us of our animality and, like de Sade, urging us to celebrate it. Even blue films, he often pointed out, were preferable for children over violent flicks that gloried in blood and gore. "Nobody ever dies in blue movies," he pointed out—although only a few years down the line, the snuff films would make us all question that one.

A few days before he left England (never to return, in fact, because once his narcotic riots had become known, the Home Office barred his reentry),

I asked him what lay ahead. "The same," he said, "ballbusting and brickbats." He didn't say it sadly but with a wily, almost eager smile on his face—as if for him, battle was the quotidian and he could no sooner avoid it than expect to be awarded an Emmy for Outstanding Services to Family Values. In fact, he had been consulting regularly with Stanley Kubrick and was eager to write a film they had been discussing—yet another ambition that was doomed to fizzle out in the endless array of drug busts and court cases that would torment him for the remaining four years of his life.

Lenny was the closest thing we had to a Zen comic in that era when Zen was being vigorously rediscovered and regularly proselytized: a direct descendant of those mad monks whose lunacy is depicted in the early Zen drawings. Out of an astonishing relaxation such as we find only in the finest jazz musicians, Bruce pursued his riff to the furthest borders of rationalism and then winged across. Without warning, he could thrust us into a world no longer confined by logical positivism or dulled with conventional associations. True Zen country, where new frames were added to the mind and the Third Eye not only opened but popped, rolled, swiveled, and hung out on a stalk.

It is often said that it was Lenny who opened the gates for the contemporary crop of American comics. What a dubious distinction! To have paved the way for foul-mouthed buffoons like Shecky Green, Buddy Hackett, and Joan Rivers! No, the fact is that Lenny's tradition died with him. There were no descendants at all. What was bequeathed was only the license for which Lenny paid such heavy dues, a license that is now blithely exercised by no-holds-barred club comics and vulgar Las Vegas headliners.

Despite his own insistence that he was merely a child of show business, Lenny can only be appreciated when compared to the advances of literature in his time. He was the comedic counterpart of Kerouac, Burroughs, Ginsberg, Corso, and Southern, and to fully appreciate both his style and his content, reference has to be made to the best that was being written and published in the '50s and '60s.

In his amorality and civil disobedience, he was something akin to Joe Orton; the moral and political repercussions were merely spin-offs from what both these artists took to be their professional vocation. In each case, as they were made conscious of larger social implications, they tried to arrogate them into their work and make them part of their personalities but in both cases, it was after the fact. The Lenny who said, "I'm not a comedian. And I'm not sick. The world is sick and I'm the doctor. I'm a surgeon with a scalpel for false values. I don't have an act. I just talk. I'm just Lenny Bruce," had gradually absorbed the implications of his own press clippings. Toward the end, when his unbearable routines were filled with self-conscious poetry about Adolf Eichmann and the injustices of the American judicial system, the old Lenny had been almost totally erased both by his champions and his tormentors and was unrecognizable. If personal hardship hadn't sunk him irretrievably into heroin, there would have been a few more luminous years—although it is inconceivable that he would have found any real refuge in society. He was too hip to its deceptions ever to play the game for long and, as his soberer critics always said: "No matter how much you liked Lenny, if you listened to him long enough, there'd come a time when he turned you off." The image of a smug, balding, buttoned-up, and respectable Lenny Bruce being given a Lamb's Club roast is simply unthinkable. Lenny was perhaps the first of the *comic-maudits*—John Belushi was in the same tradition; so was Andy Kaufman and Sam Kinison and, if we're very, *very* lucky, there will be others.

Lenny, *the musical, was revived in London in the summer of '99, and recreations of Bruce tended to pop up regularly on both sides of the Atlantic. Contemporary comics always seemed to use Lenny as a measuring rod, but after the death of Kinison, there weren't too many dangerous comics around. Mainstream comedy, despite its Bruce-brokered freedom to use obscenity and profanity, became curiously tame in its subject matter. The exceptions were the new black comics who, irreverently mixing race, sex, and politics seemed to continue where Lenny left off.*

★★★

37

THE EXONERATION OF ELIA KAZAN

When I was growing up in New York in the '50s, the liberal-leftist microcosm that was my world had one unmitigated villain: Elia Kazan. It didn't matter that he was the miraculous midwife who had brought Arthur Miller's *Death of a Salesman* and Tennessee Williams's *Streetcar Named Desire* to fruition, he was a "squealer," a "rat," and a Judas who had turned in his communist comrades and therefore deserved to be hung, drawn, and quartered.

The animus against Kazan began shortly after he became a cooperative witness before the House Un-American Activities Committee and has not abated in forty years. Shortly after learning of his testimony, Arthur Miller came out with a play (*The Crucible*) about an accused man who refused to "name names." Originally earmarked for Kazan, Miller publicly broke with the man who had virtually established his career, and the play was directed by Jed Harris. Some years later, a reconciliation of sorts occurred and Kazan did direct Miller's *After the Fall* at New York's Lincoln Center, but by then the gleam of notoriety had somewhat faded on both men.

After condemnation from the Left, Kazan's career went on, if not imperturbably, at least steadfastly. There were movies like *On the Waterfront, East of Eden, A Face in the Crowd, The Last Tycoon,* and a number of novels of which *The Arrangement* was probably the most successful. But despite the success of this considerable oeuvre, "the old comrades" remained bitterly unforgiving and for them, everything Kazan touched was morally tainted.

His massive autobiography could not redeem him because it did not contain enough "mea culpa" to satisfy the liberal Left. The fact is that Kazan's disaffiliation with American-styled Soviet communism was actually a genuine disenchantment with a treacherous, mean-spirited, and obnoxious political philosophy to which too many impressionable liberals had been drawn in the '30s and '40s. But, of course, it wasn't the ideology that was at issue. The more salient point was that people who were "named" were economically ruined, and so, the ostensibly honorable ritual of repudiating communist doctrine carried with it the stigma of destroying the lives of former friends and comrades.

Last October in L.A., the four major talent guilds produced a commemorative evening for survivors of the blacklist at the Academy of Motion Picture Arts & Sciences. It was a heartwarming evening and just about four decades overdue. Obviously, the homage paid to the victims of the hearings that blighted so many lives did not, and could not, extend to those who, like Kazan, had been partially responsible for the creation of the blacklist. I, like so many of my morally indignant friends, smoldered with resentment against Kazan through the '60s and '70s but must confess that gradually, by means of a painful and torturous circumlocution, I reached a new plateau of understanding about both the man and his times. I feel now that what is significant about Kazan, and what posterity will honor him for, is his creative genius, and that is right and proper. To amend Marc Antony's line: The good that men do live after them. It is the evil that is "oft interred in their bones."

Kazan wasn't simply "a brilliant director," he was an artist who left his stamp on a generation of other artists and the man who raised social and psychological realism to a plane where it had never been before. He was a sorcerer, in that he conjured magical performances out of performers such as Marlon Brando, James Dean, Rod Steiger, Julie Harris, et al., that these artists rarely achieved again. He did it by refusing to play the role of old-styled director in jodhpurs and boots, bellowing abuse at trembling actors but by quietly whispering hints and provocations into their ears, which radically transformed their sense of characterization and often electrified the material on which they were working. No ploy was too low or too conniving not to be employed to win the "gold" of a spectacular performance. No tactic too shoddy or too cruel if it jolted the imagination, thereby astonishing both the audience and the artist.

In retrospect, it could be argued that his influence on playwrights such as Arthur Miller, Tennesee Williams, and William Inge is even greater than that stamped upon his actors. Williams acknowledged his debt to Kazan openly and, before the split, Miller did so privately. Kazan was the shaman and silent manipulator who simultaneously winnowed out and sharpened the work of America's finest playwrights turning torturous "rewrites" into startling "mise-en-scène." We are all, in a sense, living in the Age of Kazan, and our idolatry of artists such as Brando and Dean, Malden and Steiger, Miller and Williams is in no small measure due to the directorial intelligence that colored the public images of those highly-esteemed actors and playwrights.

In justifying his decision "to testify" rather than "take the 5th," Kazan, exploring the moral circuitry that separates the "informer" from the "silent accomplice," fashioned a cinematic masterpiece in *On The Waterfront,* scripted by that other "friendly witness," Budd Schulberg. That film was torn from the guts of a man in a state of agonizing ambivalence. Can one really argue, forty years after the fact, that the moral dilemma painfully exorcised in that work was not worth the effort? Regarding his testimony, Kazan has never expressed any public remorse, and it may simply be my introjection that tends to believe he felt it in private. But should our appreciation of an artist's achievement mainly be determined by the flaws in his character? By that measure, we would have to derogate Brecht, Ibsen, Strindberg, Celine, Von Karajan, and dozens of others.

Every year doting prize-givers commemorate those artists who have enriched their profession. Even poor abused Chaplin, spurned by his adopted country and branded as everything from a lecher to a Red, was rehabilitated before his peers, sobbing in his wheelchair as he received a Special Oscar, which was due him at least thirty years before. It is bad enough that prophets are never honored in their own country but is a truly dismal spectacle to see mediocrities regularly lauded in one hyped-up award ceremony after another while supreme artists languish in neglect.

Surely, it is time to honor Elia Kazan's unsurpassed mastery—not his moral character or his self-justifying sense of ethics, but the potent imagination with which he fertilized some of America's most treasured playwrights and inspired many of its greatest performers. If Russia can rehabilitate nonpersons such as Meyerhold and Solzhenitsyn, surely America can acknowledge the troubled and besieged man who provided both theater and film with some of its most enduring achievements.

★★★

Not that I believe there was any connection between the two, but in March 1999, one year after I wrote the previous article, Kazan was awarded an Honorary Oscar by the Academy of Motion Picture Arts & Sciences. It stirred an enormous amount of controversy and when the statuette was awarded, many at that ceremony sat with hands stubbornly clasped on their laps while others only mildly applauded. Kazan will never redeem himself from the bitterness of the McCarthy Years, but future generations, who may not be quite so vindictive, will marvel at the work.

★★★

38

ROBERT LEWIS: AN APPRECIATION

Of all the stalwarts of the Group Theater—Harold Clurman, Lee Strasberg, Cheryl Crawford, Elia Kazan, Clifford Odets, et al.—Bobby Lewis was the most unorthodox and, in many ways, the most endearing. While everyone else was following the aesthetic party line, which in the '30s was the Stanislavsky System (soon to become under Lee Strasberg "the Method"), Lewis was experimenting with a variety of non-naturalistic styles, broad theatricality, and other innovations that did not endear him to the Group rank-and-file. Dubbed "Trotsky" because of his revisionism, unlike his namesake, he didn't leave the fold to create an alternative methodology. Instead, Lewis extended Stanislavsky's teaching and in the process directed some of the finest productions of the '40s and '50s, including the hallmark Group Theater production of William Saroyan's *My Heart's in the Highlands,* John Patrick's *Teahouse of the August Moon,* Lerner and Loew's *Brigadoon,* and a score of others.

He had a lethal wit. His bullshit-detector was always on and ticking. Confronted by pretentiousness or sophism, he placed the offending artist on his well-lubricated rack and gently proceeded to break all his bones. In the last years, he was sick and tired of being thought of merely as the Boswell of the Group Theater years and the docent of the turbulent '30s. He had other fish to fry, plays to stage, and ideas to try out. Like many artists too firmly associated with one period, he became, in the minds of many, inextricable from his defining era. But for those who knew him, it was clear that his mind was constantly surfing the web of these pre-millennial years and finding a variety of new networks to explore.

His film career was spotty; he was invariably cast as Orientals because of those lurid slant-eyes. My most indelible memory of him on screen is in that Fred Astaire "Limehouse Blues" sequence in *Ziegfeld Follies.* Without dialogue and in only a handful of frames, he brilliantly evoked the cruel and possessive sugar daddy of Lucille Bremer.

From the '60s onward, his greatest strength was as a teacher. He had served as head of the acting department of the Yale School of Drama under Robert Brustein, co-founded the Actors' Studio, and was one of the most persuasive voices raised against the separation of acting and vocal technique, arguing that only the seamless integration of both truly served the actor's needs.

His unfailing good sense was a tonic to the young and a bracing snifter to the old. In an interview I conducted with him in 1986, I asked him what it was that distinguished the performers of his generation from those of today. "They all had voices," he said. "Remember in *Sunset Boulevard* Gloria Swanson says, 'In those days, we had faces.' Well in those days, we had voices." Questioned about democracy's role in the creative process, he said, "I don't think democracy has any place in art. You can vote from morning to night but nobody can vote anything artistic." He was a firm believer in the centrality of the director's role and, despite his Group orientation, quietly recoiled from the idea of "collectives."

Lewis had a vast and cherished collection of theatrical memorabilia. These were the tokens, icons, and sacraments of the theater's illustrious past. It was clear that his reverence for them and what they represented is what conditioned his own attitude to his art. It was Jean Louis Barrault who said, a man has to respect what he professes to love. Lewis's love of the theater was like that of a superannuated Romeo who, having had every extramarital affair conceivable, was still true to his first love and could think of no better place to expire than in her arms.

39

JERZY GROTOWSKY: AN APPRECIATION

The death of Jerzy Grotowsky in Pontedera, Italy, on January 14th, 1999, is a jolt to many of us who were involved in the wave of theatrical experimentation that swept through Europe and America in the '60s and '70s. The conspicuous innovators were the Living Theater, the Open Theater, and the work of Eugenio Barba and Peter Brook, but it was Grotowsky who emerged as the most spiritually dedicated and, in many ways, the most revolutionary.

While many practitioners were assimilating the technological advances in multimedia, Grotowsky was leading a personal crusade to create a theater in which the actor—refertilized and retooled—would regain his centrality. His kinetic experiments in productions such as *The Constant Prince, Dr. Faustus, Akropolis,* and *Apocalypsis Cum Figuras* were shattering revelations of what the human body could express when it connected with the deepest reaches of the human psyche. The textbook theories of acting seemed to have ended with Stanislavsky, Brecht, and Artaud—until Grotowsky arrived to write a whole new chapter.

In the '70s, there were literally hundreds of Grotowsky-styled troupes scattered over three continents, many of them travesties of the work that Grotowsky began in his "Theater of Thirteen Rows" in Opole in 1959 and then moved to Wroclaw, the city in which his Laboratory Theater was institutionalized. But the foreign tours that began in 1966 made actors and directors dramatically aware that there was a whole new vocabulary of dramatic expression that (astonishingly) had been honed in a nondescript town in Poland.

It was in Holstebro, where I'd brought my own work, that I first encountered Grotowsky. He had been described to me as a guru and an egomaniac, and, in a sense, he was both. His commitment to developing a new dramatic language based on an extension of the actor's physical means of expression made him intolerant of the "let's pretend theater," which merely reshuffled prevailing clichés. He exhorted actors to go deeper and deeper into creating acting alternatives and thereby extending the possibilities of the art form. This reinforced his reputation as an egomaniac. And it was the remarkable results he wrung from the withers of young actors experimenting with new sounds and movement that gave him the status of a guru. To a man on a holy quest for a new theater rooted in ritual, conventional theater practice was as alien as Sunday School would have been to an early Christian martyr.

He had been on his deathbed for almost six months and had written farewell letters to many of his closest friends. His death was attributed, appropriately, to an enlarged heart. During his stint at the University of Irvine, which began in 1984, and in workshops with student actors in Santa Cruz, Santa Barbara, and Berkeley, it was that grandiose heart that transformed their professional lives and made them see acting not so much as a "career choice" but as the highest calling an artist could pursue. That such a swelling heart should have ultimately burst was only to be expected.

40

HOWARD STERN AND THE BODY POLITIC

Why are the Jews so ashamed of Howard Stern?

It is an embarrassment reminiscent of the attitude they used to display toward Lenny Bruce (née Leonard A. Schneider). Bruce "talked dirty" and that was, and remains, a big "no-no" among conservative Jews. Stern not only indulges in profanities, he revels in salaciousness. He leers, he leches, he is obsessed with mammary glands, female posteriors, and the calibrations of sexual relations. He wears uncouthness as if it were the *Legion d'Honneur* and dispenses a style of raunchiness that, deplorable as it may be to many, has become widely accepted as a legitimate form of media entertainment.

That, of course, is what makes certain Jewish elements recoil. Respectability, frequently disguised as "good taste" or a determination "not to give offense," is an underlying principle among many Jews and, judged by that standard, Howard Stern is the quintessential *trombenik.* Publications like *The Jewish Journal,* where you might suppose he would be atomized with analysis, cannot even bring themselves to discuss him. But even in the face of disparagement and ridicule, "Sternism" remains a national phenomenon—a lip-smacking appreciation of vulgarity that garners ratings, sells books, produces films, and encourages fierce loyalty among a large horde of fans.

Of course, pornography, whether graphic, literary, or wholly "unredeemed by any social or artistic merit," has always had its following. Its classier big sister, Eroticism, has been the staple of great art from ancient times to the present. It has produced its own special icons: for example, Boccacio, the Marquis de Sade, D. H. Lawrence, Henry Miller, Anaïs Nin, Jean Genet, and so on. But "Sternism," a guiltless combination of scurrility and voyeurism, is very much a contemporary development. One can discern its flavor in less flamboyant forms such as Geraldo, Sally Jesse Raphael, Jerry Springer, and Rickki Lake; the deification of gossip in publications such as

The Star and *The National Enquirer;* and even, I suppose, in the eagerness with which the general populace sops up sexually explicit congressional reports from independent counsels like Kenneth Starr.

There is about Howard Stern the whiff of junior high school-gym-locker-stag-party prurience redolent of our blotchiest adolescence, when the secrets of sexuality were first being divulged to us in the form of girly magazines, strip shows, copped feels, nocturnal emissions, and masturbatory fantasies. Those sensations were, for many of us, inseparable from "coming of age," and although, in maturity, we look back on that period with a kind of mellow tolerance for the callow youths we once were, the intensity of those experiences is rarely matched in adulthood. Hence, the appeal of Stern, who is a kind of Peter Pan of Unrepressed Sexuality, a revivified, walking-talking wet dream who simultaneously embarrasses us and makes us nostalgic.

Stern is an avid purveyor of adolescent fixations. In his weltanschauung, women exist to bare their breasts, titillate the imagination, or routinely provide orgasms; men, to seduce, dominate, or take revenge upon the opposite sex. When Milton Berle was his guest, Stern's overriding obsession was confirming or denying the legendary size of the comedian's male member. When he found himself opposite a taciturn Warren Beatty, virtually every question was aimed at eliciting explicit details about the actor's former conquests. This is the kind of sexual curiosity that usually characterizes pubescent schoolboys, and we all recognize this neural itch since most of us have grown out of it by the time we are nineteen.

To sustain these adolescent fantasies on an almost nightly television program, it is essential that Stern surround himself with an entourage whose arrested development matches his own. Robin Quivers, his politically correct Ed McMahon–figure, employing indiscriminate laughter and automatic jollity, confers a certain normality to the proceedings. Her presence implies that the lurid subject matter and anatomical preoccupations are par for the course, and everyone should enjoy them as much as she does. Those rollicking male companions who mindlessly yok it up for Howard also reinforce normality.

Since nothing in the show is ever allowed to become conceptualized or rise above the level of barrack-room banter, uneasy viewers can readily persuade themselves that what appears to be lewd or gross is really rather harmless and amusing. But nothing destroys adolescent frolics faster than the arrival of a mature, critical intelligence, and so Stern and his producers ensure that guests, staff, and interviewer continually maintain the horny larkiness that is the unflagging tone of every show.

But Sternism is in no way restricted to the capers of the shlock-jock himself. It is a state of consciousness that, at the twilight of the century, has thoroughly permeated American life. Call it the Tabloid Mentality or the Victory of Voyeurism over Discretion, or what-you-will, the fact is that society insists that there can be nothing so private that the public should be barred from relishing its exposure. All journalism has become *investigative* journalism; all of politics, a preoccupation with suppressed scandal; and Stern, to his credit, doesn't attempt to gloss this over. He wants to see what's bouncing around inside your blouse or dangling down your inside trouser leg and to refuse him is to take refuge in a modesty that, in a Sternian universe, is almost unbecoming.

The great complaint in America has always been that the two major political parties were indistinguishable from one another, but since the House Judiciary sessions on impeachment, that is no longer the case. Clearly, the Republicans are the party of rampant Puritanism and sexual obsession, and the Democrats are those who believe lying is constitutionally protected free speech and that it is the birthright of every American husband to have a little pussy on the side. Here, too, what is fascinating about President Clinton is not his political credo but his libido. Beneath what the Republicans see as the salaciousness of his private life is the widespread American belief that a man who screws is more to be trusted than one who suppresses his sexual appetite. In this, of course, the instincts of the American people are bang on. They instinctively recognize that a man who operates from the Punishment rather than the Pleasure Principle is capable of committing dire human atrocities. Again, a validation of Howard Stern's worldview.

It is silly to treat Sternism as if it were a threat to the national welfare. And to flay it with moral indignation somehow cheapens both morality *and* indignation. It is a wart on the body politic, like thieving HMOs, shyster lawyers, and dissembling used-car dealers, but, over time, we have learned to live with all these moral shortfalls. Howard Stern, caught in an act of marital infidelity, would never "parse words" or claim executive privilege. "I did it, and it was great," he would say, smacking his lips and patting his groin. If only Clinton, caught red-handed, would have adopted the same tactic, he might have endeared himself to an even greater segment of the American public and destroyed the ethical fantasy that holds that politicians cannot have peckers. Had it all played out that way, Howard Stern might be viewed as presidential timber in the year

2000 and the true nature of the American republic allowed to surface from four centuries of sexual hypocrisy.

Stern rose to prominence around the time of the O. J. Simpson saga and reached his pinnacle during the Clinton-Lewinsky scandal. He is clearly a graffiti-sign of the times. The times conjured him up and made him their representative. To malign the man without recognizing the dynamics that brought him into being is to misunderstand a social phenomenon.

Howard is the great, hulking brother of Anna Nicole Smith and John Wayne Bobbitt, who lost his pecker to his wife's rashness. He has been nourished by the steamy, backroom atmosphere of crooked politics that threw up lechers like Senator Bob Packwood and convicted extortionists like ex-Governor Edwin Edwards. When you have a Reign of Terror, the society produces terrorists, and when you have a Reign of Vulgarity, it produce vulgarians. The roots of this problem are social, moral, and political and have almost nothing to do with the entertainment media.

41

JOHN GIELGUD: THE LAST EDWARDIAN

In October of 1953, while he was rehearsing for N. C. Hunter's play *A Day by the Sea* at London's Haymarket Theatre, John Gielgud was arrested for importuning a young man in Chelsea and was booked at a local police station. It being Gielgud and a knight of the realm, the news made all the papers, creating a mixture of embarrassment and hostility directed mainly against a law that many Brits thought was antediluvian and, given the roaring trade in female prostitution, cruelly one-sided.

Once the legalities had been disposed of, Gielgud was scheduled to open his play. Even after the Wolfenden Report changed the law in 1955, legalizing consensual sex between males, British homosexuality was always conducted with great discretion, and so the actor was clearly in a high state of agitation about appearing in public. "Let's play the thing as quickly as we can," he urged his co-star Sybil Thorndyke on the opening night, "to avoid any barracking from the house." As he stepped shakily on stage for his first entrance, the entire audience burst into applause and gave him a standing ovation. In their own idiosyncratic way, that audience was registering a protest against the government's repressive attitude toward gays and giving a resounding vote of confidence to one of their most treasured artists.

Being gay was somehow an acceptable feature of working in the theater. When I was at LAMDA in the late '50s, I had a gay classmate who was consciously farmed out to Gielgud, then rehearsing one of his many *Tempests,* this one under Peter Brook at Stratford. The gift was bestowed by the school's principal in very much the same way an American director might cast a young nubile lady into his company on the tacit understanding that, whatever her stage duties might be, she was primarily there to bestow sexual favors.

Kenneth Tynan underestimated Gielgud's talent when he wrote in 1959 that Sir John was "the finest actor on earth from the neck up." The more salient truth was that listening to Gielgud play Shakespeare was like hearing silver liquid being poured into golden goblets. It wasn't simply "The Voice Beautiful," it was a sound textured with exquisite intelligence and reverberating with psychological nuance. It didn't matter that he lacked Olivier's physicality or Richardson's gregariousness; he had a vocal diversity that was equal to anything the other theatrical knights could field.

When the new Drama was flourishing and writers like Arnold Wesker, John Osborne, and David Storey had put paid to the theater of Coward and Rattigan, Gielgud thought of himself as something of a relic, particularly when Olivier, with Osborne and Tynan in tow, took over the National Theatre and pointedly froze him out. But with performances in Storey's *Home,* Pinter's *No Man's Land,* and Albee's *Tiny Alice,* Gielgud virtually created a new stage persona for himself; quirky, acrid, cynical, and refreshingly modern.

His greatest gift, that syrupy-textured voice, was also his greatest handicap. As an actor he was fixated on text and virtually oblivious to subtext. That didn't mean that things weren't going on underneath the lines. In acting, they always are. But it does mean that whereas a different kind of actor would methodically organize the emotional substructure of a role, Gielgud instinctively relied on language to activate his feelings.

Lyricism was a constituent not only of his acting but also of his personality—which is why he was so successful as Hamlet and Richard II and incapable of roles like Richard III or Iago. The pampered upbringing, the tendency toward stylishness, the reverence for elegance—all of these qualities predisposed him to success in parts like pompous Jack Worthing in *The Importance of Being Earnest,* prissy characters like Malvolio, or hierarchical types like Prospero. But he turned his limitation into a strength and, in the main, veered away from parts that were too earthy or too remote from his own Spartan character.

His face was a scowling Japanese mask, but his character was gentle and adorably fey—like one of those traditional British eccentrics who inhabit the Mayfair clubs and are forever awash in anecdotage. Even with all his later forays into the avant-garde, he always remained a kind of stranded Edwardian dandy, reminding one of an earlier and more elegant era.

★★★

42

TOM STOPPARD: A LITTLE LIGHT MUSIC

In the summer of 1965, when I was little more than a fledgling director myself, I was asked to "enlighten" a group of up-and-coming British writers buoyed up by a Ford Foundation grant at a retreat in Wansee, a suburb of Berlin best remembered as the site of the Wansee Conference at which Hitler's "final solution" was casually ratified.

It was here that I first met Tom Stoppard—tousle-haired, droopy-eyed, sucked-in cheeks, looking more like Mick Jagger than Jagger ever did. My most vivid memory of him is when, in conversation with other members of his group (which included Piers Paul Read, Derek Marlowe, and Peter Bergman), he blithely and unself-consciously referred to himself and his cohorts as "the coming men." How refreshingly conceited, I thought to myself, to already know with such certainty that one was "a coming man." But Tom was quite correct. He "came on" very rapidly after that.

Toward the end of the seminar, each writer had to present an excerpt from some work in progress, and I was expected informally to adjudicate. Tom's excerpt, unquestionably the weirdest of the lot, concerned two minor characters from *Hamlet* who spent a lot of time tossing coins in the air and receiving visits from a hoary old self-denigrating gent called King Lear. It struck me as an unsalvageable piece of academic twaddle, and I remember thinking that Stoppard, whom I knew as a sometime-reviewer in London, would probably be more gainfully employed knocking out copy on Fleet Street.

Two years later, rejigged and refined, Lear deleted and a slate of new material inserted, the play emerged on the stage of the National Theatre as *Rosencrantz and Guildenstern Are Dead*. It was like a retarded child making such a miraculous recovery that he was now ready to take up his duties as dean of linguistic philosophy at Oxford or Cambridge. As I lacerated my palms expressing my enthusiasm, I had a disturbing little flashback to the tiny Berlin stage where I had seen the play gestate and, downgrading my powers of perception several notches, marveled at the transmutations of which art was capable.

In one of those curious flip-flops that often occur between members of the same generation, Tom was assigned to write a review of *The Trigon,* one of my early productions at In-Stage, a company I had founded in London. It concluded with the words: "After sitting in acres of plush watching the worse two-thirds of London theater, it is slightly eerie to sit in that ridiculous little attic and watch something so polished." A few years later, I was reviewing *Travesties* and, subsequent to that, preparing a profile on him for the *New York Times.* In those days, journalistic incest was par for the course. It hasn't changed.

Now enthroned in a vast house in Slough (that most un-Stoppardian of all London suburbs), we jockeyed around trying to determine the latitudes and longitudes of our altered relationship. Having known him in the grubby Fleet Street days, I thought I sensed a slight embarrassment as he showed me around the sumptuous garden of what in my memory looms as "the Baronial Manor." He was as dry and witty as he had been when knocking out notices for his newspaper in Bristol, but his manner seemed to imply that both his property and his status were the result of some incredible spin-of-the-wheel that he could not properly explain and that, in any case, would shortly be reversed.

His philosophical curiosity was as alive as ever, but the new acquisitions—both of property and status—had removed that nervy edge of questing that had made him both narky and ratty several years before. Some part of him suggested that he wasn't really entitled to his newfound prosperity, but that was aggressively countered by another part that defiantly asserted its claims in the teeth of all self-doubt. If I had just been an anonymous journalist on assignment, I am sure he'd have been able to muster an appropriately diffident air, but being a director and critic with an indelible memory of his earliest days, I think he was slightly discommoded, as if my knowledge of his grungier self in some way subverted the successful persona he had now formulated.

What was always arresting about Tom's work was that "outside-looking-in" perspective that enabled significant events—such as the Russian revolution and rise of Dada in *Travesties* or the central action of Hamlet in *Rosencrantz and Guildenstern Are Dead*—to be glimpsed, as it were, through the wrong end of the telescope. Paradoxically, Stoppard, who in *Jumpers* larked his way through classical philosophy, seemed to be most airborne when carrying the heaviest freight—and the consequence of this paradox is that his deepest concerns often appeared trivial, a word that became affixed to him as impermeably as the number scorched in the flesh of an Auschwitz inmate.

In '75, in that *New York Times* piece, I asked whether it was true to say he had no strong political feelings: "I'm not impressed by art *because* it is political," he replied. "I believe in art being good art or bad art, not relevant art or irrelevant art. The plain truth is that if you are angered or disgusted by a particular injustice or immorality and you want to do something about it—*now*—at once, then you can hardly do worse than write a play about it. That's what art is bad at." However, in recent years, Stoppard, like Pinter, appears to have developed a Johnny-Come-Lately political awareness and, in works such as *Professional Foul, Every Good Boy Deserves a Favour,* and *Night and Day,* has foisted a new aspect of his literary personality. For my money, most of these works fail to convince as "political statements," but in a romantic comedy like *The Real Thing,* Stoppard's talent and subject matter magically coalesce. Treating subjects such as infidelity and the hunger for genuine, as opposed to delusional, experience, he has found his truest voice. Heard in the fullness of its range, it is the voice of an incisive, skeptical, bemused observer of human foibles (more Marivaux than Molière) who uses comedy to agitate social and psychological insights.

In that same earlier interview, he said: "I think to be amusing and entertaining about a serious subject is a reasonable objective." Acting on this principle, Stoppard seems recently to have become the Bard of the Hampstead and Highgate Set, those upwardly mobile, slightly paunchified yuppies whose gospel is the Sunday Supplements and who find in sexual promiscuity and political activism an antidote to social ennui. The wellspring of many of Stoppard's characters (here, too, he resembles Pinter) is boredom. One feels that they are not motivated by conviction so much as the need to amuse, divert, or reanimate themselves. And the same observation could be applied to the playwright. Sizzling social and political issues are (if you'll pardon the mixed metaphor) the meat out of which Stoppard makes his cucumber sandwiches. To hear him address subjects such as the enslavement of East Europe or the brainwashing of political prisoners in the USSR is to hear Rudy Vallee belting out excerpts from "Der Gotterdamerung" through a megaphone.

In our time, the compulsion of comic writers to deal with serious issues in a serious way has flattened out Woody Allen, hamstrung Neil Simon, attenuated Alan Ayckbourn, and dehydrated Tom Stoppard. None have been done permanent harm and, in some cases (as in the film *Manhattan* or the play *Henceforward*), a judicious balance has been struck. But on the whole, the Pagliacci syndrome has gone against the grain of a talent whose natural tendency was flighty, capering, and wholesomely trivial. As if Comedy could not accommodate every idea consciously crammed into the Serious Drama.

Stoppard's verbal alacrity, which is the outward flourish of an irrepressible inner wit, gives everything he writes an almost blinding sheen. It's not that he is not profound (he's one of the few contemporary playwrights who can converse authoritatively on Wittgenstein and Schopenhauer), it's just that his temperament often engulfs his intellect, and just as Wilde described *The Importance of Being Earnest* as being "A Trivial Comedy for Serious People," so everything that Stoppard touches feels like "A Serious Comedy for Trivial People."

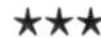

43

RACHEL ROSENTHAL: ENDANGERED SPECIES

Rachel Rosenthal, her bald pate gleaming with sweat and her stark features grooved like pissholes in the snow, looks like a female Eric Von Stroheim—who let's face it, could himself have been a woman in drag. Short, stubby, Teutonic, and with the kind of wracked expression one imagines Rimbaud wore after his season in hell, she could just as easily be the commandant of a Nazi death camp as the most senior and compelling Performance Artist in California.

In fact, she is the latter and for some forty years has been experimenting with a mix of Dada, surrealism, Artaudian metaphysics, and social activism. A photo of her in 1963, before she shaved her head and wound gold earrings into her brow, reveals an attractive, lantern-jawed young lady with sensuous, devouring lips and large, mesmerizing eyes. The updated Rachel Rosenthal is clearly an artifact consciously designed by the artist for public consumption and intended to be an amalgam of all the aesthetic influences that shaped her over the years. A kind of animated abstract of postmodernism, she combines the grittiness of Brecht with the mania of Artaud and appears to be permanently impaled on "the cutting edge."

She is a rare bird. One couldn't begin to conceive of anyone more un-American. Drenched in European aesthetics and committed to performance dynamics that radically go against the grain of conventional theater, she plies her trade like an industrious mole groveling away inside the body politic. Like all individual artists, she, too, has had her NEA grant withdrawn but soldiers on in a small loft-space off Robertson Boulevard, surrounded by a loyal and talented cadre of performers who have clearly been infected by her brand of rabid counterculturalism. She should be on the Endangered Species list because there are very few like her around, and once they disappear, the performing arts will be severely impoverished. People like Rosenthal inhabit a tiny, usually remote inlet where alternative practices challenge the pounding surf of the mainstream, offering that rarest of all virtues: an aesthetic alternative to mob culture. It is an inlet previously inhabited by artists such as Baudelaire, Joyce, Jarry, Picasso, Artaud, Rauschenberg, Cage, and Cunningham and is invariably where the freshest and most dangerous ideas are incubated, the ones that subsequently influence and ultimately transform the mainland.

One of her more recent works, *Tohubohu,* a Hebrew term denoting "chaos, confusion, and hubbub," grew out of loose patterns and a few fixed musical rhythms but was entirely improvised and improvised differently each night. The subject matter was ecological, social, and philosophical and most effectively so when language was kept to a minimum. In it, Rosenthal essayed a short piece in which the sixty-nine-year-old artist alluded to a recent fracas at Highways, a performance art venue in Santa Monica, where Joan Hotchkiss scandalized an ostensibly hip audience by discussing the sexual cravings of sexagenarians. Rosenthal played off that mini-scandal with fantasies of her own, which forcibly reminded us that, though their contemplation is anathema to the mainstream, the sexual organs of people in their sixties are still wigglingly alive. The uniqueness of her company lies in the fact that, out of a well-lubricated mechanism, Rosenthal has created a living organism and one that, with practice and support, could turn into something quite extraordinary. Which brings us back to the subsidy question.

The puddin'-headed conservatives of both parties who view all art as a threat and all subsidy as a hand-out are directly responsible for extinguishing the exciting potentiality of artists like Rosenthal and her company. Monster musicals and straightforward commercial plays are not dependent on subsidy and may well be able to make their way through the quagmire of the marketplace, but small-scale, experimental activity, which ultimately nourishes mainstream art, must always be helped by patronage—private, corporate, or governmental—and every civilized country in the world except America understands that.

Rosenthal's venue at Espace seats about forty people. The subsidy it requires is a moiety of what is annually raised for the Music Center or the regularly hoopla'd, invariably tedious L.A. Arts Festivals. She is involved in the kind of research Bill Gates was doing in college before he came up with Microsoft, and although Performance Art will never dominate the culture the way computers do, it may well influence the direction that all the performing arts, particularly dance and theater, may take in the future. To turn an artist like Rosenthal into an endangered species is to negate the whole conception of a cultural environment. You don't back research because it is spectacular or successful but because it is the devotion out of which spectacular and successful work of the future evolves.

Fifty years from now people in L.A. will be saying, "Did you ever happen to see the work of Rachel Rosenthal?" and octogenarians will fondly compare indelible memories. It would be disgraceful if in that surge of nostalgia they also said, "Yes, and isn't it sad she was never really supported in her lifetime? What marvels could have come about, if she had been!"

★★★

III

ON THE PAGE

44

JACOB ADLER: A LIFE ON THE STAGE

A Memoir by Jacob Adler

Translated and with Commentary by Lulla Rosenfeld

To those who never experienced its *Sturm und Drang,* the Yiddish theater, which flowered in America from the turn of the century to the early '50s, will seem to be little more than an ethnic oddity. It consisted of a score of playhouses in which domestic melodramas, folksy song-and-dance, and truncated versions of European classics regaled audiences made up largely of working-class Jewish immigrants who fondly recalled life in the *shtetl* and wept openly at the social and familial cruelties of the New World.

Shund, meaning "trash," was the pejorative most often applied to the repertoire, and without being tuned into the religious beliefs that were tacitly understood and frequently challenged in these plays, they would appear to non-Jews as quaint and incomprehensible as Noh dramas or Balinese dance.

But the Yiddish theater was a powerful moral force in the lives of its public, much more so than the American theater was to English-speaking audiences during the same period. It not only gave instructions on ethical conduct and espoused Enlightenment for its people but produced some of the most magnetic performers of the century: Paul Muni (née Muni Weisnenfreund) for instance, and Anna Held, Menasha Skulnick, and Molly Picon and, in its earliest phase, Boris Thomashevsky, David Kessler, and Siegmund Mogulesko. Not names that would necessarily ignite the memories of the general public, but awe-inspiring icons among Jewish theatergoers, who saw the turmoils and tendernesses of their lives mirrored in their performances.

Yiddish theater originated in Romania under the aegis of Avrom Goldfaden, the first Jewish hyphenate: writer-composer-director-producer-actor. In its Russian incarnation in Odessa, it was wrenched into being by a little-known con man called Risrol Rosenberg, who had the good sense to recruit Yankev Pavlovich Adler, who, as Jacob Adler, became the most celebrated Yiddish actor of his generation.

Adler's memoirs originally appeared in the Socialist newspaper *Die Varheit* in 1916 and nine years later, in 1925, were resumed in the *New Varheit.* The late Lulla Rosenfeld, who provided both the translation and the illuminating commentary, is responsible for unearthing a genuine *objet trouvé:* an autobiographical chronicle of Adler's life that parallels the rise of the Yiddish theater, both in Russia and America, and at the same time evokes the world of the *shtetl* in Czarist Russia more vividly than any other record of this period I have ever read.

Adler was an actor from the top of his imposing dome to the tips of his terpsichorean toes, and so this is no intellectually astute, socio-psychological exegesis of the period. It is unashamedly the recollections of a man who spent his life touring half-obliterated towns such as Kishinev, Yelizavetgrad, Zhitomer, Lvov, and Novomirgorod; fleeing pogroms, feeling the constant pinch of poverty, suffering through internal intrigues with fellow-players and unspeakable brutalities at the hands of heartless Cossacks and marauding police.

The whole of the first half of this memoir feels like the kind of silent film epics that D. W. Griffith and Eric von Stroheim used to turn out in the '20s. It is heady, melodramatic, sensational, disaster-prone, and elevating—very much like the plays that Adler actually produced and appeared in. It is only when one stops to realize that these devastating events actually occurred that one begins to appreciate the fact that the late nineteenth century was a world so hazardous and primitive that it is almost impossible to grasp it with a twenty-first-century sensibility.

Like the early Elizabethan stage, the Yiddish theater in Adler's native Odessa is mounted in tents, in barns, in warehouses, playing to peasants and illiterates who nevertheless find a childlike affirmation in the experience of watching a play. Gradually, it moves into playhouses, developing extraordinary performers, even producing playwrights such as Joseph Lateiner and Jacob Gordin who, though no Marlowe or Shakespeare, begin to assemble workmanlike scripts that reflect the lives of the people who make up their audience. Then, in the '20s, after less than fifty years, one looks around and sees that something quite unique has been created: a Yiddish theater that is both as naturalistic and as expressionistic as anything produced by Andre Antoine or Max Reinhardt.

Adler's earliest years in Odessa were wild and unruly. He ran with a delinquent crowd, drank to excess, patronized bordellos, and gained his first kudos as a boxer in the bohemian Molodovanka district of the city. It was through the influence of Yisrol Rosenfeld that he gradually discovered his true vocation in the nascent Yiddish theater and, once found, it transformed him utterly.

Adler's first breakthrough performance was in Karl Gutzkow's *Uriel Acosta,* a nineteenth-century German play that rapidly got appropriated by almost every Yiddish theater in Europe, but his most fertile work occurred when he began a dynamic collaboration with Jacob Gordin, the true father of Yiddish drama even if he did come a decade or so after Goldfaden. Gordin's *Yiddish King Lear* was something of a harbinger of Adler's greatest triumph as Shylock in 1903, which was brought to Broadway with an English-speaking cast, Adler alone playing in Yiddish. Here was a production of the overtly anti-Semitic *Merchant of Venice* that, paradoxically, was fervently embraced by Jews since, for the first time since Kean, the character emerged not as a scoundrel or a buffoon but as a proud Jew wrongfully trampled down by a society of bigoted venture-capitalists. In affirming the latent dignity of Shylock, Adler virtually dissolved all of the role's negative connotations and, in so doing, exonerated a character that for three centuries had been regularly maligned. That is more than delivering a great performance; that is bestowing a racial benefaction.

Technique, in Adler's day, was largely a matter of assimilating externals. He talks about learning how to apply greasepaint, wear the costume, regulate his vocal range, alter his posture. The lessons of Stanislavsky had not yet been transcribed or assimilated. But it is clear that he disdained actors who merely duplicated the effects of previous interpretations and constantly sought to strain character through the sieve of his own sensibility. His explanation of what he tried to do with Uriel Acosta, with Lear and Shylock, are the simplistic descriptions of an artist constantly striving to be fresh, original, and true to his own nature—which is a lesson that antedates Stanislavsky and virtually every other theatrical theorist.

The second part of the memoir, being written almost a decade later and one year before Adler's death, feels foreshortened, but Lulla Rosenfeld's commentary goes a long way toward filling in the gaps and providing the rounded portrait that the author was too weary and too ill to furnish.

What emerges at the close of this remarkable book is the confirmation of a truism. A great actor, goes the old saw, is forged by great experience. Adler's suffering in Russia, then in the pathetic slums of the Whitechapel district of London before emerging full-blown in New York in the 1890s, turned the man into a living repository of emotional memory that nourished all the work he created on the stage. The cliché that art is distilled from suffering was never more dynamically confirmed than in the work of the mature Adler.

When he died in 1926, over a hundred thousand people followed the funeral cortege to the Williamsburgh Bridge en route to its final resting place in Mount Carmel. In the main, these were the immigrants whose lives had been shaped and memorialized by the man who had spent fifty years on the stage dramatizing the vicissitudes of their American experience.

The bulk of this autobiography was written over eighty years ago. Its publication is like placing a headstone at a grave that has remained unmarked for almost a century.

★★★

Although generally assumed to be a relic from the distant past, there are, at this writing, two Yiddish-speaking theaters in New York alone: the Folkesbiene and a breakaway company, the Yiddish Public Theatre. Not to mention the English-speaking Jewish Repertory Theatre at the 92nd Street YMHA. All have roots traceable to the theater of Jacob Adler. His children Luther and Stella were pillars of the Group Theater, and Stella became a charismatic acting teacher whose prize pupil was probably Marlon Brando. Frances, the eldest daughter, was also a well-established actress and teacher in New York.

★★★

45

THE SMART SET: GEORGE JEAN NATHAN AND H. L. MENCKEN

by Thomas Quinn Curtiss

Between about 1910 and 1939, no one in the theater made a move without consulting George Jean Nathan. In the midst of scriveners, hacks, and stringers, Nathan was the real thing: an erudite theater critic with more than twenty books to his credit, a fabled association with H. L. Mencken behind him (they co-edited *The Smart Set*), and a range of European-bred tastes that gave him a sophistication that few of his colleagues could rival. He not only encouraged the early Eugene O'Neill but was a close friend of the playwright's and became his staunchest champion. He elucidated G. B. Shaw for the masses and created the appetite that eventually established Sean O'Casey.

Nathan has recently re-surfaced as a result of two new publications from Applause Books: *The Smart Set,* Thomas Quinn Curtiss's lively history of the magazine that between 1914 and 1923 mockingly declared war on American philistinism; and *The World of George Jean Nathan,* a reissue of Charles Agnoff's 1952 chrestomathy of material drawn from the author's collected works.

The fate that, from the '40s onward, befell H. L. Mencken somewhat hobbled Nathan as well. After three decades of pervasive influence as a critic, seer, and pundit, Mencken was relegated to the role of superficial wiseacre and dispenser of once-fashionable-now-passé cynicism. Nathan, whose literary style was almost the mirror-image of Mencken's, was likewise downgraded. Although he beat the drums for O'Neill and European playwrights such as Hauptmann, Schnitzler, Maeterlinck, and the Capeks, by mid-century many of these same playwrights had lost their allure. Even O'Neill got taken down several pegs, and today a fierce controversy still rages as to whether he is really America's most prodigious playwright or a brooding Strindbergian clone who never quite managed to master either language or dramaturgy.

The Mencken–Nathan partnership was one of those curious unions based on ostensible incompatibility. Mencken was a proud Teuton, admirer of the Kaiser, bigoted against blacks, casually anti-Semitic, and a devotee of beer and burlesque; Nathan, a dandified Jew who emulated Oscar Wilde and "art for art's sake" and a shameless hedonist who didn't care a fig about politics. They both shared a fanged sense of humor and allied themselves against what Mencken liked to call "the booboisie": bible-thumping Philistines, Comstocks, and Babbits.

In one of his early credos, Nathan wrote:

> What interests me in life is the surface of life: life's music and color, its charm and ease, its humor and its loveliness. The great problems of the world—social, political, economic, and theological—do not concern me in the slightest. I care not who writes the laws of the country so long as I may listen to its songs. I can live every bit as happily under a king, or even a Kaiser, as under a president. . . . If all the Armenians were to be killed tomorrow and if half of Russia were to starve to death the day after, it would not matter to me in the least. What concerns me alone is myself, and the interests of a few close friends. For all I care the rest of the world can go to hell at today's sunset.

Thomas Quinn Curtiss in *The Smart Set* contends that this was Nathan merely projecting a histrionic image of himself, but everything in his oeuvre tends to bear out the sentiments expressed.

Harold Clurman disdained Nathan (ironically, he was the first recipient of the George Jean Nathan Award for Drama Criticism), but then Nathan disparaged Clifford Odets and most of the repertoire of the Clurman-Strasberg Group Theatre. When, in the '30s, the American stage was veering irreversibly toward social realism, Nathan was still championing Continental elegance and artificiality. One of the curious contradictions in his character is that although he espoused "high art"—O'Neill, Shaw, Ibsen, and Shakespeare—he had an insatiable weakness for frivolous musical comedies, vaudeville, and strip-tease. He was perhaps the first to fully appreciate the genius of Florenz Ziegfeld, and his encomium on Ziegfeld from 1921 is one of the most astute essays ever written on that exceptional showman.

Nathan's great strengths as a critic were his erudition, his wit, his clear-cut statement of aesthetic principles, and his ability to stick to them—even when they might have been gainfully re-thought. Perhaps because of his iconoclastic years with Mencken, he was always anticipating encroachments from the Vulgarian, the Philistine, and the Yahoo. He was so prone to tilt against windmills of his own making, that he was often blind to the real virtues of a writer, a play, or a movement. Withering put-down became a reflex action and, as any critic will tell you, it's always disastrous to go to the theater cutlass in hand.

What he lacked was the gift of incisive analysis, a sense of dramatic structure beyond obvious observations about "a weak second act" or "an unsatisfactory climax." His spirited defense of O'Neill, triggered by Eric Bentley's sharp, deflationary criticism of the playwright, is more like that of a booster than a cagey intellectual defender mustering unassailable arguments. No matter how impressive Nathan the Critic ever becomes, he is constantly subverted by Nathan the Dandy: the man who is more concerned with witty badinage and flip cynicism than he is hard, critical reasoning.

But, then, neither Kenneth Tynan nor Frank Rich were exactly intellectual heavyweights, and critics like Alexander Woolcott and Brooks Atkinson were such lightweights that beside them, Nathan looms like a Tunney or a Dempsey.

The overriding fact is that Nathan was utterly saturated in the arts and throughout his life fed off them like an insatiable gourmet, and so all his copy seems to come from a sensibility that is thoroughly habituated to a wide and fertile cultural terrain. Perhaps in the long run that is the only characteristic of the true critic that counts: that he be a man who cares passionately about standards and their maintenance, and that he conveys that passion in every word he writes.

★★★

46

LOLA MONTEZ: A LIFE

by Bruce Seymour

To some extent, we all invent ourselves. Inspired by early prototypes, compensations for personal inadequacies, and tendencies to romanticize the more prosaic facts our backgrounds, we create a persona, costume it accordingly, and project it to the world as a flashy substitute for the less spectacular men and women we happen to be.

In some cases, the effort is transparent and the disparity between what we imagine and what we are, glaringly evident. In Hollywood, for instance, aided by legions of PR-men and spin-doctors, there are countless men and women living inviolable psychotic lives: figments of their own imaginations that, ironically, become figments of the public imagination as well. In fleeting, undeluded moments of clarity, these people probably catch a glimpse of their true selves, but since such insights tend to subvert their fabricated identities, those glimpses are immediately suppressed.

We have terms with which we disparage this widespread practice of fictionalizing ourselves. We call such people "phonies," we say they suffer from "delusions of grandeur," that they are not "living in the real world." But since "none" of us are living in the real world and we all need to be fortified by contrived personality traits, we tend to accept each other's cover story and adapt to the fictions as if they were facts. The "illusion" of reality is as close as we ever get to the real thing.

Lola Montez, born Eliza Gilbert in Limerick, Ireland, in 1820, was an entirely created character but, once created, so totally inhabited by her maker that virtually no vestige of the original woman remained. Socially nondescript by birth and upbringing, she was instinctively drawn to the superstars whose realm she was determined to inhabit. Franz Liszt was one of the most glittering of those superstars, and in 1844, Lola swooped down upon him. Although he quickly tired of her quixotic temperament, he did introduce her to the *haut monde* of Paris and effectively launched her social career. Over the years, with the unquenchable zeal of an unreformable star-fucker, Lola seduced (or was seduced by) Robert Peel, eldest son of Sir Robert Peel, the ex-British prime minister, and hob-nobbed with the likes of Alexander Dumas and a great clutch of influential journalists and aristocrats. She inveigled herself into the lives of many distinguished, affluent men and finally, in 1846, caught the brass ring in a private audience with King Ludwig I of Bavaria. Shortly after that first meeting, the rumor spread that Ludwig had pointed to Lola's curvaceous bosom and inquired: "Nature or art?" at which point Lola took up a pair of scissors and cut away the front of her dress, revealing the Montez boobs in all their natural splendor. It probably never happened, but already the legends that would envelop her life had begun to circulate and, as time went on and Lola herself fabricated events that also never happened with people she never actually knew, the myth grew to gargantuan proportions.

King Ludwig, who probably only slept with his mistress three times in three years (but who had a weakness for taking her unwashed feet into his mouth), was Lola's prize catch, although she turned out to be the bane of his existence. He built her a sumptuous palace near the royal castle so that he could avoid the inconvenience of meeting her at her hotels, plied her with jewelry and money (an estimated $3 million over a two-year period), and eventually hoisted her into the aristocracy by making her Countess of Landsfelt. In return, she caused all his top ministers to resign en masse, created a revolution in Bavaria, and eventually forced the abdication of King Ludwig himself. This didn't deter her appetite for royal sustenance and, in a number of nakedly exploitative letters, she begged, implored, and extorted money from the frail king (he was in his early sixties, she in her late twenties) so that she could continue to live in the style to which he had accustomed her. Eventually, her infidelities, lies, and temperamental outbursts brought a certain enlightenment to the hearing-impaired monarch—although he never quite got the dancing girl out of his system. When Lola died at the age of forty, a convert to Christianity, repenting a life of sin and mendacity, he probably emitted a great sigh of relief—as did all the other men she had hounded and harried throughout her turbulent life.

Spoiled, arrogant, volatile, petty, and a congenital liar, Lola started as a bogus Spanish dancer (her specialty was the "Spider Dance," in which she exhibited her legs and thighs in a violent Flamenco-styled attempt to seek out and destroy the poisonous insect that had secreted itself among her private parts) and went on to play in Sheridan and custom-made plays, the most successful of which was *Lola Montez in Bavaria,* a kind of docu-melodrama that dramatized (and falsified) her tempestuous relationship with King Ludwig and the Bavarian nobility. Although everyone was taken by her striking beauty, the critics invariably put down her dancing and were only a little kinder to her acting, but the real lure was simply seeing the notorious Lola Montez—after Queen Victoria, the second most talked-about woman in the nineteenth century. When she got too long in the tooth for stage performances, she became a lecturer on fashionable feminist topics; the fees she commanded were higher than those of Charles Dickens.

A few years after her death, she spawned a fascinating clone—namely, Ada Menken, who was also neither a dancer nor an actress but who achieved international fame as Mazeppa, "the naked lady." (In fact, her nakedness was a kind of stage mirage produced by pink, skin-tight leotards that left nothing to the imagination and therefore gave the impression of total nudity.) Like Lola Montez, Menken smoked cigarettes, cut her hair short, and toured the world on notoriety rather than talent. She, too, challenged enemies to duels and harassed newspaper editors with indignant letters intended to boost her popularity. She, too (even more so than Lola), was the intimate of cultural superstars: in Menken's case, Algernon Swinburne, Walt Whitman, Bret Harte, Mark Twain, and Alexander Dumas, and she openly acknowledged the influence of Lola Montez on her lifestyle.

What Montez did (in our time Brando, Dean, and Monroe did it as well) was to create a new personality mold to which highly impressionable acolytes fitted themselves. We get flashes of Montez's personality from media-whores such as Zsa-Zsa Gabor, Anna Nicole Smith, and Demi Moore, and the lessons learned from her have been instinctively assimilated by innumerable nonartists who use hype to fuel careers that would otherwise go nowhere. So the mythos generated by Lola is very much part of our times and clearly demonstrates how deeply rooted hype is in the American character.

There are those who view Montez as a proto-feminist, but her main concern was her own independence, not that of any imaginary sisterhood—and the same was true of Ada Menken, who, despite her bobbed hair, cigarettes, and proselytization of free love, was only concerned with realizing her own rampaging individuality.

Bruce Seymour, whose only former claim to fame is having won over $300,000 on *Jeopardy,* which enabled him to write this biography, has plunged boldly into the archival depths and mythical murk of his subject. But in the case of Lola Montez, a woman who consistently obfuscated the facts of her life, research is like the Black Hole of Calcutta. Seymour, in *Lola Montez: A Life,* has clarified some of the more outrageous prevarications about his subject but is regularly blown sideways by speculation and hypothesis, never conclusively separating fact from fiction—a virtually impossible feat with someone as unpindownable as Lola Montez. But the narrative sweep of the Bavarian years is excellent, and the lurch from one lover to the next, consistently enthralling.

But Seymour writes like a quiz-show winner rather than an astute historian, and one often rankles at the baldness of the exposition and the steady accretion of unwinnowed details. He unearths facts but doesn't convincingly place them into a dramatic perspective, as, for instance, Richard Ellmann did with Oscar Wilde or Leon Edel with Henry James. Yet Lola is a compelling character, and Seymour is obviously hooked on her, which, most of the time, makes up for a pedestrian literary style.

The great value of a myth is that, unlike a detective thriller, it can never be unraveled at the end. We still don't really know about Lola Montez: what made her tick, swing her pendulum from scheming adventuress to repentant sinner, from selfish psychotic to would-be saint. No biography can ever fully de-mythify someone as fundamentally untraceable as this, and part of the joy of reexperiencing her life is getting the full brunt of the contradictions and anomalies. Who would want to read a tell-all biography of Sappho or Aphrodite?

47

TRUE AND FALSE: HERESY AND COMMON SENSE FOR THE ACTOR

by David Mamet

David Mamet, I suspect, has a pretty hairy chest. He comes from Chicago, which was the hometown of other tough guys like Al Capone and "Bugs" Moran. Judging by his writing style, I would think he's pretty well-hung. Certainly, *"he"* thinks so, and his demeanor seems to suggest that testosterone was as mother's milk to him. I'd hate to tangle with him *mano a mano;* he'd probably level me with one blow and then, to drive home his point, kick me in the nuts. He's one tough "mother," and his book *True and False: Heresy and Common Sense for the Actor* is a kind of mini-monument erected to his brawn.

As a playwright, in razor-sharp works such as *American Buffalo, Glen Gary Glen Ross, Speed the Plow,* and *Oleanna,* Mamet has built a reputation for himself in the past three decades that is almost the equivalent of that created by Arthur Miller in the '40s and '50s. His plays are canny, cynical, probing, acrid, and stylistically distinctive. His book, on the other hand, is fatuous, sophistic, grandstanding, and moronic.

Although it begins by proclaiming: "The Stanislavsky Method and the technique of the schools derived from it, is nonsense," it constantly regurgitates Stanislavskyian principles (e.g., playing actions, employing units and objectives, using "the magic If," finding the throughline, etc.). What seems to have dawned on Mamet rather late in life is that the Method (viz. Strasberg's Freudian fudge) is generally in disrepute and *has* been for something like fifteen years. "Stanislavsky," Mamet reminds us, "was essentially an amateur." But so was Andre Antoine, so was the Duke of Saxe Meiningen. So is every groundbreaking artist at the outset. And so, fulsomely, is Mamet when he forsakes playwriting and assumes the mantle of Mohammed.

Mamet's mentor, of course, was Sanford Meisner who, though he deviated from many of Strasberg's principles, was still cut from the same cloth (Stanislavsky via the Group Theatre) and simply made action-playing, rather than emotional memory, his stalking-horse. Most of *True and False* is Mamet rehashing Meisnerisms, but he seems to be oblivious to the fact that today even the dogma of action-playing is being seriously questioned and that boiling scenes down to "one simple objective" is considered by many to be crass reductionism and an approach that denies the complexity and contradictory nature of human behavior.

The secret hero of *True and False* is the playwright. "It is the writer's job to make the play interesting," says Mamet. "It is the actor's job to make the performance truthful." Which only prods memories of a thousand ill-written plays that were enhanced, sometimes rescued, by the intercession of great acting. The whole history of "vehicles" in the theater is the history of rotten plays like *The Bells* and *The Jest* transformed by the alchemy of actors such as Irving and the Barrymores. But again and again, Mamet is drawn back to the lodestone of "the author." If *only* the author will be trusted, if *only* his words will be respected, if *only* actors wouldn't mar those precious lines with mugging, and "characterization" and what he calls "funny voices," how blissful the theater would be!

"The only reason to rehearse," says Mamet, "is to learn to perform the play. It is not 'to explore the meaning of the play'—the play, for the actor, has no meaning beyond its performance. It is not to 'investigate the life of the character.' There is no character. There are just lines on the page."

Literary content is the gold bullion, implies Mamet, and the actor's job is merely to haul it up out of the ground, making sure he doesn't drop any in the process. But if "character" is not inherent in that literary content, then what is? *Hamlet* may be "lines on a page," but a succession of actors, from Burbage to Barrymore, from Olivier to Branagh, have incarnated those lines according to the lineaments of their own personality. "Lines on a page" are *only* "lines on a page" when they don't provide the foundation on which characters can be created. Mamet's argument is similar to that floated by classical scholars of the '30s who believed all of Shakespeare's plays were simply "poems" and not the predicates of flesh-and-blood performances that, from generation to generation, could be radically rethought.

Sometimes, Mamet's "advice to the actors" sounds like a parody of those drippy acting manuals from the last century. "Here again, is your job," exhorts Mamet, "learn the lines, find a simple objective like that indicated by the author, speak the lines clearly in an attempt to achieve that objective." Which is alarmingly close to Noel Coward's dictum to British rep actors: "Just speak the lines, darling, and try not to bump into the furniture." As if the quest for a true objective was "simple" or that it must invariably be that "indicated by the author" or that the author was the sole arbiter of a play's meaning. If a play could be reduced to such formulae, no dramatic work would ever possess ambiguity or be susceptible to endless reinterpretation.

Mamet the Theorist is like the child who, having learned to rattle the bars of his crib, is persuaded that he is actually making music. The intellectual poverty of his writing is, if anything, superseded by his secret glee in creating controversy. "I will take every established belief, every sacred notion, every conventional truth, and stand it on its head," says Mamet the fearless shit-stirrer "and that'll show them!" And who is *"them"*? Why the actors who have had the temerity to impose "characterization" on his lines or uncalled-for emotion into his situations. Despite his deference to actors and his adulation of "the profession," *True and False* is essentially a vendetta against the creeps, crumbs, and Method-bums who, over the years, have insinuated their own personalities onto his plays, thereby, in his view, traducing their integrity. The book fairly bristles with hostility and, although he would be hard pressed to admit it, it is hostility against performers. Much of it may well be justified, but to disguise this aggression as Messianic criticism is to render Mamet himself guilty of the same moral transgressions that he so hotly impugns in others.

I don't want to suggest that every page of this book is intellectually odoriferous. It isn't. When Mamet weighs into the phoniness of acting teachers, one wants to shout, "Right on!" But that doesn't nullify the teachings of people such as Stanislavsky, Vakhtanghov, Meyerhold, or Michael Chekhov. Nor does it invalidate the notion of personalized wisdom lovingly handed down from master to disciple. Does Mamet rank Herbert Berghof with the charlatans? Uta Hagen? Stella Adler? Jerzy Grotowsky? His own revered Sandy Meisner?

The most disturbing message coursing out of Mamet's writing is the idea that acting, so long as you winnow out all the intellectual chaff, is actually very simple. That is perhaps the most deadly oversimplification in a book chock full of oversimplifications. The truth is the opposite. The best art is agonizingly complex and, of all the arts, acting, over the centuries, has suffered the most from the notion that it can be reduced to a formula and made pat. By sneering at characterization, belief, analysis, and conceptualization, Mamet, in an obvious grandstand play, is coaxing the art of acting back to the nineteenth century.

Although you cannot judge a book by its cover, you can often get a good idea of its hype from the blurbs. This one has drooling eulogies from charter members of the We-Think-Mamet-Is-The-Greatest-Thing-Since Sliced-Bread Society, such as Joe Mantegna and William H. Macy, and a squib from that formidable pundit and outstanding theatrical theorist Steve

Martin. "I agree with almost nothing Mr. Mamet says in this book," says Alec Baldwin, for contrast, "and encourage you to devour every word. Mamet is a genius." Which seems to me to raise serious questions about Mr. Baldwin's mental probity. If he can be so rhapsodic about a work with which he almost totally disagrees, God defend us against the writers he approves of.

True and False is like a sermon delivered by an angry cleric whose secret desire is to shove his notion of God down the throats of misbelievers. Its passion is misplaced; its exhortations, woefully unresearched; its bias, so blatant as to be embarrassing. It has obviously been calculated to produce precisely the kind of prickly reaction reflected in pieces like this, so I imagine the author is satisfied with his result. I doubt anyone else will be.

48

BERNARD SHAW THEATRICS

Edited by Dan H. Laurence

There is something positively salubrious about Bernard Shaw. Returning to him after an extended absence is like "taking the waters" in an elegant spa-town like Bath or Baden-Baden. The renewed exhilaration reminds one that simply being in the presence of a first-rate mind is sometimes tonic enough. Whatever verbosity and polemics we may complain of in Shaw (and, God knows, he was always trying to prove one proposition or another), when we return to him we invariably feel the cool breeze of his omnifarious intelligence fanning our brows. With Shaw, it is never hot air. It is either the bubbles from champagne or the heat of sulfur.

Toward the end of last year, I re-encountered *Major Barbara* in a sprightly revival at A Noise Within in Glendale. In many ways, it is one of the most lopsided plays Shaw ever wrote. It so crackles with dialectical fireworks that even in that stalled last act, where all the characters do is stand around a munitions factory and dispute the morality of capitalism, one sits enthralled the way one might at the last set of a Wimbledon final or a TV debate where political candidates throw off the gloves and go at each other with naked fists.

In *Bernard Shaw Theatrics,* a selection of Shavian correspondence on sundry theatrical matters edited by Dan H. Laurence, one constantly hears the crunch of Shaw's steel-trap mind impaling one adversary after another. To a director of St. Bartholomew's Hospital who had the temerity to assemble an unauthorized charity production of *Arms and the Man,* he writes: "I do not know whether the Governors intend to offer their guests any refreshments, and if so, whether they are asking the caterers to supply them gratuitously, but if so, they are treating me worse than the caterers because the 2,000 persons, being fed, will be as hungry as ever next day, whereas their appetite for the play may be so satisfied that the next manager who offers them a performance of it on the usual terms will offer it in vain."

It is edifying to see someone of the stature Shaw had obtained by the 1920s trying to snowball an actress like Edith Evans into a revival of *Mrs. Warren's Profession* or, earlier, trying to persuade Ada Rehan into a role in *Captain Brassbound's Conversion* that Ellen Terry had made her own on an American tour. It makes clear that no matter how successful playwrights become, the courting of star-names is one of the profession's inescapable indignities. Through the collection, one sees the practical side of Shaw coldly negotiating terms: "What is this you say about Grove? Does he want an article? Will he pay? How much? I will see him boiled in hissing hell sulphur before exhibiting my dialogues to him; but for greed of gain I do not mind writing for his pestiferous rag, ruined as I am by days spent in proofreading of Fabian essays & Sundays in spouting to raise the wind for the dockers. . . . "

The other minor revelation of the correspondence is Shaw's eagle-eyed, spot-on notes to actors and actresses in the kind of detail that often sends performers up the wall—notes often given on the same day as an opening or immediately after an exhausting dress rehearsal. He was tough on stars who, in his view, took liberties with his stage directions. To Maurice Evans, he wrote:

> Somebody has told me that at the end of *Man and Superman* you altered my stage business by making Ann sit down and distract the attention of the audience from yourself, thereby stealing the end of the play from you. She and everybody else on the stage should not stir a finger during your speech about the wedding presents and be entirely forgotten until she gives you the cue for the last word "Talking!"—If you really made such a blunder you are hopeless as a producer. Engage a competent specialist and stick to acting, which is your job and sack him if he changes my business in any essential particular. My plays flop in the hands of duffers who think they know better than I do.

By this time, 1947, Shaw's egoism was already cast in marble. He had spent more than half a century dickering with mediocrities and opportunists who tried to get the better of him. He had reached that point of cantankerous self-righteousness that many great men achieve in the last stanza of their lives. But with Shaw, it was always a perfectly justifiable arrogance and never the crotchetiness of someone out of touch with the world as, for instance, was the case with Sean O'Casey. As much as he claimed to be an ailing old man, Shaw's wits were resilient to the very end. Ironically, his greatest complaint in the last years was that the still-flickering flame of that unquenchable spirit that had sustained him for over ninety years simply would not permit him to die.

Despite his flirtations with Stalinism, his almost adolescent adoration of Strong Men, his quirks, and his quiddities, his oeuvre demonstrated that the theater was a place where Mind and Spirit could successfully coalesce. After Shaw, we would always feel shortchanged if we encountered wit without intellect.

★★★

49

NOEL COWARD: A BIOGRAPHY

by Philip Hoare

The upper-middle class characters in the plays of Noel Coward are as imaginary as the lower-working class characters in the plays of Clifford Odets. No one ever spoke like the couples in *Private Lives,* and the diction of the characters in *Waiting for Lefty* is also pure fabrication. But interestingly, in Coward's case, after he had concocted the dry, brittle patter that became the hallmark of his characters' style, a whole stratum of English society *began* to talk like them. Coward's great achievement was not so much in the artistic realm as in the social. His works provided a model of behavior and a demonstration of attitude among a certain class of society that, before his arrival, had to make do with the diction bequeathed by Oxbridge and the stodgy mannerisms that were a legacy of the Age of Victoria. As his biographer points out, Coward's play *The Vortex* "started a whole new form of conversation—until November 1924 nobody called anyone 'darling' except as a declaration of love."

What was the Coward type?

A facetious, uptight, artificially restrained young man given to camp outbursts and snide bitchery, more concerned with the pursuit of pleasure than the world around him. Narcissistic; consumed with trivia and self-gratification; apolitical and anti-intellectual; addicted to cigarettes, drink, and travel; excessively loyal to those friends who qualified for his "set" and disparaging of those who did not. A prig masquerading as a snob. A homosexual disguised as a straight. A conservative in social matters, a libertine in regard to morality; a working-class sensibility glossed over with middle-class pretensions and flattered by the attentions of the aristocracy. An inveterate social climber for whom royalty was tantamount to deity and the sumptuous weekend house party in the country, the acme of social accomplishment.

In short, someone very much like Noel Coward himself.

The paradox is that this haughty, arrogant, supercilious, predatory, and trumped-up man-of-mode was also one of the most brilliant playwrights of the first half of the twentieth century. If one had only *Private Lives, Design for Living, Hay Fever,* and *Present Laughter,* Coward's niche would be secure. One could blithely dismiss the crass jingoism of *Cavalcade* and *In Which We Serve:* the wet, murky, class-conscious melodrama of *The Vortex* and *Post Mortem;* the short fiction derived in tone, and often in subject matter, from writers such as Somerset Maugham, P. G. Wodehouse, and "Saki," without his literary reputation being in any way diminished.

Philip Hoare's biography *Noel Coward* is a warts-and-all, in-your-face (and in-his-bedroom), biography of what his sycophants were prone to refer to as "the master." It succeeds in painting an egregious portrait of the sexually vulnerable human being from which the master craftsman and inspired comedy writer emerge unscathed. You are appalled by the gross vanity of the man, even as you are impressed by the fastidiousness of the artist. The book delves into the nitty-gritty of Coward's neurotically camouflaged sexual persona, enumerating every infatuation, orgy, and one-night stand in which he ever indulged. It tells you everything you always wanted to know about Coward and a lot more you could have done without. Although it never quite tells you where he stands in the English drama—that is, in relation to contemporaries such as Terence Rattigan, St. John Ervine, Somerset Maugham, and his American counterparts, Philip Barry and S. N. Behrman. It is both exhaustive and exhaust*ing.* If one views theatrical biography as a kind of odyssey of openings, closings, tours, parties, affairs, and teeming society gossip, it perfectly captures the carousel-like life of its subject. If, however, one expects a biography to interpret a life, as well as to detail its splendid and sordid sides, it leaves something to be desired.

The arc of the career is a familiar one in the British theater. A childhood apprenticeship in musicals and pantomimes; a dazzling early success with a sensational drug-addled family drama (*The Vortex*), followed by a period of ripe and well-deserved successes in the '20s and '30s; a fallow and uncertain period during the Second World War marked by ostentatious bursts of patriotism (diluted by social condescension); a final spurt of creativity in the '40s and '50s, leading to decline and incompatibility with a society forever changed by the convention-busting '60s, culminating in a nostalgic recrudescence and revival of interest just before the subject expires in 1973.

In the '60s, Coward and other writers of his ilk (Terence Rattigan, N. C. Hunter, Ronald Duncan, etc.) represented the "enemy": the morally bankrupt, cup-and-saucer brigade that playwrights such as John Osborne, Arnold Wesker, and John Arden set out to demolish in the era of the Angry Young Man. Coward, understandably, abominated the New Wave, its pugnacity and willful lack of elegance. The only exception was Harold Pinter, whose perfectly crafted language-constructs, despite the difference in social milieu, actually resembled Coward's own exactitude. Of all those writers, Osborne was the only one who refused to put the boot in. He quite rightly saw Coward as a man who had reinvented himself, and as Osborne had done the same thing (and from similar working-class roots), he felt an affinity.

Coward, who probably described himself best in the short lyric that contains the lines "but I believe that since my life began/the most I've had is just/a talent to amuse," was one of the deftest lyricists of the period, his true genius flowering in Cochran revues such as *On with the Dance, This Year of Grace,* and *Words and Music.* His melodic gifts never quite matched the intricacy of those crackling internal rhymes to be found in songs such as "Mad Dogs and Englishmen," "Could You Please Oblige Us with a Bren Gun," and "Uncle Harry." It was because his greatest work of art *was* the creation of "Noel Coward" that he scored such a great success at Las Vegas, singing songs and projecting the blasé personality he had constructed over a period of some forty years. As for his appearance, there, too, he said it best when he described himself as having the look of "a heavily doped Chinese illusionist."

The enigma of Noel Coward (it is also, up to a point, Tennessee Williams' as well) is by what devious circumlocutions he managed to arrive at a series of successful heterosexual comedies that cunningly camouflaged and re-routed the impulses and experiences of an inveterate homosexual. It is this very sense of "outsiderness" that gives his characters such a peculiar reverberation in the straight world they appear to be inhabiting—although in plays like *Present Laughter* and especially *Design for Living,* the gay eddies often swirl up through the straight surface.

Hoare's book is thorough, prodigious in research, and eminently readable. The bad taste in the mouth comes, to a large extent, from his subject, and only when one washes it down with great lashings of Coward's oeuvre does it entirely disappear.

★★★

50

JOHN BARRYMORE, SHAKESPEAREAN ACTOR

by Michael A. Morrison

"Ham," "Poseur," "Alcoholic," "Lecher," and "Has-Been" are some of the epithets that were directed at John Barrymore in his day. Others used words such as "genius," "our greatest classical actor," and "the true descendant of Booth and Irving." Barrymore provided good grounds for each of them. No actor had ever flown so high or suffered such an ignominious descent.

In the '20s, with groundbreaking portrayals of *Richard III* and *Hamlet,* he single-handedly brushed the cobwebs off the mustiest of Shakespearean traditions. In collaboration with European-influenced artists such as Arthur Hopkins and Robert Edmond Jones, swept up in the wave of modernism that washed away those crabbed, Victorian notions of art that had overlapped into the first decade of the new century, Barrymore brought the first intimations of what was to become contemporary classical interpretation: highly conceptualized Shakespeare (in his case, heavily influenced by Freudian theory), conversational renderings of the verse that still managed to preserve the weave of the poetry and kinetically vibrant portrayals of Shakespearean characters that banished the oratorical renderings of traditionalist actors such as Johnson Forbes-Robertson, E. H. Southern, and Walter Hampden.

Barrymore's Hamlet was not merely a new interpretation, it was like the resuscitation of a divine creature who had been frozen in ice for over a hundred years. It had youth, vigor, sensitivity, humor, and physical beauty and translated what had become Elizabethan platitudes into the vivid and muscular language of a new cultural era. It was, along with Picasso, Braque, Eliot, Joyce, and Fitzgerald, couched in the diction of the iconoclastic '20s and, as such, instantly comprehensible to the new generation. It was also, as Michael A. Morrison rightly points out in *John Barrymore, Shakespearean Actor,* the harbinger of the innovative interpretations of actors such as Gielgud and Olivier, which, through osmosis, influenced later artists such as Richard Burton, David Warner, and Nicol Williamson.

For those people who recall Barrymore only when he was a self-parodying buffoon, guying himself as an inebriated matinee idol in trashy potboilers like *My Dear Children* or indulging in painful self-mockeries on Rudy Vallee's radio programs, it is difficult to realize how powerful and unparalleled a force he was on the American stage two decades earlier.

The decline began in the '30s when Barrymore, who found it impossible to sustain a performance over a long run, was seduced by the emoluments of Hollywood. That, and a series of catastrophic marriages to wayward women like Blanche Oelrichs (a.k.a. Michael Strange), Dolores Costello, and Elaine Barrie (née Jacobs), plus an inherited alcohol problem, ultimately cooked his goose. Toward the end, he was playing the only persona anyone wished to see—the empty shell of the man who had once been John Barrymore. By the '40s, the elegant and eloquent artist who had brought Shakespeare alive for a new generation of theatergoers was so effectively dissipated, one would have had to consult the archives to believe he had ever existed.

My own memories of him, vivid though dating back to my childhood, are as the snorting, histrionic windbag on the Rudy Vallee radio series the *Sealtest Hour.* I visualized him then as a rambunctious, broad comedian sending up the pretensions of the barnstorming ham-actors of an earlier day—never realizing that in the prime of his life he was as far removed from that as any actor possibly could be; that far from being a bombastic windbag who rolled his r's and tore a passion to tatters, he had, in fact, been an actor of exquisite sensitivity who actually brought the reign of the ham-actors to an end. Only years afterward did I discover that before becoming a distinguished classical actor, he had been a gifted and highly successful light-comedian.

Michael A. Morrison's chronicle gradually evokes the greatness on which the subsequent parodies were based and scrupulously recreates the achievements of that great triumvirate—Arthur Hopkins, Robert Edmond Jones, and Barrymore—which brought the theories of Gordon Craig and the practice of Max Reinhardt into a culturally arid American theater. Although he explicitly restricts himself to the circumlocutions of Barrymore the Shakespearean actor, Morrison, in a series of insightful flashes, illuminates the whole history of the man and his pitiful descent into degradation and death. Although expressly not a biography, by following the swings and roundabouts of the performer's capricious career, he unintentionally limns a life story that is as gripping as anything written by Gene Fowler or John Kobler, Barrymore's official biographers.

My only quibble is with the inordinate length of Morrison's detailed, scene-by-scene reconstruction of the actor's 1922 *Hamlet*—a futile exercise because, no matter how meticulously one tries to evoke the reading of a line or the shading of a nuance, no amount of fastidious verbal description can recreate the shape and feel of a performance or the calibrations of an actor's interpretation. In a handful of personal reminiscences by colleagues and close friends, one learns more about the *geist* of Barrymore's performance than in all the sixty-some pages that attempt to describe precisely how it looked and sounded.

The great value of Morrison's work is that it cuts through the fog generated by eighty years of scandal and gossip about the outrageous Barrymore personality and forces us to concentrate on the nature of the greatness that so rapidly and pathetically dwindled into self-parody. It brings to mind the willful alienation of Chaplin in the '50s and the callous treatment heaped upon Orson Welles in his latter Hollywood years. It is the classic fable of the way in which an omnivorous American commercialism consumes, diminishes, and ultimately disgorges genius.

51

METHOD ACTORS: THREE GENERATIONS OF AN AMERICAN ACTING STYLE

by Steve Vineberg

One of the great fables of the American stage is the rise and fall of the Group Theatre, that reverberating 1930s acting-ensemble spearheaded by Harold Clurman, Cheryl Crawford, and Lee Strasberg, and its *leitmotif* is the discovery and dissemination of the Stanislavsky System, which, under Strasberg's alchemy, became the American Method. We have all heard and read how Stanislavsky's disciple Richard Boleslavsky passed the torch to Strasberg in the late '20s and how Strasberg proceeded to turn the Russian's earliest theories into a magical formula for two generations of actors that included legends such as Lee J. Cobb, John Garfield, Marlon Brando, James Dean, Montgomery Clift, Kim Stanley, and Geraldine Page.

Method Actors, Steve Vineberg's encomium to these and other disciples, makes us aware that we are now in the midst of a third generation and what, in the '30s, seemed a pretentious foreign import and in the '50s a mystical form of self-therapy has now become the acceptable stage-grammar of training programs in colleges, universities, and theater schools all over America. Originally, a series of techniques and precepts devised by Stanislavsky to help coax the inspiration that, though the gift of great actors, came only infrequently to average actors, the System became, in Strasberg's hands, mainly a "method" for engendering true feeling based largely on the use of emotional memory exercises and other self-inducing psychological stimuli. Today, of course, the Method is something of a generic title that doesn't begin to describe the variations, extensions, and even reversals of the original doctrines, which, were Stanislavsky to return today, would probably make him disown those stalwarts who palpitate most fulsomely in his name.

Vineberg believes there was a natural affinity between the thrust of this acting theory and the American temperament, that its preoccupation with Freudian psychology and adolescent rebellion made it the perfect medium to express the duality of American life and the repressiveness of American youth. John Garfield, Marlon Brando, James Dean, Paul Newman, Robert di Niro, and Jack Nicholson, Vineberg argues, are all united by a certain renegade stance that a conformist society secretly admires. Playwrights like Clifford Odets, Arthur Miller, and even Tennessee Williams (all popularized by Method actors and directors) have perpetuated this strain of rebellion, and the Method is the aesthetic by which it was effectively conveyed to the public.

So immersed is Vineberg in the minutiae of the Method that he finds parallels everywhere. John Garfield's "sunken look" at the end of *Body and Soul* is seen as prefiguring "Brando's in a similar moment at the end of *On the Waterfront*." Sylvester Stallone's performance in *Rocky* is a "composite" formed out of the work of Brando, Anthony Quinn, and Ernest Borgnine. And even Tennessee Williams's preoccupation with animal imagery in *Streetcar Named Desire* is attributed to the animal exercises Strasberg inherited from Maria Ouspenskaya in the '30s and incorporated into the work of the Actors' Studio.

This is not persuasive cross-referencing, it is merely delusion and stems from Vineberg's larger delusion that every advance in contemporary acting owes something to the permutations of the Method, as it evolved from the early Strasberg days to the present. It blithely bypasses the fact that creative new performers with distinctive personalities find original ways of expressing themselves whatever their orientation. It isn't the Method that produces staggering "moments" on the screen and stage; it is the sensibility of forceful new actors who embellish whatever their basic training may have been, with nuances derived from their own unique character.

When an actor's performance slips, as Paul Newman's did in Tad Mosel's TV play *Guilty Is the Stranger,* it is because the Method has failed him. In Newman's case, Vineberg writes, "You can sense the Yale Drama School (which he attended before taking classes at the Studio) and Broadway (where he played the rich fraternity boy in *Picnic* in 1953) lurking uncomfortably beneath every line."

So staunch is Vineberg for his subject that even his put-downs have a way of doubling back on themselves. To write of Dustin Hoffman playing Shylock, ("surrounded by classically trained English actors" in Sir Peter Hall's Broadway production of *Merchant of Venice*), that "his limitations were infinitely more interesting than their range," is to turn special pleading into sophistry.

Occasionally, and begrudgingly, Vineberg admits to certain limitations in the approach. "The real failure of (Kim) Stanley's acting" (in the ill-fated

Actors' Studio production of *The Three Sisters*) is that "it doesn't illuminate the character or explain the text. She's too preoccupied with her own feelings to pay attention to the relationships between dialogue and action, action and motivation, character and context. . . . " Indeed, this has been one of the Method's pitfalls since the late '40s, that actors mesmerized by its methodology were able to delude themselves that rigorously following its rules was tantamount to achieving artistic results.

Vineberg is a true zealot and that zeal pulsates audibly beneath the text of *Method Actors,* but it also blinds the author to the fact that the cul-de-sac realism that he celebrates has produced more bathos and deadly treacle than the melodramatic fustian that it banished a century ago. While in Europe, the Orient, and many parts of America, artists are assiduously trying to escape the clutches of a cloying psychological realism, it is a little daunting to find an American critic launching a jamboree in its honor.

The Method's blind-spots are given short shrift. The fact that it is ludicrously inapplicable to the classics, for instance, is never seriously dealt with, and the Actors' Studio production of *The Three Sisters,* which was its most conspicuous failure (paradoxically, in a play where it should have yielded its most striking results) is never adequately explained. If the Method is this magic lozenge for psychological truth, what happened when the cream of the Studio under Strasberg's own direction rallied their forces to convey the interior world of Anton Chekhov? If, as Vineberg admits, it was "one of the great theatrical follies of our time," does it not say something devastating about the relation of theory to practice?

Despite the headiness (or perhaps because of it), Vineberg is excellent in analytical cameos on Clifford Odets, Arthur Miller, and Tennessee Williams and in showing how the tentacles of the '30s spread into the succeeding five decades. His admiration for these actors and his descriptions of how certain off-the-wall choices finesse their performances generate some of his finest prose. He is right on the button describing how actors like John Garfield or Jack Nicholson achieve their effects and the way that audiences tune in their subtly coded messages. He loves and reveres the Method so much that he manages to find its vestiges even in self-proclaimed non-Method actors such as Jason Robards. (His "process," writes Vineberg, wishfully thinking, "may be a subconscious-instinctive application of the Method.")

I share his appreciation for the towering alumni of the Actors' Studio but am not so myopic as to believe that every time one comes across a great actor (i.e., Olivier, Paul Scofield, Charles Laughton, Ralph

Richardson), one is automatically encountering Method technique unconsciously inculcated. The great paradox of the Method is how actors like John Barrymore, Paul Muni, James Cagney, Edward G. Robinson, Spencer Tracy, and Bette Davis exemplified it without knowing of its existence.

★★★

52

LIFE, THE MOVIE

by Neal Gabler

The pundits of the next millennium looking back at our own century may well conclude that the lure of films and TV was responsible for a drastic change in human consciousness. The obsession with celebrity, they may conclude, was the motive for some of our most atrocious crimes, and the tendency to fictionalize our lives, egged on by media that permeated our culture, encouraged a state of mind that confused our identities and distorted our goals.

Actually, we don't have to wait for the next millennium for this judgment to be made, as writers such as Neil Postman, Daniel Boorstein, and Richard Shickel have already made it. And now, to put the boot in, we have Neal Gabler's *Life, the Movie*, the subtitle of which—*How Entertainment Conquered Reality*—says it all. Gabler has taken a widespread perception about the way in which films and TV have colonized the collective imagination and turned it into ideological Grand Guignol.

That many of us are no longer content to sit on the sidelines and view Life as a spectator-sport, that we crave to be cast in the juicy roles that heretofore have been reserved for the chosen few—the stars and superstars—is a fact that gets confirmed daily in our newspapers, in our talk shows, and in the way that politicians, journalists, televangelists, attorneys, authors, models, and designers have become part of the new performing elite. What we see, and privately fantasize, has produced the dominating role models on which many of us, consciously or unconsciously, fashion ourselves.

Indisputable as this is, and Gabler provides persuasive and meticulous research to drive home his points, I have a niggling suspicion that it was ever thus. In the Middle Ages, priests, soldiers, courtiers, and troubadours were the fashion-plates and encouraged multitudes to follow in their footsteps. Christianity proffered numerous role models, and hordes of deluded clergymen and nuns were prepared to starve, die, and gamble for immortality because they swallowed whole the "movies" of their day, viz. the teachings of the Church.

Shakespeare provided a whole slew of role models, from Hamlet to Richard III and Juliet to Lady Macbeth, which undoubtedly influenced the behavior of Elizabethan men and women, giving them social goals and character types to emulate. During the Restoration, the rake, the fop, the gallant, and the aristocrat were copied by impressionable persons of both genders and all ages. And we know from history that if there were suicidal Werthers wandering through the eighteenth century, it was because Goethe had established the prototype and encouraged a horde of young men to clone his tragic hero. When Shakespeare said, "All the world's a stage and the men and women merely players," was he not preempting Gabler's entire thesis?

No, Gabler would probably answer, because the theater was not so pervasive and ineluctable an influence as the movies are today. For Gabler, the saturation of sensibility that movies and television promote makes them indigenous in a way that no other art form can quite equal. We get our morals, our ambitions, our fashions, and our language from the movies and the immersion in movie mythology is so total that we ourselves now star in what Gabler dubs *lifies*—existential simulacra of the fictional concoctions of filmmakers.

But for this to be a convincing argument, we have to believe that the earlier arts of literature and poetry, theater and opera were merely diversions that conditioned neither our behavior nor our mores. That *Don Quixote,* for instance, was not inspired by the sagas of chivalry on which he patterned himself but was simply an aberrated old gentleman. Literary influences, it is true, were not as pervasive then and not everyone could read or attend the theater, but everyone saw and heard about everyone else, and admirations led to emulations and imitations.

Another of Gabler's overarching points is that we now expect everything—crime, sport, finance, fashion, politics, law, religion, you name it—to be "entertainment," and because of this expectation, practitioners in all these fields labor to satisfy the public taste. In so doing, of course, the true nature of all these fields is distorted or demeaned. What can we say of a nation that finds the same kind of diversion in soap opera and Movies-of-the-Week as it does in impeachment proceedings and nationally televised murder trials? Gabler's reply: That differentiations are no longer made between these diverse spectacles and, consequently, life and entertainment have merged into a kind of marathon movie, the one indistinguishable from the other.

Whatever reservations one might have about Gabler's thesis, he is squarely on the money when he argues that the hunger for celebrity is an outgrowth of cinematic and televisual identifications. The desire, as he puts it, to "get on the other side of the glass" is overpowering and fully explains the temptations of ordinary people to expose the darkest and most shameful secrets of their lives to modern exorcists such as Jerry Springer and Sally Jesse Raphael. What was significant about Andy Warhol's dictum that in the future everyone would have their fifteen minutes of stardom was not the brevity of their fame, but the fact that virtually everyone really craved those fleeting moments in the spotlight. Social visibility has become, in some magical way, a confirmation of "being," and before the advent of movies and TV, this simply was not the case.

In one sense, Gabler has written a fascinating and highly readable tract about the ways in which entertainment has become the standard for all social efficacy, and in another, he has mustered a number of elaborate arguments to prove a truism. The more authorities he cites and the more he adds sinew to his thesis, the more one feels it was a position to which everyone already subscribed. A horde of psychologists, sociologists and media-mavens were there, to paraphrase Henrik Ibsen, Aheadà Gabler.

In the final chapter, Gabler makes clear that his motivation has been interpretive and not didactic. He bluntly refuses to be bricked up in "some grand conclusion," explaining that readers will have to resolve these knotty issues for themselves. "One can understand," he writes, "why many people—especially those who read and who take ideas seriously—reflexively recoil at the idea that life is a movie and all of us performers in it. Even as these critics participate in the spectacle, they assume that the transmutation of character into personality, of the life unself-consciously lived into the life calculatedly constructed, is a horrible thing." But by then, Gabler has already demonstrated through opinions and statistics that for those people who have exchanged disagreeable facts for comforting fiction, life is often happier and more fulfilling. His desire to remain impartial, justified as it may be intellectually, badly smacks of cop-out. For if life *has* been abducted by the moviemakers and TV shamans, if human values *have* been subsumed by artistic alchemies, then some instinct in us wants the author to indict the witch-doctors guilty of casting such a spell and to assert the primacy of Life over Art and human beings over fictional creations. In refusing to do so, Gabler is merely saying: Isn't it fascinating the way technology and illusion have filched our souls? But brilliant speculation notwithstanding, some deeply ingrained part of our natures wants an author who has brought such sweeping charges to stand up and be counted.

Given the implications of his tract and the way he presents it, Gabler invites us to view him as one of those very people who are performing a *lifie* based on cinematic models. Is Gabler, in the deepest labyrinths of his own unconscious, Paul Muni in *The Life of Emile Zola,* exposing the crimes against Dreyfus? Is he Gary Cooper standing up to the evil capitalists in *Meet John Doe?* Or Jimmy Stewart battling for democratic principles in *Mr. Deeds Goes Town?* If so, the force of his argument is considerably weakened and we put down *Life, the Movie* feeling it has succumbed to the very evils it has so entertainingly exposed.

★★★

53

LAUGHING MATTERS

by Larry Gelbart

Should you have any doubts about Larry Gelbart's status as a writer and "TV Great," the first pages of his book *Laughing Matters* will banish them. Before you even reach chapter 1, there are three pages of glowing film, TV, and radio credits followed by two and a quarter pages listing his awards, which include Tonys, Emmys, Peabodys, and trophies from the Writers Guild of America. Should some small doubt still linger in your mind regarding his greatness, you are directed to Alan Alda's paen of praise in the preface and/or editor Sam Vaughan's seven-page encomium that follows.

But let us assume that for some perverse reason, you are still not convinced that Gelbart is Mark Twain, S. J. Perelman, and Robert Benchley all rolled into one. In that case, you need only consult the book jacket, where the likes of Jack Lemmon, Neil Simon, Carl Reiner, Mel Brooks, Bob Hope, John Gregory Dunne, Norman Corwin, Stanley Donen, and Hal Prince assure you that, comedically speaking, Gelbart is not only the greatest thing since sliced bread, he is, as it were, the quintessence of flour, yeast, and poppyseeds as well.

Does this bespeak some insecurity regarding self-esteem? Or is this blurby elephantiasis some kind of newfangled publishing technique devised by Random House to program reader's responses before they are foolhardy enough to make up their own minds? It's hard to say. All one can say with any certainty is that hype of this order is like immersing a subject in the light of a spotlight so powerful it can also double as a death-ray.

That said, I have to admit that Mr. Gelbart is, in fact, a very funny man. He drops one-liners faster than a molting cockatoo drops feathers and looses barbs as if they were packed in the magazine of a Sten-gun. His professionalism is unassailable. He has written for comic legends such as Bob Hope, Red Buttons, Sid Caesar, Art Carney, Danny Kaye, and Marty Feldman; been involved in writing, rewriting, or rewriting-the-rewrites of commercial projects such as *M*A*S*H, Tootsie,* and *Oh God* and been responsible for theatrical hits such as *A Funny Thing Happened on the Way to the Forum, Sly Fox, Mastergate,* and *City of Angels.*

Curiously, he always seems to be most creative when bouncing off the erstwhile creations of other men. *M*A*S*H,* as he readily admits, owes its progeny to Richard Hooker's novel and Robert Altman's film; *A Funny Thing* consists of ingenious extrapolations from Plautus's comedies; *Sly Fox* is indebted to Ben Jonson's *Volpone* (although Gelbart admits he found the original too prolix and foraged instead through Stefan Zweig's more simplified adaptation); *Tootsie* was a casserole in which traces of Don McGuire, Murray Schisgal, Elaine May, and many others could be discerned, and *Oh God,* George Burns's nonagenarian potboiler, began life as a novel by Avery Corman.

Still, none of this diminishes the metamorphoses wrought by a first-rate creative mind. Shakespeare, as I needn't remind anyone, owed most of his inventions to Plutarch, Boccacio, Livy, Ovid, Spenser, et al.—not to mention assists from contemporary collaborators such as Thomas Kyd and John Fletcher. For my money and despite its linguistic overkill, Gelbart's most inspired piece was *Mastergate,* wherein he was able to indulge his obsession with word play and his bitter sense of parody. For the fact is, behind the prolific, sweet-scented gag-writer, one may easily detect a whiff of Swiftian disgust. Disgust with Man, Society, Money, Pretension, and so on. Given his milieus—radio, TV, and films—there was no ready outlet for what might well have been Gelbart's most natural impulses: political invective and moral repulsion. Only when he turned to the theater did he have the freedom to follow his true bent, unmitigated by sponsors, air-headed producers, and timorous advertising executives terrified at giving offense.

I have to inject a personal note here, as it would be equivocal not to do so.

Several years ago in London, I directed Larry Gelbart's comedy *Jump* in the West End. Throughout, Gelbart was the thoroughgoing professional—weighing, probing, modifying, replacing bits without a moment's hesitation or the slightest whiplash to his ego. Like a Geiger-Counter, he assiduously tested the material for any trace of flab or redundancy. It was not so much the playwright adding or subtracting as it was the work itself issuing tacit demands that Gelbart faithfully followed for the sake of *its* integrity. The comedy was intrinsically American in both diction and temperament and therefore not easily palatable to British audiences. It won no awards and set no performance records, but for me, it was an illuminating crash-course in comedy construction and a salubrious insight into the mind of a meticulous craftsman.

The book, part-souvenir, part-sampler, part-autobiography, is a fast and mellifluous read, laced with witticisms like Hershey bars dipped in strychnine. Gelbart is extraordinarily perceptive about the art of comedy and clearly adores comedians. (The feeling is obviously mutual.) He rightly attributes the decline in current film output to the debasing influence of television and its deplorable lapses of taste. Like all writers sucked into movies, he recounts Hollywood horror stories, now become commonplace nightmares, almost cozy in their irredeemable fatuousness. Ultimately, one feels that Gelbart himself has fallen victim to the cultural anemia that he so rightly impugns and that in another country, in another culture, he could truly have become the great artist his publishers would have us believe him to be.

If he ever needed an epitaph that precisely sums him up, an excerpt from his chapter "On Writing" would perfectly fit the bill. "I agree with Dorothy Parker. 'Wit has truth in it—wisecracking is simply calisthenics with words.' Unfortunately," writes Gelbart, "I have spent much of my life doing verbal aerobics."

You're still alive and kicking Larry; high time to leave the gym.

★★★

54

BLABBERMOUTH

COLERIDGE: "DARKER REFLECTIONS": 1804–1834

by Richard Holmes

The dramatizing biographer, as opposed to the nonspeculating chronicler of unadorned facts, became something of a fixture toward the end of last century. Both Ronald Reagan (Dutch) *and Bill Clinton* (Primary Colors) *were extensively fictionalized and, of course, show business celebrities, whose lives were always something of a fiction to begin with, continued to be heavily fabricated. The leading "dramatist" and one of the most successful was Richard Holmes, who empathized his way into the lives of Shelley, Samuel Johnson, Richard Savage, and Samuel Taylor Coleridge (twice). By 2001, the practice was very much under attack and critics like John Barrell bluntly asked biographers like Holmes whether "he has the right to speak for his subjects." The fineness of the fine line between imaginative biography and imaginary biography continued to grow ever finer.*

★★★

The most devastating comment on Samuel Taylor Coleridge was probably made by Max Beerbohm in his deadly cartoon entitled "Coleridge Talks On." There we see the great poet and mystic-philosopher seated at a dinner table, his head bent, chasing down some elusive, metaphysical subtlety, while ten guests with petrified yawns on their faces lie racked together in a stupor of boredom.

"Above all things," said De Quincy in 1837, three years after S. T. C.'s marathon soliloquy had finally come to rest, "I shunned as I would shun a pestilence, Coleridge's capital error which through life he practiced, of keeping the audience in a state of passiveness. . . . This eternal stream of talk which never for one instant intermitted, and allowed no momentary opportunity of reaction to the persecuted and baited auditor, was absolute ruin to the interests of the talker himself . . . the poor afflicted listener . . . returned home in the exhausted condition of one that has been drawn up just before death from the bottom of a well occupied by foul gases; and, of course, hours before he had reached that perilous point of depression, he had lost all power of distinguishing, understanding or connecting." Madame de Staël put it more succinctly. "Avec M. Coleridge, c'est tout fait un monologue."

But Beerbohm's was a brittle wit and the man himself something of a dandy, and so it is understandable that his mind might wander during a Coleridgian discourse, and de Quincy, a very early disciple, so tanked up with opium himself, is not the most reliable of judges. Madame de Staël, however, is usually right on the money, and in fact, innumerable witnesses attest to the fact that once Coleridge got going, there was no stopping him. But there were just as many who, far from complaining about "the foul gases," were mesmerized by the eloquence and riveted by the mixture of encyclopedic knowledge, literary whimsy, and stratospheric imagination.

Richard Holmes, in the second part of the massive Coleridge biography entitled "Darker Reflections," clearly implies that our celebration of Coleridge owes more to the magnitude of his mind and the complexity of his character than the weight of his oeuvre. Apart from a handful of poems ("The Rime of the Ancient Mariner," "Christabel," "Kubla Kahn," "Dejection: An Ode," etc.) and books (*Biographia Literaria,* two volumes of *The Friend* and *Aids to Reflection*), one has to measure the greatness of the man more from his jottings (four double volumes of Notebooks) and his recollected aura than from any tangible works of art or criticism.

Being "a talker," his most natural outlet was the lecture platform and from the remains of his talks on Shakespeare, Philosophy, and Literature, it is clear that here he sucked up the ether and exhaled ambrosia. A lecturer is *supposed* to be set apart from his public and expected to orate, theorize, and intellectually perambulate, all of which Coleridge did with ease and to astounding effect.

But more riveting than his opinions or his theories (many of them antedating Freud, the New Critics, and even certain modern scientists) was the emotional quagmire bubbling inside the man. Enamored of his much-fantasized Asra but never consummating his passion, championing Wordsworth whom he revered and was then callously alienated from, imprisoned in an airless marriage to a wife who would whittle him into domesticity and from whom he took every opportunity to be separated, doting on his favorite son Hartley, in whom he saw a homunculus of himself, and then having to suffer the agony of loss when the son, revealing the intemperate traits that paralyzed the father, abandoned Coleridge in early manhood just when the writer most needed the filial support—these personal disasters, coupled with finagling publishers, scabrous critics (like Hazlitt), and the grinding poverty, created a pressure that virtually no nature could withstand. The opium taking became the double-edged sword that both enabled him to cut his way through the spiritual flak of his life and, simultaneously, sapped his energies but, from all accounts, never weakened his mind. To the end of his days as the Sage of Highgate, Coleridge could hunt down the universal in the particular and make startling connections between the tangible world and the deeper mystery from which it sprang.

Holmes is lenient on Coleridge the plagiarist; the man who paraphrased and pilfered the ideas of Schlegel, Schelling, and Jean Paul Richter and became the leading exponent of German mysticism in England; yet articulated ideas do not move from one thinker to another by osmosis but through verbal appropriation, and though one can admire Coleridge's elucidations and enhancements of the German philosophers, the resemblances remain too striking merely to brush under the carpet. Nevertheless, Coleridge's greatest asset was that fecund, constantly improvising intellect and when his work is taken as a whole, as with Shakespeare's, the plagiaries vanish in the flames generated by the heat of the more creative artist.

But the question of his "artistry" remains unresolved even after 622 pages of Holmes's hagiography of the poet, the critic, and the mystic. Should we throw laurel wreaths on the tomb of the "lake poet," the fastidious critic, and the finicky philosopher, or merely applaud a first-class mind that bruited masterpieces but never really delivered them? That Coleridge could be a bore seems to me incontestable. I would hate to find myself at a dinner table with S. T. C. on my right and absolutely no one on my left. And even in the most original literary explorations, there is something in the digressive manner that is ineluctably tedious. But what Holmes's magnificent biography makes crystal clear is that when a man has a cast of mind like Coleridge's, the emanations themselves are often as inspiring as those gleaned from a perfect artifact. Some people create masterpieces, and some people *are* masterpieces.

The research here is like a meticulously executed root-canal job, and the empathy of the biographer for his subject makes this one of those symbiotic masterpieces where, forever after, one will see the subject through the eyes of the man who journeyed through the aeries of heaven and the labyrinths of hell to capture and reveal his spirit.

★★★

55

STILL ALIVE: AN AUTOBIOGRAPHICAL ESSAY

by Jan Kott—Translated by Jadwiga Kosicka

The trajectory of most books is from the eye to the brain and then out some imperceptible pee-hole at the back of the head. Only occasionally does something that you read enter the bloodstream and become a permanent part of your metabolism. Those are books that become so permanently lodged in the mental archives that they remain on instant recall for the rest of your life. Jan Kott's *Still Alive* is that kind of book for me. I read it, savoringly, over four or five days, and when I'd finished, found scenes and situations recurring in my dreams. An analyst would be able to provide some astute reason why that was so. He could probably prove that it connected up with personal psychic preoccupations that were triggered by the story. But a critic would have a simpler explanation. He would point out that, being vivid, subtle, graphic, and profound, the book fleshed out a world that, although known in general terms, here achieved a specificity that made it ineradicably memorable.

The book documents, in a haphazard and discontinuous way, the life of a Polish intellectual and political activist who suffered through the terrors of the German occupation and the even more terrifying reign of terror unleashed by the Soviet occupation, emerging from all these catastrophes with a philosophical detachment bordering on the Absurd. Almost every horrific wartime event is flecked with elements of black comedy. The unbearable and the absurd are constantly in tandem. First-class chronicles of the past seventy years of European history have been churned out at an alarming rate, but I know of none that captures the deracination of those decades as well as this; none that gives you the palpable sensation of actually being in the midst of the carnage, displacement, and hunger that characterized those tumultuous years. The book presumes to be nothing more than a souvenir of the past, but being peppered with irony and stewed in bemused contemplation, it gradually becomes a kind of *Paradise Lost,* with Survival taking the place of both Heaven and Hell.

Throughout the book, Kott, a university professor who rapidly became involved in the Polish resistance, allows his mind to wander from period to period, person to person, anecdote to anecdote, and yet, despite the discontinuity, a kind of thematic throughline asserts itself. As if memory, independent of chronology, had a logic of its own.

There are innumerable Polish characters with long, unpronounceable Polish names—party-workers, poets, writers, apparatchiks—far too many to achieve any recognizable identity, but it doesn't matter. The landscape itself is vivid and the gist of all the roachlike characters who inhabit it illustrate the same themes: bureaucratic oppression, ubiquitous fear of disappearance or death, threatened imprisonment, and obliteration by decree. People are constantly being arrested, tortured, murdered or committing suicide, and little by little, the sense of living in a besieged society where virtually everyone's life is poised on a knife's edge insinuates itself upon the reader. It suddenly, and powerfully, makes sense of all those hideous Second World War films where refugees and hostages were constantly being terrorized by jackbooted storm troopers.

Kott, a Jew who managed to obtain false papers to prevent his ethnicity from sealing his doom, races from one city to the next, always a step ahead of the Gestapo and the threat of imminent extinction. Miraculously, he survives the Second World War only to be submerged in the mausoleum of Soviet-occupied Poland. Here, because of his communist credentials, there is a temporary improvement in his status, but in the unpredictable political atmosphere of this postwar Stalinist society, revisionism and the unpredictable vicissitudes of political factionalism force him to develop survival skills even greater than those acquired under the Nazis. Ultimately, there is an escape to the West, where, now a highly lauded Shakespeare scholar, he settles down in Stony Brook, but the reverberations of what he has lived through never entirely subside. They condition his outlook and permeate his worldview. For Kott, the world will always be a place where the status quo can, in an instant, do a backflip; where storm follows calm and order merely precipitates chaos. This is the quintessential European experience of the early twentieth century, and Kott not only describes it, he contains and exemplifies it.

The style of the book is casually devastating. Confronted with the most terrifying circumstances, the eyes in Kott's Punch-like visage narrow, a smile plays on his lips, and the author immediately detaches himself from catastrophe and, in a widening long shot, proceeds to objectify his experience. Like the Good Soldier Schweik, Kott has the ability to be enmeshed in the most harrowing incidents and emerge relatively unscathed, his good humor miraculously intact.

In the last chapters, Kott describes with clinical precision and total lack of sentimentality the five heart attacks that, each time, almost snuffed out his life. The metabolic terror that assaults his body is like the biological equivalent of the totalitarianism that wreaked such havoc on his social self between the 1930s and the 1960s. Somehow the cardiac arrests emerge like the progeny of Stalin and Hitler, Gomulka and Jaruzrelski. They are just as irrational; just as menacing; just as impossible to counter or cope with. The clinical descriptions segue into limpid, utterly sensible contemplations that give the book its solid philosophical anchor.

What always made Kott such a distinctive critic was the way in which he was able to find in the classics, particularly Shakespeare, the living essence of contemporary forces. It was Kott more than anyone else who showed us the connection between historical power politics and their contemporary parallels; how the Kings Annointed and the modern despots shared both the same ideologies and techniques of plunder; how the so-called Grand Mechanism was hatched in the Middle Ages and acquired sophistication right up to the present. (Bosnia being the chilling, most immediate example of his thesis.) What *Still Alive* does is to spell out the experiential base from which those theories were hatched. It was because Kott lived the kind of life that he did, that he was able to have the insights he had. What made him an astute critic of Shakespeare was not reading and scholarship but converted perceptions about life's cruelties and absurdities. That is what has always lifted Kott far above his critical colleagues. They were writing exegeses; he was extrapolating from personal traumas and tragedies.

A personal note.

I first met Kott in the early '60s in England but got to know him very well when he relocated to Santa Monica in the '80s. In my many meetings with him, I would always excavate that endlessly fertile mind for insights and perceptions about Shakespeare. We almost never alluded to his personal life—the subject of this book—and when I finished it, I found myself kicking myself for my obtuseness. Instead of discussing "gender theories" or "medieval pageantry," I should have been asking him about the Polish resistance movement, the atmosphere of living under Nazi and Soviet occupation, of being displaced from one corner of Europe to another. Instead of learning first-hand about what was really vital in his life, I contented myself with critical *aperçuts.* And so, for me, *Still Alive* served a double purpose. It opened up a dimension of the man that I virtually knew nothing about and, in so doing, has given me a Jan Kott who is now even more precious than he was before. Secondly, it took the abstractions and clichés of the war years and translated them into vivid, unforgettable terms. What makes *Still Alive* such a compelling read is that from his earliest days right through the rigors of the past sixty years, Kott has always been bristlingly, electrically, unquenchably "alive," and it is the quality of that indigenous liveliness that—being *still* alive—confers such magnetism to this book.

Shakespeare, Our Contemporary displays the length and breadth of Jan Kott's intellect, but *Still Alive* is a literary microcosm that contains the soul of the man.

★★★

56

SHAKESPEARE: A LIFE

by Park Honan

The Shakespeare that emerges from Park Honan's new biography is of a good-natured fellow not prone to revelry or excessive socializing; neutral, sometimes to a fault; careful with money and punctilious about real estate, legacies, and legalities; wary of political implications in the fractious atmosphere of his hometown in Stratford—more at ease in the intellectual climate of London; outwardly respectable in religious matters but deeply agnostic within; sensual, even libidinous, but externally restrained; loyal to the actors and fellow-writers who made up his artistic circle; a man who sublimated his pessimism and pain into his art; who was unfailingly politic on the outside, though often hostile within; a conforming landowner and reliable citizen who never flaunted the uniqueness of his creative powers or ever entertained the prospect of future immortality.

By exploring the nooks and crannies of Warwickshire, the peculiarities of its rural habits, and the mundane occupations of its people, Honan manages to create a social milieu in which Shakespeare is an unexceptional figment of sixteenth-century ordinariness. Resisting the dramatic speculations that often make biography come across like E-Entertainment TV documentaries, Honan sifts prosaic facts and figures, incidents, and hypotheses that flesh out a time and a place that, like Shakespeare himself, have become *kitschified* into a kind of Disneyland theme park: "Ye Olde England," in which the "Bard of Avon" sits, plume in hand, receding forehead, ruff-collar, sober doublet, wearing an expression of inscrutable seriousness, churning out masterworks.

Honan's cast of characters, apart from star-turns like Ben Jonson, Richard Burbage, the Earl of Southampton, Elizabeth I, and James VI, contains a bevy of evocative cameos, which include vicars, schoolteachers, neighbors, physicians, distant relations, and Elizabethan oddballs—all of whom add texture to the background of his central subject. He cunningly discovers aspects in the work that can be traced back to incidents in the period, and his capsule critiques of the main plays, although sometimes opaque, are generally astute and occasionally glitter with fresh insights. Honan is steeped in Shakespearean lore, and it is reassuring to be led through the history of both the man and his times by a docent who has every historical nuance at his fingertips.

The few facts of Shakespeare's life that have been winkled out of old documents and ancient hearsay are now so familiar that the tendency of current biography is to cast the net wider in order to capture facts about the family, the locales, the social conditions, the civic context, and so on. The assumption seems to be the more details we uncover about his milieu and family environment, the more we learn about the man himself, but given the uniqueness of the subject, it seems willfully reductive to proceed on such assumptions. We don't really learn all that much about the "exceptions" by fastidiously recreating the "rule."

There is another school of thought that believes that given the length and breadth of Shakespeare's oeuvre, it should be possible to extrapolate the author's character by simply analyzing the collected works. But the anomalies inherent in the writer, the inability to pin down precisely where he stands in the hurly-burly of the issues he treats, makes him maddeningly ambiguous. We think he is a god-fearing Christian until, in a work like *Lear,* we catch the whiff of a disillusioned agnostic. We believe he is a firm believer in love and conventional morality in a play like *Romeo and Juliet* until we read *Troilus and Cressida* or *Timon of Athens* and encounter an impious cynicism that leads us to believe this author believes in nothing. The sonnets shuttle between heady sentimentality and sneering sarcasm, idealized love and thinly veiled carnality. Can we ever truly construct the psyche of an artist using the building blocks of his work? Was Hemingway a roaring macho or a troubled child compensating for a pampered childhood? Does the romantic early Ibsen bear any real resemblance to the embittered old codger who wrote *When We Dead Awaken?*

Ultimately, Honan's title—*Shakespeare: A Life*— is ironically accurate. It isn't *the* life because, despite what we have learned about his social context and his familial relations, Shakespeare remains as enigmatic as Hamlet and as remote as the Prince's dead father. Honan's achievement is to have widened the field in which we ravenously seek the man, and there's something to be said for that.

★★★

57

HOW GOOD IS DAVID MAMET, ANYWAY?: WRITING ON THEATER

by John Heilpern

In England, there is a commonly held belief that a great drama critic comes along about every seventy years. Hazlitt, in the early 1800s, yielded to George Bernard Shaw around the end of the century and then to Kenneth Tynan in the early 1950s. If the theory holds, we are just about due for the arrival of another formidable pundit. Could it be John Heilpern?

Heilpern's anthology, culled largely from pieces in both the *UK* and *New York Observers* and oddly titled *How Good Is David Mamet, Anyway?*, begs the question: How Good Is John Heilpern, Anyway? Well, as critics go, he is really quite good. He dispenses an easy, readable, lighthearted prose that reveals a congenital love for the art form and a tendency to shrug, sneer, and occasionally fulminate without becoming vulgar or bitchy or losing his verbal elegance. And he has the courage, lacking in many other drama critics, to rap the knuckles of others in the fraternity with whom he disagrees. For instance, he has the refreshing insolence to criticize Robert Brustein for browbeating George Wolfe's *Bring on da Noise, Bring on da Funk* for being "a chronicle of black oppression" instead of the celebration of black American talent Heilpern believes it to be. He even has the temerity to take the *New York Times's* Ben Brantlee to task for drooling over the splendor of diverse gay peckers instead of raising his eyes from the pelvis in order to concentrate his gaze at the heart of these entertainments. Elsewhere, he wickedly deflates another *Times* critic who exhorts his public to "read" Turgenev's *A Month in the Country* rather than see "this seriously flawed production"—although Heilpern's defense of the show is based almost exclusively on a registered difference of opinion rather than a rationalized rebuttal of the critic's argument.

He is excellent at retaining a detached calm in the face of the convulsive enthusiasm that regularly infects critics when confronted with self-promulgating blockbusters. While others lose it into their Depends, Heilpern remains smugly continent. He is, for example, appreciative of Julie Taymor's dazzling design sense without losing sight of the fact that all that overproduced ingenuity is in the service of a simplistic Disney cartoon that suffers from that ineradicable Disney curse, false naiveté.

On other occasions, Heilpern loses his cool and gives vent to effusions that neglect the analytical skills and rooted insights that occasionally elevate criticism to the level of art. He often swoons like a bobby-soxer and devotes a lot of verbal energy to noisy orgasms. Instead of adhering to the Arnoldian dictum of "seeing the object as it really is," he squanders copy trying to articulate the emotions it has aroused. The point about a critic who gushes is that although it conveys the fine frenzy of a sincere enthusiasm, it leads us to suspect he has been abducted by his feelings and is seeing more than meets the eye.

Having memorialized David Mamet in his title, the reader may reasonably anticipate an original exegesis of the inventor of Mametspeak; but in the main, the playwright is taken to task for archness, obscurity, and banality—all of which constitute the prevailing censure of Mamet's work already described by others. One looks in vain for an incisive analysis of the playwright's strengths and weaknesses, his personal flair, and his stylistic debts to writers such as Harold Pinter and Samuel Beckett. All we really learn is that Heilpern doesn't think Mamet is what he's cracked up to be. Having announced the fact that he is attired in the Emperor's New Clothes, the critic never proceeds to examine the anatomy of the naked writer—instead, he seems merely to enjoy the effrontery of deflating a fashionable reputation. We hunger for criticism and get only journalism.

Despite the fact that he is himself a Brit, Heilpern bombards the three wise men of the *New York Times*—Brantlee, Canby, and Marks—(no, they're not a law firm but given their prose style they might just as well be) for genuflecting before the glories of the British stage and unjustifiably downgrading first-class American fare that, in his view, is more socially charged and aesthetically adventurous. That is the kind of critical good sense that *ought* to be directed against American critics whose Anglophilia is often nothing more than a veiled form of snobbery.

Apart from reviews, there is a reprint of an occasional article, and the dialogue that makes up his *Lunch with Gielgud and Richardson* (that's Sir John and Sir Ralph) could easily be a brilliant parody of two old stage duffers if it weren't, in fact, a verbatim record of an actual conversation that took place in a West End restaurant. In it, Heilpern captures not only the accents of two legendary theatrical knights but an atmosphere of surreal idiosyncrasy reminiscent of both Lewis Carroll and Harold Pinter. We are forcibly reminded that the author's early prominence was as a writer of matchless profiles for the *Observer* and that anyone whose ear is so acute to the vagaries of British diction is probably going to be an excellent guide to dramatic writing.

But by and large, Heilpern writes better than he thinks; dispensing opinions rather than *aperçus;* preferring irony to exegesis; and gilding his opinions rather than marshaling them cogently to prove his case. He conjures up the "feel" of a performance better than he is able to describe the aesthetic constituents that render it valid or flawed. His gregariousness is infectious—he's the kind of person with whom you'd like to have good old pub crawl and a late-night snifter.

The book jacket is a retching example of You-scratch-my-back-and-I'll-stroke-your-ego. The close-harmony quartet serenading the author consists of Peter Brook, Tony Kushner, Natasha Richardson, and George C. Wolfe—all past recipients of the critic's fulsome praise. If editors select reviewers with an eye toward objectivity, shouldn't publishers' blurbs avoid the squeals of groupies? It may be sound merchandising practice, but it reeks of cronyism.

Many of the members of Heilpern's personal Guarachi band remark on the critic's "decency" and absence of "meanness," and it is precisely these qualities that soften an edge that should be scalpel-sharp. He *is* "decent" and without "malice," traits we wouldn't associate with George Jean Nathan, Frank Rich, or Kenneth Tynan—all of whom instinctively realized that the way to defend the theater against the *shlockmeisters* was with buckshot and flamethrowers. In this regard, Heilpern more closely resembles Brooks Atkinson, who was also "decent" and "not mean" and beloved by the theater community but lacking in the kind of vitriolic audacity we associate with great critics like Voltaire, Swift, or Mencken. In theater criticism, being "decent" almost always means pulling punches. The effective drama critic needs to be tough and dislikeable and, yes, even negative. Saying "No" to work that isn't up to scratch is the most positive act a critic can perform. If he's too naturally congenial and supportive, what should be a no-holds-barred debate turns into a meeting of the Mutual Admiration Society.

Heilpern's irritation with the bluntness of Jackie Mason's ethnic insults (unquestionably a very "indecent" and "malicious" comedian) bespeaks a prissy-prickly nature. Heilpern, having worked for both Peter Hall and Peter Brook, has shuttled between the poles of orthodoxy and radicalism. Although a staunch supporter of Brook (he wrote the chronicle of his African odyssey *Conference of the Birds*), one senses he is temperamentally more akin to Hall. The book-jacket photo reveals the face of a man-child desperately holding back tears and straining hard to scowl his way into a smile. One shouldn't try to divine character from a photograph, but there is an irresistible temptation to correlate style to personality when confronted with an expression as telling as that.

Basically, drama critics fall into three categories. There are those who employ style merely to dispense opinion; those who dissect works of art in order to *arrive* at opinion; and those who use the dramatic event to try to originate their own works of art. Great critics can inhabit the last two categories; the first produces only popular critics, most often in the newspapers and magazines. Occasionally, a critic comes along who moves freely between all three categories, but this is rare.

Heilpern belongs squarely in the first category, where he is in the illustrious company of writers such as Frank Rich, Clive Barnes, and John Simon. He doesn't have the muscularity of a Robert Brustein or the intellectual breadth of an Eric Bentley, but then he is far more entertaining than either, and what he does have, which is quite unique, is a certain irrepressible levity that makes him agreeable and accessible to an ever-increasing Yuppie population composed, in the main, of middle-brows with highbrow aspirations. The quick-fix carbohydrates of periodic journalism are not to be sniffed at just because they lack the rich protein of academic insight. A burger has as much right to peristalsis as a rib-eye steak.

★★★

58

THE ESSENTIAL GROUCHO

Selected & Edited by Stefan Kanfer

Somewhere around 1976, when I was assembling a program on Woody Allen for the BBC, an interview was arranged for me with Groucho Marx in Beverly Hills. I was informed beforehand that he was slightly loopy, not exactly senescent or "out of it," but that it might be tough going. It didn't matter. Marx was one of the earliest childhood icons, and just seeing him in the flesh would be enough for me.

Groucho, behind real glasses and wispy mustache, somewhat crumpled and a little creased, was still unmistakably Groucho. He was cordial enough at the start but about ten minutes into the interview became rather sour and even surly, as if the genial facade had been assembled just long enough for the curmudgeon to gather his ammo and come out with all guns blazing.

He was somewhat obsessed with one of Woody Allen's one-liners—namely: "I have nothing against dying. I just don't want to be there when it happens," which he repeated two or three times as a rare specimen of Allen's wit. What questions I managed to concoct were invariably derided or their premises scoffed at. The impression he gave was that someone was trying to put something over on him and I was clearly in league with the conspirators. Logic and continuity went out the window and, clearly, nothing was going to be salvaged from the taping. Throughout, his companion-nurse-amanuensis hovered smilingly, ostensibly pleased by the fact that her employer was being entertained masticating a member of the media. After about forty-five minutes of meandering non sequiturs peppered with indignation, sulks, and undisguised hostility, I was informed the interview had to be brought to a close, as Groucho needed to go for his daily "constitutional" around the grounds. As I was leaving, the comedian, unbidden, whipped out an early glossy of himself, scrawled his name across it, and gave it to me with the magnanimity of a superstar patronizing a fawning groupie.

It occurred to me afterward that his behavior, easily misattributed to advancing years, was in fact entirely characteristic of the Groucho we had all grown up with since the '20s. Groucho's stock in trade had always been effrontery, and as Gloria Stuart, the Oscar-award actress of *Titanic* (who had been married to one of his writers) pointed out: "He taught us all how to be irreverent." I had simply been turned into Louis Calhern in *Duck Soup* or Margaret Dumont in *Animal Crackers,* and it served me right for thinking I could assert orderly procedure into a maniacal universe.

The most astute criticism of the Marx brothers came from Antonin Artaud in the early '30s. For Artaud, they were the incarnate spirit of surrealism. "In *Animal Crackers,*" wrote Artaud, "a woman may suddenly fall, legs in the air, on a divan and expose for an instant all we could wish to see—a man may throw himself abruptly upon a woman in a salon, dance a few steps with her and then whack her on the behind in time to the music—these events comprise a kind of exercise of intellectual freedom in which the unconscious of each of the characters, repressed by conventions and habits, avenges itself and us at the same time.... When the poetic is exercised, it always leads towards a kind of boiling anarchy, an essential disintegration of the real by poetry."

Before we attribute too much of the Marx brothers' hilarity to Andre Breton and Robert Desnos, it should be pointed out that the kind of anarchy they exemplified was also a characteristic of American vaudeville—and indeed, an indigenous tendency in American life to be found in gymnasia and frat-houses throughout the land. The Silent Screen comedy of Chaplin, Keaton, and the Keystone Cops is pervaded by the very same surreal delirium.

Where Groucho was always different from the rest of his brothers was in his literary tendency. He made up for an abysmal lack of formal education by reading voraciously and, from the '30s onward, turning out books and articles, not to mention idiosyncratic correspondence with pen-pals such as T. S. Eliot, E. B. White, Russell Baker, S. J. Perelman, and Joe McCarthy's nemesis, Joseph N. Welch.

Although there is a certain Marxian insouciance in all of these works, he was never really a litterateur. He was an existentialist comic, and the suggestive leer, simian walk, and rolling eyes had to be seen to be disbelieved. But given his literary bent, he did exercise a salutary influence on his collaborators that, at various points in his career, included George S. Kaufman, Morrie Ryskind, Arthur Sheekman, Goodman Ace, and the aforementioned S. J. Perelman. Like any comedian steeped in the rollicking lore of vaudeville, playing and being exposed to three-a-day performances in flea-bitten theaters throughout the Keith-Albee and Klaw-Erlanger circuits, Groucho's mind became a storehouse for every pun, wisecrack, and shaggy dog story ever concocted—all of which could be adapted into zinging one-liners at cocktail parties or on his long-running quiz show, *You Bet Your Life.* The comic lore, which was his natural inheritance, was enhanced by his own searing wit, but the backlog was the vaudeville fundament from which much of it sprang.

Stefan Kanfer, in compiling extracts from the films, tidbits from the radio shows, and magazine articles by and about Groucho, slightly misleads us in his title. *The Essential Groucho* is not to be found in prose or inscribed gags. It resides forever in the persona he created on the Broadway stage and then transferred to the screen in the late '20s and '30s. His genius is not that he was an illiterate who developed a literary style roughly fashioned on the fabrications of his gag writers, but that he was the personification of insolence, a man whose natural instincts were at war with the bogus respectability of established society. When he said, "I don't want to join any club that would have me as a member," he was proclaiming the outsiderness that made him sacred to all the rest of us who were desperately clamoring for membership in that club. When he refused to appear at the premiere of a biblical epic starring a beefy, barrel-chested Victor Mature, with the excuse: "I never attend films where the leading man's tits are bigger than the leading lady's," he was disparaging Hollywood shlock more venomously than any film critic ever could.

He was, as Artaud rightly realized, the spirit of social rebellion in an age when conformity was both the prevailing virtue and the asphyxiating evil. His genius was in his style and stance. It influenced Spike Milligan and the Goons, the Crazy Gang, Monty Python, Don Rickles, Woody Allen, and Steven Wright and can still be found whenever propriety is kicked in the ass and someone reveals the embarrassing subtext of a truth that, for the sake of social comfort, is better left suppressed.

Revisiting the comic free associations of *The Coconuts, Duck Soup, Animal Crackers,* et al., is nostalgically pleasurable, but Julius Marx, apart from being one of the century's greatest comedians, was also a brooding, cranky, parsimonious, and troubled individual, and now that we have had volumes of hagiography, it is high time someone produced an unvarnished portrait of the man behind the false eyebrows and painted mustache. It might not be all that funny, but it might well be riveting.

★★★

59

BOSIE: A BIOGRAPHY OF LORD ALFRED DOUGLAS

by Douglas Murray

For just over a century, Lord Alfred Douglas, the exquisite golden-haired boy whom many held responsible for the tragic downfall of Oscar Wilde, was contemptuously relegated to the dustbin of literature. Whether he seduced Wilde or the other way round, it was that peevish, disputatious, supercilious, spoiled, aristocratic youth who was thought to have destroyed one of the most brilliant and whimsical intellects of the nineteenth century. The biographies provided nauseating evidence of the corruption, and later, plays and films only corroborated the ways in which "the love that dare not speak its name," once uttered in the headlines of the British gutter-press, succeeded in contaminating both the reputation *and* the name of the most successful playwright to emerge in England before the advent of Shaw.

Therefore, it comes as something of a shock to discover that the opprobrium of one hundred years may have been misplaced—may, in fact, be entirely unjustified. If *Bosie,* Douglas Murray's riveting biography of Lord Alfred, does nothing else, it effectively lodges a strong appeal for a judicial review of everything we thought we knew about the Wilde scandal and the man who ostensibly perpetrated it.

But rehabilitating Lord Alfred Douglas is a little like painting Genghis Khan as a genial family man with a pipe and slippers who loves dogs and faithfully attends church every Sunday. Not even Murray and his detoxifying prose can do this easily for, whatever his virtues, we are still dealing with a hot-headed, anti-Semitic, litigious, and blustering philistine who, having renounced homosexuality and adopted Roman Catholicism, became as vociferous a prig as he was a crusading sodomite.

What Murray makes clear is that there were at least four distinct stages to Douglas's life. He started as a ravenous hedonist, became an aggressive and fulminating litigant (like his father, the Marquess of Queensberry), developed into one of the most impressive sonneteers in England, and then transformed into a serene relic of the Victorian era who publicly confessed all his transgressions and labored assiduously to prepare his soul for its certain redemption in the next world.

In between, he became a highly efficient editor of literary publications such as *Plain English, Spirit Lamp,* and the *Academy*—and, having butched down his homoerotic instincts, fell in love with and married Olive Custance, who, the Wilde infatuation notwithstanding, was unquestionably the great love of his life; at least he maintained that relationship, despite ruptures and harangues, for over forty-three years.

At some point or other, Douglas managed to quarrel with almost everyone: T. W. H. Crosland, the man with whom he went into business; Olive, his doting wife; Raymond, his mentally unbalanced son; Colonel Custance, his father-in-law, Frank Harris, his devious collaborator; and a bevy of writers, including Arthur Ransome, Wilfred Scawan Blunt, and Andre Gide. The latter publicly blamed him for all of Oscar's problems, provoking the epithet: "Gide is a shit! Like a person who has an abscess on his bottom and continuously displays it to the world." His staunchest relationships were with his mother, the Marchioness of Queensberry, who never forsook him, and George Bernard Shaw, whose politics he abhorred but with whom he maintained a warm and cordial correspondence in the last third of his life.

Douglas's Jungian "shadow," the nemesis whom he loathed almost as much as he was loathed in return, was Robert Ross, Wilde's first lover, literary executor, and the man who throughout the Yellow Nineties, lusted for a privileged place beside the successful playwright. It is harrowing to read about Ross's treachery against the fey young boy who displaced him in Wilde's affections as it is blood-curdling to read of Douglas's implacable vengeance against the scheming sodomite that tried to destroy him. In *De Profundis,* Wilde eloquently pegged this destructive trait in Douglas: "Hate," he wrote, "so blinded you that you could see no further than the narrow, walled-in, and already lust-withered garden of your common desires. Your terrible lack of imagination, the one really fatal defect of your character, was entirely the result of Hate that lived in you. . . . That faculty in you which Love would have fostered, Hate poisoned and paralyzed."

Murray sagely comments: "Wilde was wrong: the hatred Douglas had felt for his father was equaled by the love he felt for Wilde." Despite a vicious *volte*-face after he found himself demonized in *De Profundis,* Douglas gradually came around to acknowledging that what was far more deeply rooted in his nature was his unquenchable love for Wilde and what the writer had meant to him in his most impressionable years.

After his imprisonment, it was Bosie who sustained Wilde on the Continent with both money and loyal companionship, although in communiqués to Robert Ross, the self-pitying exile sang a very different tune. Wilde emerges from these well-documented episodes as a two-faced, opportunistic dandy who, despite the professed affection for his lover, coldly places self-interest before ethical behavior. For the Wildeans, these may be disagreeable revelations, but throughout the entire Douglas-Wilde saga, the cards were always stacked in Oscar's favor. Even in his ignominy, he achieves a kind of posthumous Grand Slam, whereas Douglas is always forced to fold. Murray is the first writer to have dealt both men a straight hand.

Throughout his middle age, when Douglas was not actually waging libel actions, he was fighting windmills. He brought a suit against Winston Churchill, alleging that, when First Lord of the Admiralty, he had conspired to murder Lord Kitchener. (Douglas lost.) He was also the star witness in a trial that allegedly concealed the names of 47,000 English perverts whom he believed posed a massive threat to national security (shades of McCarthy) during the First World War. (He won that one.) He was generally despised both by the British political establishment and by many in his own aristocratic circle, who felt too close a proximity might compromise their reputations. Douglas, the descendant of William ("The Black") Douglas, the renowned thirteenth-century warrior and close friend of Robert the Bruce, never dropped his guard or lowered his cudgel. He took umbrage the way other men took afternoon tea. Gradually, as we watch him hurtle from one court battle to the next, his untiring pugnacity inspires a grudging kind of admiration in the reader. Here is a Lord who doesn't give a damn whom he alienates in the process of espousing causes in which he fiercely, albeit wrong-headedly, believes.

Much of the strife in Douglas's life grew out of a series of vindictive homosexual bitcheries, the kind of tumult one associates with drag queens dissing each other in public, and a perfectly understandable loathing of England's class-ridden, hierarchical society. The real *vice Anglais* is not so much flagellation as it is an all-devouring philistinism that uniformly punishes both sexual and social deviations. It rigorously upholds a bogus standard of Good Taste that loosely translated means: everything should *appear* respectable and be unthreatening. It is widespread among the upper classes, and Douglas got more than his share of it from vindictive aristocrats and upper-middle-class snobs who were not so much opposed to homosexuality as they were to it being publicly revealed. To champion it vocally and unashamedly and argue that although possibly a sin, it should not be considered a crime, was to court certain ostracism. Douglas died long before "The Wolfenden Report" decriminalized homosexual practices in England, but as editor, writer, lecturer, and example, he was in the vanguard of that reform. Today, he would be a hero of the gay and lesbian lobbies everywhere and probably win a parliamentary seat in Brighton.

In the '20s, when poets like Eliot, Auden, and Pound were replacing the strict and elegant versification that Douglas and others of his generation typified, he railed at their modernity, their lack of formalism, and renunciation of traditional poetic techniques. Even in the '40s, when the modernist taste had more or less established itself, he never stopped railing at them. He was so deeply embedded in the aesthetic into which he had been born that he couldn't countenance a view of poetry that abandoned strict meter and a celebration of the Beautiful. His biographer mounts a strong campaign for including Douglas in the pantheon of great English poets, but for me, the samples of his sonnets that he includes reveal a somewhat frozen and studied lyrical approach to poetry that resembles Wilde at his wettest.

Paradoxically, in his declining years Douglas lost his exquisite beauty, acquiring a bulbous nose, tight-hard wrinkles, and a permanent grimace—as if the portrait of Dorian Gray, forsaking its hiding place in the attic, had come to life and begun to move among us. Hugh Kingsmill, Frank Harris's biographer (and never a striking beauty himself) sought him out in the '30s and wrote of a "Douglas wizened and bowed; his nose jutting out from beneath his soft hat. If anyone had been told by God (he would not have accepted it from lesser authority) that one of these two men had been the handsomest man in England in his youth, he must have picked me out." To paraphrase Nietzsche: "Whom the gods destroy, they first make plain."

Author Douglas Murray is a twenty-one–year-old undergraduate at Magdalen College, Oxford, and, judging from the book-jacket photo, precisely the kind of willowy youth Douglas would have made a beeline for in his own Magdalen days. He has clearly been seduced by Douglas's poetry and in this biography has produced a brilliant piece of reconstructive surgery. He never allows his sympathy toward his subject to influence the case he is making. He bleaches but doesn't entirely remove some of Douglas's blemishes, presenting a convincing picture of a man who was more sinned against than sinning and who, whatever his character flaws, openly renounced his worst faults and, toward the end of his life, made a 360-degree turn. Douglas has been obscured in the formidable shadow cast by Wilde, but Murray, by shining an equally bright light on him, reveals him as an independent entity whose life undergoes an almost Shakespearean transmutation—an Osric who changes into a kind of persecuted Richard II, only to emerge as a benign Prospero offering reconciliation to all his former enemies.

Forcing us to reconsider opinions long cast in stone is what good biography is all about, and that's precisely what *Bosie* succeeds in doing admirably.

★★★

60

DADDY DEAREST

Dream Catcher: A Memoir

by Margaret A. Salinger

In the '50s, J. D. Salinger's meteor landed with a great thwack in the dead center of America's literary heartland. For the next half-century, the man himself disappeared into a black hole from which no one could extract him. Eventually, tentative biographies began to appear but always somewhat speculative and dubious. Apart from legally disputing Ian Hamilton's use of his personal letters in that author's unauthorized biography, Salinger remained largely incommunicado. Then in 1998, At Home in the World, *Joyce Maynard's account of her affair with the writer, was published and that was followed by the largest peephole of all, a tell-all memoir by daughter Margaret. Despite the furor, Salinger maintained an impregnable silence and, if anything, became an even greater subject of gossip and speculation than he had been fifty years before. Beckett was camera-shy, but Salinger was virtually agoraphobic, and so the agony caused by the memoir must have been unbearable.*

In *Dream Catcher,* Margaret A. Salinger, tortured daughter of J. D., has written a piece of Grand Guignol ingeniously disguised as a memoir of her life in the Salinger household.

Redolent of *Justine* and other Sadean works in which innocent young ladies are relentlessly tortured by pitiless male monsters, the author describes a reclusive childhood in a remote Cornish retreat, barred from normal human contacts, where, subjected to her father's subtle brainwashing, she learns the Salingerian Doctrines of asceticism and aloofness. The author, his literary reputation already beginning to blossom, is enthralled with a variety of arcane pursuits that include Zen Buddhism, Vedanta, Yogananda's Church of Self Realization, Christian Science, Scientology, Homeopathy, Macrobiotics, the theories of Edgar Cayce and Wilhelm Reich, sitting in orgone boxes, speaking in tongues, and drinking one's own urine. One's sympathy is immediately aroused for this captive daughter, for whom "the man who came to empty our garbage" and the remote postman "who only came by in person if there was something my father had to sign" represent the only social alternatives to the Frankensteinian father, molding her into an antisocial monster very much like himself.

Throughout, Margaret Salinger, egged on by her mother, Claire (another subjugated acolyte), views herself as a typical victim of cultism; the cult being, in this case, founded on the Salinger Gospel of living spiritually while disparaging life. The book is sprinkled with footnotes from analysts and ex-cult members that confirm, in the author's mind, the extent to which she has been brainwashed by a possessive and exploitative ogre disguised as a loving dad.

Things do not improve when our persecuted heroine manages to escape her rustic incarceration and is sent off to a variety of private schools. She finds her father is niggardly in providing subsistence, despite a slew of health disorders that may well have been attributable to his denying her conventional medical treatment as a child. When, in her twenties, ailing and desperate, her disability payments are suddenly terminated, she pleads to daddy for help, but he sends her only a copy of Mary Baker Eddy's *Science and Health with Key to the Scriptures* and urges her to stop believing in the "illusion" of her sickness. At which point, writes the author: "What began to crack was my belief in the illusion of my father."

After therapy, bouts of bulimia, hallucinations, Chronic Fatigue Syndrome, and an abortion, the daughter experiences an epiphany. All her life she has been the product of "someone else's dream" and the revelation is blinding. "One of the first things I took a look at were all the Salinger 'thou shalt nots.' Thou shalt not dabble in the arts unless a born genius, thou shalt not study religion unless in a sackcloth at the foot of some foreign guru. Thou shalt not set foot in the unclean Ivy League. And for God's sake, never take an English class. Thou shalt not do anything unless it's perfect, thou shalt not be flawed, thou shalt not be woman, thou shalt not grow up."

Epiphanies are liberating, but how to sweep away the accumulated debris of the past?—Why, with a book, of course. A book in the Great Tradition of Getting Even with the Parents, such as Christine Crawford's *Mommie Dearest,* Gary Crosby's *Going My Own Way,* Barbara Davis's account of mother Bette Davis in *My Mother's Keeper,* Susan Cheever's *Home Before Dark,* Aram Saroyan's biography of his all-devouring father, William—etc., etc., etc.

It seems to me entirely justifiable for put-upon sons and daughters to wreak a posthumous (or even nonposthumous) revenge against the parent who abused their psyche or their soma. "Tit for tat," although not enshrined in the Constitution, is a profoundly treasured right among American citizens. But questions of taste also apply—and just as "the lady protests too much" makes us question "the lady's" sincerity, so a flood of undefended indictments makes us wonder if fair play is being observed.

Having personally dealt with members of the Salinger family (Matthew and Claire), I am prepared to believe that J. D.'s influence *was* noxious and soul-destroying. The evidence is everywhere. Nevertheless, there is something repellent about the ex-wife finding delight in her daughter's decision to write a tell-all book about "Daddie Dearest." ("When I decided to talk to my mother about what I was considering, she put her hand over her mouth like a Catholic schoolgirl and, with eyes wide, said: 'That's sacrilege!' When she dropped her hand from her mouth, though, she was smiling.")

But the daughter still had certain misgivings about publicly trashing her father, and so she sought advice from a close friend of hers who was a psychic. "A few months later," reports the author, "she called me and said that a woman had appeared to her in a dream and told her to tell me that I should do it, that it would be important to my son. The point I am making here isn't about psychic phenomena, but rather that I needed that *kind* of reassurance."

Bolstered by her psychic's permission, Margaret proceeded to chronicle her father's manipulative guile, her mother's rampant promiscuity, and her own bewildered attempt to come to terms with a dysfunctional upbringing. If all of this was for the sake of her son, I would question how, in later years, he will take it. Will he not, like objective readers, wonder how much of this story has been distorted by an afflicted sensibility, filtered through a series of kooky theorems every bit as weird as those ascribed to her father, and quite possibly motivated by commercial gain? And what disturbing questions arise about the taste and character of the woman who felt the need to write it?

Bombarded with this litany of moral crimes against J. D., the reader's natural instinct is to become tacitly defensive—especially as one becomes increasingly aware of his daughter's sudsy diction as opposed to the crystalline clarity of her father's style. Much of *Dream Catcher* is concerned with drippy reminiscences of childhood crushes, schoolgirl-crises, dreary camping-trips, and heated affairs that flower and fade at the speed of stop-action photography. Essentially drivel. The author, unconsciously self-indulgent and tediously egoistic, tends to forget that the only reason anyone has picked up her book is to penetrate one of the great mysteries of modern times: the Secret Life of J. D. Salinger, the very subject that has prompted her memoir in the first place. Once you have succeeded in attracting avid voyeurs to your lurid Web site, it is sheer effrontery to regale them with your medical records or snapshots from your high school folio.

The book concludes with an explosive telephonic denouement, in which Salinger berates his newly pregnant daughter for bringing a child whom she cannot support into this "lousy world" and suggests an abortion. This finally shatters Margaret's protective shell. "I don't know where I found the courage—perhaps because I was a mother whose child was being attacked—but I'm proud to say that, for the first time in my life, I let him have it, straight from the gut, unedited." All the grievances from childhood to motherhood came flooding out in a great tsunami. Margaret goes on to say: "As soon as I hung up, or rather slammed down the phone, I'm not quite sure why, but I wrote down the conversation verbatim." Any two-bit Freudian could have told her why. By then, the unconscious desire to wound him where she knew he was most vulnerable, the neurotically guarded area of public exposure, had already been formed and all that now remained was to gather her weaponry and take aim.

Margaret Salinger now works as a hospital chaplain, giving aid and comfort to distressed children and adults. It is as if she has converted all the parental disdain that she describes so graphically into a new persona that will in some way compensate the emotional deprivations she has had to suffer. Here, too, there is a characteristically Sadean conclusion to the story; a retreat to a kind of monastic life in which Virtue will erase the obscenities of the past—at least, until the next horror comes along.

Our insatiable thirst for gossip encourages books like *Dream Catcher* but, like all shameful cravings, makes us feel cheap afterwards. Too many great writers have been monsters for us to throw up our hands in horror over J. D. Salinger's moral shortcomings. If he must join the ranks of Balzac and Villon, Hemingway and Mailer, Faulkner and Celine, so be it. It seems these days a tarnished character only enhances the polish of a writer's reputation.

★★★

IV

THINK PIECES

61

TWO CHEERS FOR BROADWAY

Frank Rich, forgotten but not gone, continues his one-sided love affair with Broadway. From the op-ed pages of the *New York Times,* he recently celebrated "the three consecutive smash hits that are rapidly bringing the era of the British megamusical to an end: *Rent, Bring in da Noise, Bring in da Funk* and *Chicago.*

Without in any way disparaging the achievements of each of those splendid entertainments, it seems to me that Broadway should be setting itself a higher goal than trying to outpoint Andrew Lloyd Webber and the elephantiasis of his megahits. Another way of looking at Rich's selected "smash hits" is that they exist in a context clogged with eight revivals and a number of appalling potboilers such as *Beauty and the Beast* and *Once upon a Mattress.* If Broadway had not imported Peter Hall's *An Ideal Husband* and relied on the drawing power of Noel Coward's *Present Laughter,* there would be virtually no classics to speak of.

Where, in this revivified Broadway season that so enthralls Mr. Rich, is there an American company essaying an Elizabethan, Jacobean, or eighteenth-century classic? Where is the transmogrified revival of Ibsen or Chekhov that is so often the highlight of a London season? Where are the courageous managements risking investment on rich new American writing that reflects the social and political quandary in which the country now finds itself? Veteran director Hal Prince pours all his bubbling energy into retreaded musicals such as *Showboat* and *Candide,* and an exciting new director like Julie Taymor becomes the opulent captive of the Disney Corporation. (Is a glittering and gargantuan stage version of the asinine *Lion King* really where the gold of the American theater is to be minted?)

In European playhouses where the theater is both subsidized and respected, there is no dichotomy between the boulevard and the "serious theater." Shakespeare, Molière, Schiller, Ibsen, Chekhov, and Brecht bed down with Franz Lehar, Johan Strauss, and Jacques Offenbach and, in the smaller houses, the work of new and challenging writers is regularly mounted. The larger stages even accommodate the great American blockbuster from time to time, but they never scant the perennial classic, the rethought revival, the more chancy, experimental work. In America, there is up-market Broadway where half a dozen monopolistic managers call the tune and set the standard, and Off-Broadway where "the serious plays" can usually be found trying to eke out a living.

"For the moment," swoons Rich, "it's enough to celebrate theater artists who are liberating Broadway's stages from theme-park culture even as it erupts on the streets all around them." But can three smash-hit musicals in a theater scene devoid of serious new plays or resourceful classics really be called "a liberation"? Surely, it is part of the old colonization of Broadway by commercial promoters peddling "glitz" and "pizzazz" in whatever old or new containers come to hand. "They keep alive," says Rich, "the dream that the new Times Square, like its fabled predecessor, may yet be a place where anything can happen." But so long as Broadway is sustained only by the next "hot ticket" and the next "smash hit," it will remain what it has always been: a magnet for facile, remorselessly commercial (usually revived) musical-comedy successes, a theater that depends desperately on infusions from abroad and bigger and better spectaculars at home. A theater that has neither the patience nor the interest to develop serious native artists and the long-range permanent ensembles that nourish themselves on the masterworks of the past.

The 42nd Street renaissance that so excited Mr. Rich might be encouraging if it didn't look and feel like an appropriation from a corporation (Disney) whose values and goals are antithetical to serious theater. It is ludicrous to view this as a revitalization of the Broadway scene when it is so apparently a corporate take-over in the name of larger and even more simplistic pop entertainment. It is, in effect, an encroachment on the independence of Broadway, which, whatever its faults, has always displayed a Catholic taste. But the Disney Ethic is rooted in sentimentality, simplification, and the crudest elements of what we now smirkingly refer to as "family values." Disney has a vested interest in avoiding controversy, side-stepping complexity, and expunging ambiguity—the very qualities that occasionally produce something memorable in the American theater.

The object of the Broadway stage should not simply be to "bring the era of British megamusicals to an end"—as if chauvinism was the driving force behind theatrical endeavor—but to consolidate some of the gains of the past eighty years by mounting first-class revivals of durable straight plays as well as musicals and by laying the foundation for rigorously trained professional companies, the best of which should become the keystone of a national theater. This, of course, is in addition to the never-ending quest for relevant new plays that should find their way on to the Broadway stage in numbers at least equal to those of the musical revivals.

Whenever Broadway has a good season, dewy-eyed Stage-Door-Johnnies like Rich immediately start throwing kisses and rhapsodizing about a renaissance. But the Broadway theater, unlike London's West End, the Parisian Boulevards, or the German and Scandinavian *staatsteaters,* is without the fundament of a serious theater: a resolve to maintain a classic repertoire; a commitment to new and pertinent plays, whether formulaic or not; and the establishment of ensemble companies to enable the best of the old and new work to be performed with consummate skill. And so long as that remains the case, the cycle will remain unbroken. Broadway will continue to warm itself with the heat of "hot tickets" and get its kicks out of "smash hits."

62

"WERE YOU THERE WHEN THEY CRUCIFIED OUR PLAY?"

On October 8th Matthew Shepard, aged 22, an openly gay student, was pistol-whipped and lashed to a fence-post outside Laramie, Wyoming, for eighteen hours in near-freezing temperatures. He went into a coma and died five days later.

A few days earlier, the House of Representatives voted to proceed with an impeachment investigation against Bill Clinton for the heinous crimes of equivocating before the Grand Jury and the country about a sexual liaison with a White House intern.

Although the two facts would appear to be unrelated, there is a kind of tendon that runs between them both. The moral admonition against homosexuality, energetically fostered by the Religious Right, is a strain of the aggressive Puritanism that is bred in the American bone and has recently been served up in massive quantities, by both the media and the politicians. Jesse Helms and Newt Gingrich are only Cotton Mather and Anthony Comstock writ small, and, for the past year or so, the rough-riders of Moral McCarthyism have been galloping into our private lives and raising an almighty cloud of dust.

More significant than the Manhattan Theatre Club's reinstatement of Terence McNally's *Corpus Christie* was the pusillanimous instinct that initially withdrew the production because of bomb threats. On the face of it, it appears to be an entirely reasonable course of action. Is *any* play worth endangering innocent ticket-holders and risking the demolition of one's theater? One obvious answer is No, and another, just as obvious, is: It is unthinkable that an independent arts organization would succumb to such threats by lamely suppressing artistic expression.

Critical reservations of Terence McNally's passion play are entirely irrelevant to the issue that recently brought the play to national prominence. The symbolic martyrdom of gay victims in a homophobic society is as valid a premise for a play as the anti-Semitism that ultimately brought on the

Holocaust. The larger question here is, should theater artists allow themselves to be intimidated by bigots—even when those bigots claim to represent established religions or impressive congressional districts?

One of the most irksome positions in the theater is having to defend imperfect work for the sake of a principle that is far greater than any individual product. Yet all that awkward squirmyness is not only worth the discomfort but is part of one's bounden duty if the iniquity of censorship is effectively to be countered. The unconquerable enemy in art has always been Establishment morality—what the majority of people feels is "right and proper." It is in the face of that, that artists have to put up their strongest defenses so that when social conditions become tyrannous and insupportable, those avenues of communication remain open to us. By permitting flag burning, we may avoid Jew burning. By allowing the Profane to be heard, we may avoid the greater profanities of Inquisitions, witch hunts, and blacklists.

Critical reservations notwithstanding, I would rather see a hundred *Corpus Christie*s on American stages than have one theater boarded up by the Moral Crusaders or a single subsidy pulled because of the self-righteous indignation of the Guardians of Good Taste.

When the Catholic League for Religious and Civil Rights (an oxymoron, if there ever was one) objected to McNally's work, it was not on aesthetic grounds. They weren't raising the kinds of objections drama critics might raise. They had decided for themselves, and wished then to decide for us, what was irreverent and therefore suppressible. Those are precisely the kinds of impulses the Constitution was created to guard us against and, for good or ill, it is the artists who traditionally serve in the front lines against such incursions.

Of late, it seems to me, there have been a lot of drowsy sentries manning these barricades. Repressive political and religious leaders have made greater inroads in the past ten years than creative artists have made in the last fifty. With minimal backchat, we have tolerated the dismantling of the NEA and the withdrawal of grants to artists for what politicians believe to be subversive or obscene work. There is a new kind of permissiveness in the nation today—very unlike the one we associate sneeringly with the '60s. This is the permissiveness of people who seem too weary to fight City Hall; are too busy with their "personal agendas" to affirm the moral imperatives of a public agenda; are more inclined to keep their noses clean than to get them bloodied in a controversy that might threaten their economic well-being. Yes, the American Way will field some resistance to the Catholic League pickets outside the Manhattan Theatre Club, but, by and large, people are too concerned with the fluctuations of the stock market or the latest wrinkle in the Clinton-Lewinsky affair to bother their heads overmuch about threats to free expression. Meanwhile, the moral zealots organize, flame, fulminate, and increase the size of their lobbies.

"The best lack all conviction," wrote Yeats, who, from his perch in the Pantheon, could be commenting on the situation created by *Corpus Christie,* "while the worst are full of passionate intensity."

63

THIS WOODEN "O"

Sam Wanamaker's obsession with recreating Shakespeare's Globe Theatre near the site where it originally stood in Southwark was one of the most inspiring and tragic events of the mid-twentieth century. Inspiring because it is always exhilarating to see a man totally committeds to a Herculean task with all the fiber of his body and fire in his soul. Tragic because when, after innumerable frustrations and stonewallings, it was finally standing on the South Bank, Sam never saw it. If the theatrical history of the century is ever written, Sam Wanamaker would deserve an encomium all to himself—but even then, it would never begin to express the gratitude he is owed by the government, artists, and citizenry of England—not just for getting it built but for infusing it with a practical and contemporaneous love of Shakespeare.

★★★

I had a boundless and long-entrenched affection for Sam Wanamaker, the American actor-director who spent over twenty-five years trying to create the Shakespeare Globe that now flourishes on Bankside. It was an affection in no way diluted by the fact that I thought his obsession was wrongheaded and, in many ways, reactionary. "Once the replica is completed," I told him, "you will have created an irresistible temptation to restore a Shakespeare tradition we have spent four hundred years trying to overthrow." Sam would reply with a quiet, snickering laugh, the subtext of which was: "If I had several years at my disposal, I'd try to dissuade you but for the moment, let's just agree to disagree."

When I actually saw the theater on a recent visit to London, I have to admit I was unexpectedly choked up. The accuracy of the construction, the sense of being back in a milieu that was genuinely Elizabethan and overpoweringly "Shakespearean" made me feel there was an incontestable point to the whole project: namely, the evocation of a venue that, before its replication, existed merely as a kind of a treasured theatrical legend based on a sketchy drawing and a lot of tantalizing historical gossip.

Then I was told the prevailing attitude to the Globe was that it mustn't be a Heritage-site, a kind of cultural Lourdes to which devoted pilgrims would journey merely to worship and venerate. It must also be "modern" and capable of producing contemporary versions of Elizabethan and Jacobean classics. But that would necessarily involve disguising the historical character of the theater and what then would have been the point of meticulously recreating it? The Globesters continually shuttled between appreciating its traditional virtues and anticipating the innovations that would occur there, without sensing any contradiction in those attitudes.

The first production I saw there was Richard Olivier's *Henry V* and the disparity between the venue and the quality of that performance was grueling. Within the framework of a startlingly recreated sixteenth-century ambiance, there was the kind of undercast, plodding revival that one normally associated with second-rate British reps and the RSC on a bad day. Unconsciously, I was expecting the vigorous, thrusting, larger-than-life theatrics that one has always associated with that salty, unself-conscious, ebullient period when the Renaissance came into full flower. In this perfectly reconstructed Elizabethan setting, my inner voice was telling me, one would finally see something resembling the gusto and vitality of the Age of Shakespeare.

If, the inner voice continued, one is really trying for a reasonable facsimile of the earlier era, let there be nut-sellers and ale-merchants, cutpurses and swindlers, a gaggle of trollops available for pre- or post-performance assignations, the cries of bear-baiting drifting in from outside the portico, horses relieving themselves on the cobblestones, and squads of agitated Puritans railing against the teeming immorality of everything connected to the playhouse. If you're going for period authenticity, go all the way! But then, of course, one would have created a perverted, Disneyesque theme park, and the efforts of all those scholars and pedants, architects and designers would have been for naught.

The *Henry V* had a studied quality that was redolent of the archaeologically correct productions we associate with the late nineteenth century, as if assiduously researching what had "really happened back then" would in some way provide a startling insight into what the play meant to spectators today. This is what one might call the Beerbohm-Tree Fallacy, and it is as intellectually bankrupt as the period from which it stems. Having had the jingoistic version of this play in the Olivier film and the "coming of age" version of the recent Branagh epic, we now look for different nuances and unexpected emphases, and they are unquestionably there. The deadly chauvinism of the French and the English conflict powerfully reverberates through the Baltic and Russian strife now raging in those parts of the world.

By which, I do not mean we need a stage filled with Serbs and Croats, Albanians and Bolsheviks, but there is a thematic vein in the play that could be isolated and fashioned into an interpretation that would make audiences feel, as ever with Shakespeare, that a historical situation still rebounds with contemporary allusions. Instead, we got a lot of self-conscious, garrulous British types booing the French and cheering the British, as if *Henry V* was some kind of up-market melodrama like *Uncle Tom's Cabin.*

The physical space seemed to be proffering an invitation toward boldness and panache, which the company appeared to be respectfully declining. This, the Globe architecture seemed to be saying, is where it can all happen again: the zest, the vigor, the dizzying variety, and multiplicity of styles that made England the standard-bearer for theater in the post-Renaissance world. This, the puttering company seemed to reply, is the kind of acting we do in England today.

Is there an irreconcilable contradiction between contemporary Shakespearean production and the physical confines of the Globe? And if there *isn't,* does it mean we must simply conceal or ignore the historicity of the theater in order to continue to stage classics in what has now become the postmodernist tradition?

My own feeling is that the existence of the Globe replica is a tantalizing opportunity to come up with a revivified acting style, bolder, more daring, and less psychologically conditioned than the one that has served us over the past fifty years. Turning one's back on the historical imperative of the theater would be both fatuous and hypocritical. Pretending it was nothing more than "another space" for freewheeling, classical reinterpretations would be an insult to the integrity and perseverance of its founders and architects. But rethinking the whole notion of the Shakespeare Tradition from the standpoint of the nontraditional stagecraft that is our contemporary legacy is a challenge that has not even been articulated.

The question that needs to be asked, it seems to me, is pretty basic: Who is the Globe for? If it's for the tourists, that dictates one clear set of priorities and any huckstering efforts that draw them in will be commercially justified. If it's for theatergoers, whatever their country of origin, and based on an underlying assumption of cultural seriousness, then a very different direction has to be taken. At the moment, the Globe is not so much fallen between two stools as it is leaping from one to the other in a frantic effort to have it both ways.

We can't "go back" to former times or, given the period-physicality of the theater, pretend they aren't implied in the design. The theater and its promotion deafeningly proclaim the theater's historicity. Nor is it simply a matter of dredging up the sixteenth- and seventeenth-century plays we associate with the period in which the Globe came into being; that, too, would be a bloodless academic exercise. The challenge is directly to "playing style," to reconsiderations of acting technique, to creating a performance dynamic that, like the building itself, can bridge the gap between our time and Shakespeare's.

For those of us who both championed and fretted with Sam Wanamaker as he worked to realize his dream, that is an intriguing challenge. The last thing we need in England is, to use a disparaging pun, a "wooden 'O.'"

★★★

64

WHAT'S IN A NAME?

Whatever reservations one may have about *Rent,* I derive a keen satisfaction from the fact that Broadway's newest and noisiest blockbuster is the work of a group of unknown actors essaying the work of an equally unknown playwright and composer.

Is there anything more antithetical to the Hollywood mentality, where the celebration of "names" is a kind of incense-strewn holy ritual, and virtually no major commercial project feels able to proceed unless it is studded with established reputations and the cozy reassurance of known quantities?

A few weeks ago in one of those conferences where the established truisms of theatrical success are reiterated like the rat-a-tat-tat of a woodpecker's beak on a log, I found myself arguing that a qualitative result in theater could draw the town even if it was totally uninhabited by name performers or established writers. I was vigorously assured that without the charisma of either a star or the lesser incandescence of relatively established leading actors, an ambitious venture would never get off the ground; that without the high octane of familiar and sought-after personalities, the theater was simply a mug's game doomed to the kind of piddling anonymity that characterizes Off-Off-Broadway and the L.A. waiver scene.

One tends to forget that before people such as Orson Welles, Joseph Cotton, Agnes Moorhead, and George Colouris became national luminaries, they were the fervent rank-and-file of a WPA-sponsored company called the Mercury Theater, which virtually no one had ever heard of. And before one was dazzled by the considerable talents of Harold Clurman, Lee Strasberg, Elia Kazan, John Garfield, and Clifford Odets, these people slogged away in nondescript country retreats, plying their craft in unhallowed obscurity.

The noisy coronation of stars tends to obliterate the unremarkable past from which they have emerged, just as anyone looking at Venus through a microscope would find it hard to believe that, light-years ago, it may only have been a conjunction of gaseous vapors from which no light emanated at all. A truism, you might say, and yet one that is fiercely disregarded in the arts—and especially in film and theater, where failing to secure the services of a TVQ-hot celebrity is a powerful deterrent both to money and to initiative.

At a certain point in the careers of established stars, an inverse ratio sets in. The best of them start to falter and grow predictable, despite (or sometimes because of) their long-standing reputations. The eye is drawn to the rising, relatively unknown talent, and it is only after he or she has received the full measure of approbation that his or her qualities are generally acknowledged—despite the fact that these actors existed in full measure years before such general recognition. (Nathan Lane and Anthony Hopkins are recent cases in point.)

The almost junkie-like obsession with name recognition is perhaps that sickness most unique to our times; our reverence for the recognizable and the familiar, a deplorable indication of our lack of imagination and the crowning proof of our susceptibility to indoctrination.

It is enough for genial nonentities such as Kato Kaelen, Anna Nicole Smith, John Wayne Bobbit, and Divine Smith to achieve notoriety for us to accept them into our pantheon of stars. That same familiarity that used to breed contempt now breeds adoration. Our "heroes" require only constant exposure to cameras and print to win a place in our hearts, and once there, we are prepared to revere them no matter how incongruous their transmutations. Heidi Fleiss, designer and talk-show panelist, obliterates the bordello madame. Kato Kaelen, DJ and model, erodes the memory of the star-fucker and unemployed actor. Eric Menendez, if his jailhouse songs acquire a recording contract, may well blur our memory of him as a double murderer. All the major and minor players in the O. J. Simpson extravaganza are capitalizing not on their skills as authors or even attorneys, but merely on their familiarity as characters in the most over-exposed TV series of the century. There is no national villain, no matter how grotesque, to whom we cannot cozy up.

Since the fundamental connection between quality and fame has been severed, we now have an entirely different criterion for reputation. Exposure is the basic constituent; recognition, the product; fame, the reward. We have reached that point of unique decadence where people can become famous for nothing more than being famous—which is why the phenomenon of someone like Angelyne is so indicative of our times. Angelyne, as you may or may not know, is a glaringly undistinguished jobbing-actress whose billboards are plastered all over Hollywood Boulevard, proclaiming the earnest wish-fulfillment that she be considered a star. And in a society where notoriety is the basic requisite of stardom, who is to deny that Angelyne is *not* a star—or leastwise any less a star than John Wayne Bobbit, Anna Nicole Smith, or Tanya Harding, all high-profile personalities the media have wedged so far down our windpipes we cannot oscillate but breathe their names.

The horrific consequence of all of this is that by blurring the distinction between notoriety and earned approbation, we steadfastly worship nonentities under the delusion that they are in some way significant. The consequence of that is that our scale of values becomes permanently lopsided and our powers of discernment deplorably debased. The consequence of *that* is that by acquiring this irresistible weakness for chimeras, we rapidly lose our sense of reality. By swallowing whole the bogus values the media impose upon us, we start to undervalue quality and overestimate hype. Our brains become addled and our values corrupt. Our culture effectively *deculturizes* us and we become, more rootedly and unsalvageably, the mind-manacled people we already are.

65

PRIVATE WORLD, PUBLIC WORDS

The following address was delivered at a Playwrights Conference entitled Inventing the Future, *sponsored by the Audrey Skirball-Kenis Center in Los Angeles and attended by playwrights, actors, and directors of many persuasions and ethnic backgrounds. It went down, as they say, like a cup of cold sick. Many at the conference felt antagonized by its sentiments and, after it was delivered, I had the rare experience of being frozen out by almost everyone in the room. Multiculturalism was a very touchy issue throughout the '90s, and ethnic playwrights in particular took it very seriously. It was a buzzword for inclusion and so, obviously, those who felt themselves excluded often took umbrage. Obviously, I stand by everything I said at the time, although I realize it will never change the minds of the dissenters.*

★★★

At a political convention, the delegates and speakers confirm their party's position on the issues. There's no real inquiry or investigation and no breaking of ranks. This, thank God, is not a political convention, but there's one way in which we resemble the politicians and that is in rehashing clichés, buzzwords, and emotive catchphrases—all of which impede true inquiry. There were quite a few phrases yesterday that made me squirm and I'd like to suggest we put them out to pasture.

There's *multiculturalism*—which is a word that tends to put the active part of the brain to sleep. There has always been multiculturalism. In the past the cultures were French, Italian, German, Russian, and Scandinavian. Now they're Hispanic and Black and Asian American. Fine. That's a "given," and to dispute it is like disputing the law of gravity.

Empowerment is another dud word that fudges the issues. It implies the acquisition or appropriation of power by an essentially powerless faction, but writers have the greatest power of all—the power of the written word—and if dictators, generals, United States senators, and the Ayatollahs of Iran feel the need to pass injunctions against the written word, I think that bespeaks the real power that it has.

As for *Eurocentric paradigms,* if that means excluding writers of color, women, and gays, I think everybody in this room would be against it. But if it means dumping the heritage of Western drama of the past four hundred years—Shakespeare, Molière, Ibsen, Chekhov, and Strindberg—I have to admit I am unbudgeably Eurocentric.

The greatest of all the dud words is, of course, *the truth*—because, as we all piously say to one another, all we artists ever want is to write the truth, the whole truth, and nothing but the truth. Then how is it that so much false garbage gets conveyed in the theater? Is it because speaking the truth has to be harnessed to the ability to communicate the ambiguities and contradictions that make the truth almost impossible to convey? If that is so, then we should be talking not about being truthful but about writing well—because writing well is the closest we ever come to the truth. Being "truthful in our art" is probably the greatest truism of all and as such should be retired from service.

There was a lot of politics talked here yesterday, and although politics are important, I'd like to start talking aesthetics, which, in the theater, are what give politics their edge.

All the most valuable public works begin in private. That's certainly true of plays, but I think it's also true of political theories, philosophical insights, and scientific discoveries. The irony is that the playwright, after meticulously baking his loaf in the intense heat of his private oven, discovers that in order to serve it up to the world, he has to relinquish his isolation and become a collaborator. Once the dough has been mixed, it is kneaded into shape by the director, made to rise by the producer, sprinkled with poppyseeds by actors and designers, masticated in the jaws of the public, and finally belched out by the critic. But the fact remains that it was the solitude of the writer that first produced the work and, a lot of people would contend, the more that solitude is respected—especially by the director—the better the texture and flavor of the final product.

There are no formulae here. A good director extends and expands a writer's work out of all recognition, often to its good. Ask Williams or Miller about Kazan. A bad director is as corrupting as a pedophile and sends the writer on a detour from which he may never return. Ask Jon Robby Baitz about Gordon Davidson.

There are two underlying questions at this conference. The first one concerns the Means of Creation: What's the most effective way for the playwright to turn out the best script his talent can create? And the other has to do with Means of Production: Under what conditions can the playwright's work best find its way into the marketplace? The playwright has some influence in regard to the first question, but I don't think he has virtually any in the case of the second.

We all know from bitter personal experience that a hastily assembled stage reading (and L.A. has fast become the Staged Reading Capital of the Western World) often produces only one dimension of the work in hand. A reading, by what it's obliged to leave out, can often create a highly misleading impression. It can make a flawed play seem amusing and entertaining, and it can make a great play look gauche and unfocused. There are some plays, strong on subtext and physical subtlety, that simply languish in reading situations. There are others, plays almost fully realized in their language (Shaw's *Don Juan in Hell* comes to mind, as does David Hirson's *La Bete*) where a reading does justice to almost all of the original work. But most plays, like most houses, can't stand very well if all they have is a facade.

The writer has to gauge whether it's worth his while to present only the facade of his work. Whether that does more harm than good. Whether the "gesture" to play production, which is essentially what a reading is, isn't simply a gross insult to both his work and the work of the actors. For after this one-dimensional performance has taken place, directors, producers, and dramaturgs, proceeding on very partial insights, begin to reshape, revise, and redevelop the play—and that's a little like deciding to marry a girl whom you know only from a computer-dating print-out.

Yet the greatest danger here isn't the process itself but the often mindless and fatuous people who are supervising the process—the directors and dramaturgs who, being neither creative writers nor canny entrepreneurs, unconsciously foist other aims and other values onto material they take to be "up for grabs." And that's the worst thing about a work in progress. Everybody feels he or she is entitled to dictate the direction it ought to take, and the author, who is often vulnerable and uncertain, finds himself being led up a variety of garden paths where he is stroked, petted, romanced, and ultimately gang-raped.

The assumption that a playwright is a kind of lost child who has to be helped on his way by directors, actors, and dramaturgs is fairly recent. Ibsen went off to foreign countries to write his plays and, when he was finished, simply sent the scripts off to his publisher. Chekhov didn't pick Stanislavsky's brains or anyone else's when he was writing his plays. And all Strindberg was ever concerned with was the clarity of his own hallucinated vision. O'Neill was notoriously isolated when he wrote a play and pretty cavalier about changes. (When his producer told O'Neill he had to cut forty-five minutes out of one of his interminable dramas, the playwright's answer was: "Chop out two intermissions.") The idea that these playwrights needed "development," in the way we use the phrase, would be ridiculous to the writers in question. But today, the general consensus seems to be that without input from an army of kibitzers, pundits, Ph.D. graduates, and bearded second-guessers, the writer would be lost. If we're talking about the playwright *Inventing the Future,* maybe a good first step is to just leave him alone to invent his own play.

The best workshop in the world is the private sanctum of the writer's own imagination—the place where he and his instincts try to dope out the best course of action for his work. Which doesn't mean he must resist all input and criticism. What it does mean is that he must be the final arbiter as to additions or deletions, as to whether or not to import newer and more fancy weaponry or to just stick to his guns. And that involves dismantling the notion of the Svengali-director, which, depending on the power of the particular Svengali involved, is sometimes hard to do—and what's even harder is resisting the temptations of big bucks, reduced risks, and Sunday features in the Arts Section, held out by that even greater menace, the Svengali-producer.

The paradox is that the private world in which the work was conceived has to have the courage to resist the allurements of the public world for which it is theoretically destined.

On the other side, one has to point out that if you are a talented new writer in the 1990s, you probably have more opportunities than your counterparts had twenty or thirty years ago. New Play programs have become part of the new Political Correctness—and if you're Black or Hispanic or Asian American, you're not quite the disenfranchised creature you were two or three decades ago. The pendulum (which you'd be right in saying you never knew existed) has swung decidedly in your direction. To be white and talented is a good thing in today's marketplace—but to be ethnic and talented means the world will beat a path to your door. That simply wasn't the case in the 1950s or '60s. That is a dramatic change and a welcome one.

A playwright's conference—any kind of inbred assembly of artists—tends to encourage peculiar kinds of fantasy. It gives people a sense of power that they don't actually possess. For example: asking playwrights to, and here I quote the conference brochure, "explore the primary issues facing playwrights" is not only a waste of time but a misunderstanding of artistic process. Each writer is going to be drawn to his own issues, and it is wrong to assume that a consensus can decide which are more pertinent than others. The breakup of the Soviet Union or the problems in the inner-cities may be obsessive concerns to some writer or other, but don't tell me that the theater exists dramatically to regurgitate the daily headlines because I don't believe that. Just as I don't believe that Movies-of-the-Week have a bounden duty to rehash the dilemmas of the Menendez Brothers, O. J. Simpson, or Charles and Di.

And as for talking about "conclusions being mandated by playwrights" (the brochure again), you can't have a mandate when you represent a group of people, all of whom have very different interests and opinions, when there is no consolidated power bloc behind your mandate. And the fact is, in the theater, the writer is too dependent on the wheelers and dealers and too remote from its capitalist mechanisms really to affect its day-to-day operations. A strike happens when labor decides to pit its power against management. There have been actors' strikes and stage-hands' strikes, musicians' strikes and screen-writers' strikes, but there has never been a playwrights' strike.

We all want more outlets, more platforms, and more productions, but the theater-public also has wants; it wants more finished articles and less practicing on its time. The public wants more works of art and less works in progress.

All of these vital issues get fudged by the trendy catchphrases I mentioned earlier that consistently confuse art and politics. To be "politically correct" may be important for a politician, but being artistically correct is what's important for a playwright and it is pretty clear that if you impose an outside agenda—even if it contains a Code of Fairness—it militates against good work. Like Harold Pinter once said: "I'm opposed to all propaganda—even propaganda for life." The playwright always has to combat the Philistine Mind, whether it's Jesse Helms's or Jeremy Collier's—but that fight belongs to the Playwright-as-Citizen—not as artist.

If these remarks have any thematic point at all, it is that the playwright lives in a private world, and isolation is both his curse and his strength. And no writer has ever become a better writer by being part of a collective, a syndicate, or a conglomerate. The Guilds and Unions are there to hammer out the best terms and the highest fees, and I salute all their efforts and dutifully pay my dues, but I know in my heart of hearts that what may be for the collective good is not going to make me a better writer. That essentially, I have to go back into my cave, or my study, or yes, even my ivory tower, and grapple with my personal demons if anything useful is going to transfer from my private world into the public world.

The Writer-as-Citizen has to involve himself in all those issues. The Writer-as-Artist has to realize there is a danger of mixing up social gains with artistic progress, a temptation to use the power of collective organization to compensate for personal weakness. It's when we strengthen our own personal fiber as playwrights, increase our own personal power as artists, that we confer some real benefit to the community—and we do that by becoming better writers, not necessarily by becoming greater activists.

66

"IT'S A BARNUM & BAILEY WORLD"

It takes a special kind of insensitivity to appreciate the Ringling Brothers-Barnum and Bailey Circus: an ability to withstand humiliation and ignore cruelty.

Picture a dozen elephants upended one upon the other or led around a Big Top, their trunks looped to the tails of the elephants in front. What can such a spectacle do but remind us that magnificent pachyderms have been not only subjugated and "trained" by allegedly superior beings but demeaned in a way that desecrates their very animal nature? To watch half a dozen lions perform debasing parlor tricks before a smooth, domineering man with a whip serves only to remind us that, morally speaking, Man "is" the lowest creature in the animal kingdom, for who else would have dreamed of cruelly denaturing their fellow-creatures and then displaying the offense for the delectation of ogling adults and wide-eyed children?

But Graham Thomas Chipperfield, who has dazzlingly overmastered eleven lions and three elephants, is without shame. "No organization in the world treats animals better than Ringling Brothers," he tells us. "We have more attendants per animal, the best food, and excellent medical care." Words that could be echoed by the warden of any one of the high-security penitentiaries that guard our most wretched murderers and rapists. Occasionally, we are told, Mr. Chipperfield "finds time to rent a video or eat out with friends" or "check on the status of his stock market investments," but his true joy comes from the animals: "Animals are amazing," says Chipperfield. "I'm always learning something new." But what Mr. Chipperfield will never learn is that this subjugation of caged beasts for the amusement of paying customers is a sin that flatly contradicts his most passionately expressed love for the animal kingdom.

Animal acts encourage us to glory in Man's power to harness forces greater than himself. But they also draw attention to the fact that there are creatures with peerless grace and natural ferocity that, unlike Man, have not entirely lost their affinity to nature. In persuading us that they have, that they can be made to bow and stamp, parade and cavort, Man only displays his egotism and his innate vulgarity. If the trainer had the feline elegance of the lion he has subjugated or the gentle grandeur of the pachyderm he has taught to dance, he would rank high in the animal hierarchy. But as he stomps, screams, whirls, and cracks his whip, he merely emphasizes his lack of grace when compared to the subjects under his domination.

The circus is an object lesson in bad theater. It proves over and over again that pure skill, no matter how dazzling in itself, is intrinsically boring. Think of your own experiences at the circus. After one has gasped at the breathtaking expertise of acrobats, gymnasts, jugglers, and high-wire artists, astonishment gives way to predictability and ultimately to tedium. Just as one grows bored with an opera singer with an astonishing voice who can't act, one tires of a highly endowed human attribute in isolation and longs for it to be integrated with something more meaningful than itself.

Marguerite Michelle hangs by her hair and braids herself into a wild spin reminiscent of the whirling dervishes. An elaborate way, it strikes me, to put a curl in one's hair. Astounding, of course, as I can think of no other performer who can hang by her hair (although I can think of several dozen I'd like to see thus strung out)—but essentially, she is a freak, like the bearded lady or the man with six toes. Samson Power from Kenya lifts an oversize wooden table by his teeth—and then, in his piece-de-resistance, selects a large, heavy-set spectator, straps a leather bit around his waist, and lifts him by his teeth as well. Extraordinary, of course, if you enjoy seeing unwieldy and obese burghers hoisted by their midsections. Would that he used those mighty molars to masticate one of the animal-trainers and then spit out the pieces; that at least would have given the act a kind of Artaudian sizzle.

The "star" of the recent Barnum & Bailey edition is Airiana, the peerless Human Arrow, around whom the whole frenetic finale is based. After a long-winded procession filled with pseudo-Roman splendor and mythological kitsch, Airiana is wedged into a giant crossbow and shot into a net about fifty feet away. It is, I suppose, courageous and novel, but it strikes the sense with the dull thud of a blackjack swathed in cotton wool. Had she propelled herself through a plastic membrane, a wall of flame, or a cathedral window, the action might have generated a certain excitement. But as it is, she is hurled from her crossbow into her webbed target like a fast ball into a catcher's well-worn mitt. No doubt, it takes skill and guts to perform such a feat, but then why does it feel so "blah" when it actually happens? The answer is: The action represents pure, unadulterated skill—and that is the equivalent of a lecturer with supreme enunciation who has nothing to say.

Naked skill, like raw talent, only draws attention to itself—never to an object larger than itself that engages the imagination. That is why, I suppose, Yma Sumac is not a great singer but simply a musical freak. That is why, I suppose, Cirque du Soleil is superior to Barnum & Bailey. There, every demonstration of skill is fitted into a structured dramatic context that has allure, whether it displays skill or not.

The only dramatic factor at the circus is the apprehension of disaster. Will the high-wire artist fall? Will the "daring young man" miss his "flying trapeze" and come plummeting down to earth? Will the lion chomp down on the trainer's head when it is placed between his jaws? In true theater, suspense revolves around motive, plot, and character as well as action, but at the circus, it is simply the elementary fear of accident. These are sensations that play upon our most primitive fears. These are the impulses that underlie bear-baiting, gladiatorial combat, and Christians being thrown to the lions. They stir our lowest impulses and appeal to our basest natures.

★★★

67

PIMPS AND PARASITES

A middle-aged man who was in desperate need of a new heart was suddenly contacted by his doctor and told that two donor hearts had just become available. The first was the heart of a twenty-seven-year-old marathon runner who had just been hit by a car; the second belonged to an eighty-six-year-old Hollywood agent who had died of a combination of emphysema and old age. The patient immediately opted for the agent's heart. The doctor proceeded to make arrangements for the transplant. "But would you tell me," asked the doctor, "why it is you chose *that* heart rather than the other?" "Because," the patient explained, "the second one hadn't been used."

A group of tourists was suddenly trapped in a boat that had caught fire. The only way to survive was to plunge into treacherous, shark-infested waters and swim ashore. One tourist after another plunged into the water and was brutally consumed by the sharks. One man, however, an agent, jumped into the waters and blithely swam to safety. "How was it," they asked him incredulously, "that the sharks allowed you to escape to safety?" "Professional courtesy," he replied.

These are only two of about two hundred jokes that disparage the calling of agent. They are quite typical. In all of them, the agent is portrayed as a heartless, subhuman monster who preys on actors; a contemptible middleman, a pimp, and a parasite.

We all know there are some agents who are literate, urbane, even altruistic; who enter into compassionate relationships with their clients and carefully and caringly guide their careers. Or do we? Or is that just an assumption we make because we dare not believe all of them are remorseless bloodsuckers? Whatever we may feel about them, we have to recognize that, like the departing Nixon, we may not have them around to kick very much longer.

Just as modern technology is rapidly eliminating the bank-teller, the post-office worker and the telephone-operator, so the theatrical agent will soon be a thing of the past.

What, after all, is the agent's prime function? To provide a selection of actors for casting agents and directors assembling plays, films, and television projects. How does he do this? By submitting photos and resumes and proffering what he believes to be appropriate choices for the roles waiting to be filled. Can he influence the dynamics that determine which actor will play which role? Only in those instances where a void of uncertainty exists in the minds of directors and producers and, even there, only in the most infinitesimal way, since he is outside the creative loop of those seeking to match the right artist to the right role. Essentially, the agent operates like the race-track tout taking bets on all the runners, with a good chance that if one filly doesn't win, place, or show, another may. He has no interest in the fillies themselves—only in the odds that regularly work in his favor.

Of course, to a large extent, the function I have just described has been entirely supplanted by the packagers; these are the mega-agents (ICM, CCA, William Morris, etc.) who, controlling the services of the biggest stars, privately assemble the artist, the writer, and the director without in any way ruffling the waters of the larger acting pool. Unions like Equity can insist on "open calls" and even coerce managements into providing them, but it's all a ruse and everyone knows it. The producer, in consort with the high-powered agent, has already decided which roles are to be filled with which salable artists, and the only remaining problem is to get them on the best possible terms. While open casting is the ideal, closed casting is the reality.

In some countries, like Norway and Sweden, casting, as we practice it in America and the U.K., is virtually unknown. The milieus are smaller and so is the acting pool, and everyone tends to know everyone else. But, of course, even in America the actual acting pool is very much smaller than it appears to be from the published statistics. Perhaps 7 percent of the acting population are regularly employed for major roles, and the remaining 93 percent just provide fillers.

In the new dispensation, using video sources and CD-ROMs, directors and producers will be able to examine every shoal within the acting pool and make their choices accordingly. Not only will they be able to evaluate faces, credits, and vital statistics but filmed audition pieces and personalized tapes as well. They will be able to deal directly with whichever artist they choose and bypass the tedious snow-jobs of agents who regularly extol the virtues of one sausage over another.

The sooner that day comes, the better, for the fact is the agent has no vital function in the artistic process—even though he has vigorously concocted one over a period of some 120 years. Not only is he intrinsically inartistic in himself, he tends, because of his mindset and temperament, to degrade the art form into which he has insinuated himself. He exacts his 10 or 15 percent on the pretext of "selling" his client to prospective buyers, but he knows very well that nothing he ever says or does can alter the fact that actor suitability is a factor in a director's and producer's game plan to which no outside influence can possibly intrude. Yet the agent, needing to legitimize himself to his client, has to pretend that he exerts an influence and, in some way, helps determine the outcome.

But, I can hear the hecklers asking, without the agents, who will negotiate the contracts, hammer out the terms, fight for the actor's self-interest? The answer is: the artists themselves—or their chosen representatives. But wait a minute—"chosen representatives"?—that brings us back to agents, doesn't it? Not really, because the agent, despite the standard clause in his contract, never represented the artist *exclusively*—because he invariably represented hundreds of clients. The modern tendency of attorneys and personal legal representatives acting on behalf the artist will, in the next century, have expanded to incredible proportions. By replacing the agent with a personal legal representative, the theatrical managements, the film companies, and the mega-producers will be dealing with a very much more knowledgeable third party and one who, as in all legal matters, would be acting on the client's instructions. The actor will be obliged to develop negotiation muscles he does not now possess.

In the year 2020, there will be one casting agency. It will be plugged into every director's and producer's computer terminal, and it will provide hundreds of thousands of possibilities for employment. It will not eliminate the personal encounter and the live audition, but by cutting out all the red tape in between, will facilitate both. Will it alter the insidious practice of packaging? Probably not. But what it will have done is to eliminate a virus from an art form that, a quarter of a century earlier, had been a source of waste and exploitation.

★★★

68

BLINDED BY SCIENCE

I am regularly astonished by the paradox that the Academic Mind is capable of lunacies that almost never affect sensible persons deprived of like erudition. A five-star university education with protracted exposure to the theories, theses, and dissertations that make up the academic life are capable of producing a degree of literacy that often disguises a bottomless pit of intellectual vacancy.

I am reminded of this paradox by the recent controversy concerning "A Funeral Elegy for William Peter," a newfound piece of seventeenth-century memorial verse signed by W. S. and vehemently attributed to William Shakespeare by scholars such as Donald Foster and Richard Abrams, two English professors from Britain.

In a recent number of the *Times Literary Supplement,* a publication that has proven to be a magnet for academic eccentrics from every part of the British Isles, Professors Abrams and Foster brandish "a three-page table charting, against late Shakespearean norms, the practice of every extant writer of English memorial verse from 1610 to 1613 (including Anon) in seventeen categories." The tests analyze run-ons and feminine endings, participial compounds, irregular negatives, hendiadys, recurring suffixes, and so on. They conclude that: "Among other elegists writing between 1610 and 1613, the maximum number of correspondences with late Shakespearean norms is five. W. S. falls within Shakespearean ranges in all seventeen categories."—Ergo, William Shakespeare is the author of the "Funeral Elegy."

Computer science has also been mustered into service. "Retrieve-software" has been employed and Professor Foster's own database, Shaxicon, has been developed "to chart the occurrence and recurrence of Shakespearean vocabulary." Shaxicon can tell you whether Shakespeare borrowed from Plutarch or Holinshed's *Chronicles.* It can also tell you which Jacobean production the author might have seen that "measurably influenced" his writing. Providing a kind of astounding X-ray of the author's creative process, it can run to ground every nuance of style, grammatical twist, and syntactical idiosyncrasy of the great playwright.

I speculate that, four centuries from now, if a similar instrument were to analyze the works of Sam Shepard, Terrence McNally, John Robin Baitz, and Tony Kushner, it might conclude that all these works were actually written by Neil Simon. Despite the incidence of a few personal idiosyncrasies, grammar, syntax, and vocabulary are pretty standard—and as far as themes and received wisdom are concerned, those tend to be as common as hamburgers and Cokes. And at some point or other, almost everyone orders a Mac and a soda-pop. One of the reasons scholars vaunt Shakespearean theories about Bacon, Marlowe, de Vere, Southampton, and so on, is that all these personages swim in the same zeitgeist, and so resemblances in language, ideas, and subject matter are virtually inescapable.

It isn't the computer findings themselves that are so alarming, but the fact that people would accept such electronic rubbish as evidence in the first place. We know that computers can beat chess champions, write novels, compose poetry, and match up perfect mates. Professors Foster and Abrams are now putting forward the proposition that they can also analyze texts and yield criticism. Why in God's name should we bother to use our own brains at all? If creativity, intellect, and form are available at the tap of a computer key, then the age of universal democratization has arrived. Thanks to interactive technology, everyone can be an artist. By purchasing the relevant software, anyone can be a critic. The gulf between artist and public, regularly blurred over the past twenty years, has now been permanently obliterated. Andy Warhol's prophecy that everyone will be a celebrity for fifteen minutes needs to be amended: we can all be celebrities indefinitely—so long as our hardware is booted up and we regularly update our software.

In the case of "A Funeral Elegy for William Peter," as the skeptical Shakespearean critic Stanley Wells has pointed out, the verse is "tedious and repetitious." It lacks anything like the muscularity and unexpected turn of phrase one expects to find in late Shakespeare, but somehow the quality of the poem has become an irrelevance; its structural characteristics, a matter of paramount importance.

Just as a long-lost number by the Beatles recently became the occasion for a commercial whoop-ti-do, so the prospect of a newfound Shakespearean poem stimulates the adrenaline glands of publishers and academics throughout the nation. But just as the Beatles discovery had its fifteen minutes of notoriety and then descended into the obscurity from whence it came, so "The Funeral Elegy" will dawdle back to the archives—not because it is or isn't by Shakespeare, but just because it isn't very good. For academics, the archaeological sense dominates all others. If they can put a name and a date to a found object, they immediately take up residence in Seventh Heaven. But when the caliber of an artifact is almost entirely determined by statistical considerations, it is easy to forget that (A) Shakespeare produced a helluva lot of tripe in his career and (B) what we venerate in his works is their ability to be rethought and renewed rather than just verified.

The greatest paradox in this paradox is that there seems to be an unbridgeable gulf between the academic appreciation of this playwright's work and the virtues derived therefrom by the general public. The Ivory Tower and the Halls of Academe might as well be on the craters of the moon for all the relevance they seem to have to the living work of William Shakespeare.

★★★

69

THE IDIOT BOX

One of the most common complaints against television journalism is that it has deteriorated into entertainment. The cause, as always, is attributed to the rating wars: the need to capture the greatest number of viewers by the most dramatic and theatrical means possible. The result is that "hard news" has almost become a thing of the past, and virtually every story is hyped up for the sake of its "human interest," which in practice means falsified by oversimplification.

"Entertainment" is also the top priority of the afternoon talk shows. Here, the source of entertainment is the real or contrived conflicts of husbands, wives, families, gays, whores, strippers, cross-dressers, et al. A never-ending procession of victims or aggressors who, given their lurid personalities and bizarre attire, may well have been fitted up by the make-up and wardrobe departments of the networks for whom they parade their aberrations. This is *entertainment,* in the sense that the word was once used in England to describe public hangings, for which apprentices were invariably given the day off so that they, too, could enjoy the delights of public retribution.

The trial of O. J. Simpson was clearly a "series" in which the chief protagonists—both for the prosecution and the defense—gradually endeared themselves to the "fans." It was only after the verdict, when a sense of profound injustice kicked in, that the viewers began painfully to reassess what they had seen and tried to unravel its significance. But while it was being performed, as with any good play or movie, the public suspended its disbelief.

Conversation on television also obeys the rules of entertainment. Radio phone-in shows may suffer fools gladly, but television insists that "talk" be amusing, unpredictable, extreme, raunchy, outrageous, and, wherever possible, accompanied by lively pantomime. Bill Maher's *Politically Incorrect* on CBS is perhaps the most glaring example of just how low standards for public discourse have sunk in America.

This is the show on which a smarmy, eye-popping Maher introduces some serious subject for discussion and then, like a zoo-keeper feeding fish to seals, tosses it out to a handful of allegedly literate guests, wherein it immediately disappears without trace. The "serious topic" is clearly a ruse to enable Maher's panel to invent one-liners and comic conceits. Anyone presuming to deal seriously with an issue is immediately construed as a "party pooper," both by the audience and the panel, and relegated to the background. If you can't be funny or outrageous, the audience seems to be saying, Don't interfere with those who can!

Rigidly observing this lame format, chat never rises to the level of controversy, and the danger of climbing into a ring where combatants actually butt heads on a real issue is successfully avoided. The result is that politics, philosophy, current events, and any conviction emanating therefrom remain trapped in a cloud cover from which the sun, although occasionally glimpsed, never actually manages to break through.

Maher, as Master of the Revels, grins and smirks and puckers his lips and gives the appearance of a chicken just about to lay an egg, but after a lot of scratching and straining, hatches only a kind of Rubik's Cube. Being sober and cerebral rather than fanciful and inspired, he lacks the essential qualities of the comedian, but then, it is clear from his demeanor that he sees himself not so much as a comic but as a droll pundit—a more mischievous version of Will Rogers, who, instead of twirling a lasso, manipulates the low expectations of his undiscriminating public.

In a recent outing, Ariana Huffington, that walking monument to naked careerism, dealt with the issue "How is conservatism reconcilable with the Moslem-like morality of the Republican Party?" by simply reiterating her leitmotif that Clinton should be forced to resign. Since no one alluded to Susan MacDouglas and Huffington had her quip ("Everyone is treating her like Joan of Arkansas") already prepared, she arbitrarily inserted it into the discussion. A gay journalist and a confused actor, Mark Hamill, crossed swords with the right-wing opposition (a Bible-thumping Rev. Louis Sheldon), and the topic was successfully drowned in banter and horseplay, even to the point of irritating emcee Maher, who tried in vain to re-track it. Within the space of about twenty minutes, weighty subjects such as conservatism, impeachment, and same-sex marriages were blithely dispatched without one new insight penetrating the collective fog.

Watching the show over a period of weeks, listening to bathos disguised as profundity and levity vainly aspiring to wit, one cannot fail to reach the conclusion that Americans, whether they be actors, writers, singers, journalists, or politicians, all suffer from foot-in-mouth disease. The compulsion to be funny, or leastwise lighthearted, is so overpowering that it entirely destabilizes whatever intellect may exist among the participants. Cliché is embraced, as a life-jacket might be passionately clutched to the bosom of a drowning man.

Many moons ago, when the British Broadcasting Corporation was not quite the offspring of commercial television that it has now become, there was a program called *That Was the Week That Was,* hosted by David Frost; this is when Mr. Frost was merely an insolent commoner and not yet a pin-striped Knight of the Realm who conversed only with heads of state. For all its unevenness, the show was a genuine attempt to tackle relevant social and political issues, and guests were encouraged to discuss those issues with gravity, where appropriate, or with gravity leavened with wit where *that* was called for. "Entertainment" was derived from the fact that certain first-class minds were spontaneously grappling with pertinent issues, and the collision of divergent views expressed by articulate and educated men and women was sufficient to both divert and compel the attention of the viewing public.

Sparkling conversation by intellectually agile minds is one of the most "entertaining" things I know, either on television or around a living room. But fudged conversation by ostentatious dolts who use issues merely to score comic points or ingratiate themselves with a studio audience is equivalent to a dinner party where, instead of exchanging ideas, people dwindle into telling jokes to one another. Those are the kind of dinner parties where the effluvium of deadbeat conversation turns even the best cuisine rancid.

Programs like *Politically Incorrect,* anchored by smart alecky stand-ups who equate being well-informed with being intellectually fecund, are part of the unremitting plague that has blighted American culture. They go hand in hand with the general shrinkage of educational standards that pollsters announce with such depressing regularity and language's nose-dive into illiteracy. So long as we find ourselves "entertained" by mindlessness and regaled by bathos, we will, I fear, remain a nation of crumbums.

★★★

70

DEATHLESS *CYRANO*

Cyrano, *being deathless, enjoyed several revivals in the '90s (most notably perhaps by Derek Jacoby and Frank Langella)—and even survived an ill-fated musicalized version of the play. No actor has arisen to rival Jose Ferrer's flamboyant interpretation from the '50s, although Gerard Depardieu made a pretty good showing in a French film version. This was written around the time of the play's centennial.*

★★★

Cyrano de Bergerac, by Edmond Rostand, is just about one hundred years old—written shortly before its first production in 1897. It is an old war-horse that has weathered a lot of campaigns and seems to be well-armored for many more. No glue factory for this old dobbin.

Like most adolescents, I fell in love with *Cyrano de Bergerac* around the time I started high school. The love affair was consummated when the Stanley Kramer film starring Jose Ferrer appeared, making concrete the fanciful longings stirred by the text. When I reached the age of discretion, I thought back to *Cyrano* as one would a teen-aged romance that, though largely an infatuation, still left indelible scars. As one became aware of the riches of Shakespeare and Marlowe, Dryden and Webster, Edmond Rostand's talent became, in retrospect, brittle, even negligible. Later on, however, after one had become somewhat weighed down with heavyweight classics, one returned with a renewed appreciation for the simpler pleasures of works like *Cyrano.* In one's maturity, it became clear that art, like food, had different densities—and sometimes a burger and a milkshake were preferable to a four-course meal and provided a gastronomic high of an entirely different order.

It is Edmond Rostand's curse that one always begins by qualifying his talent and apologizing for his work—as if liking Rostand was tantamount to culturally slumming. This is an impulse that never arises when watching his play but seems to be unavoidable in critical evaluations. Yet just as Herrick and Campion need suffer no sense of inferiority when compared to Shakespeare and Marlowe, so there is no need for us to justify our liking for Rostand. In fact, to put things into proper perspective, *Cyrano de Bergerac* is a far sturdier piece of craftsmanship than *Pericles* or *The Siege at Rhodes,* confirmed by the fact that it has not been out of the modern repertoire since Coquelin first plastered on his giant proboscis almost a hundred years ago.

The last thing Rostand is interested in is the well-made play. Like his rambunctious hero, he instinctively recoils from anything fixed and prefabricated. There are whole chunks of the play that, judged by established playwriting techniques, could be deleted because they do not help the plot culminate to that point of resolution to which traditional plays usually tend.

But if one did delete them, one would be losing the pearls that give the crown its glitter. Apply the traditional yardstick to a work like *The Importance of Being Earnest* and you could reach the same conclusion—but the virtues of that play, as with *Cyrano,* are in the amplifications, the digressions, the—if you like—irrelevancies. Sometimes it is texture that determines the quality of content, and in such cases, one must revere the peculiarities of a text as one does the peculiar characteristics of an individual who, outsize and unpredictable, is, for those very reasons, more fascinating.

The play is predicated on the irresistible lie that wit, talent, and personal panache cannot only compensate a man for physical ugliness but also enable him to triumph over competition that is patently more attractive. It is the pipe dream of every acne-ridden schoolboy and tubby, balding Romeo who watches the good-looking jock waltz off with the most desirable campus queen. It elevates the idea of aesthetic worth to a height as fanciful as it is unreal. Perhaps that is why the play is juvenile in the very best sense of that word and, for a century, has been so highly appreciated by the very young. Its own intrinsic romanticism speaks persuasively to people who have not yet lost their sense of romance. It is redolent of the fairy tales on which young persons have been weaned. It is a literary extrapolation of *Beauty and the Beast, The Ugly Duckling,* and all those other fables where unprepossessing heroes improbably win the hands of fairy princesses. In other words, it nourishes the fantasy-quotient in men and women, which, unfortunately, attenuates as they grow older and wiser—that is, mundane and cynical. It is, if you like, children's theater on the very highest level because, mythic roots notwithstanding, its branches yield the succulent fruit of lyric poetry.

The hero of *Cyrano De Bergerac* is not the eponymous hero, based on the real adventurer and poet of the mid-seventeenth century, but poetry itself: the poetic notion of life as opposed to its prosaic counterpart; fancy as opposed to fact; dream life as opposed to real life. Cyrano's adventure, both in the play and in his own life, exemplified the kind of endeavor that is no longer available to us in our own lives—except through emulating make-believe heroes in books, plays, and films. That is why we continually come back to Cyrano. He represents the freedom, independence, nonchalance, and impetuosity that we barter away in order to become responsible citizens—qualities that we can never forgive the adult world from taking from us.

★★★

71

THE CRITIC'S LOT: U.S. VS. U.K.

Frank Rich, the now fabled "Butcher of Broadway," reigned supreme as the *New York Times* drama critic for over a decade. During his sway, the theater community smarted under his acrimonious notices. When he walked into theater receptions, the actors, it is alleged, walked out en masse. There were even rumors of plots against his life but, as anyone familiar with the New York scene knows, there is no tyrant as impregnable as a theater critic who enjoys the confidence of his editorial hierarchy.

After his departure a few years ago, as with the retirement of Prime Minister Margaret Thatcher, Rich became the subject of a fulsome wave of nostalgia. Reading the reviews of blander and less vituperative successors, the seizures he once caused among Broadway denizens gave way to a painful sense of loss when he went on to the Op-Ed pages. So is "Maggie" remembered today in Britain as a kind of modern-day Boadicea rather than the ghoulish misanthrope she actually was.

Rich, whatever his critical shortcomings, was cut in the Broadway mold. His blunt, acidulous, take-no-prisoners attitude was very much in keeping with the acrid climate of the city in which he worked. By and large, the New York critics are not noted for pulling their punches. The belief is that Broadway is a kind of theatrical Citadel, and critics view their job as keeping the barbarians from the gates. This often produces a harsh, unsentimental strain of criticism that yaps at mediocrity and tears great chunks out of flaccid or banal offerings. The stringency of that tone of voice is so admired, and so habitually employed, that it militates against the fine shadings and intellectual nuances that one looks for in the best criticism. But New York has always been a hit-or-flop kind of town and, over the years, reviews have tended to shuttle between the dismissive and the rhapsodic—blithely ignoring that vast gray zone in which the niceties of criticism, when they do appear, most closely resemble art itself.

The American drama critic, when he is not a failed playwright or actor, tends to be recruited from the ranks of journalists. The English drama critic comes to the live theater after an immersion in up-scale, university-bred culture. On some tacit level, playgoing in England is always viewed as the more vulgar expression of literature. But being better read and better educated than his American counterpart doesn't always ensure a more sensitive response to the act of theatergoing. Too often larger, and largely irrelevant, issues becloud his judgment and his mind is constantly distracted by generalities that are part of a political agenda, an elaborately wrought aesthetic or merely the legacy of an overeducated intellect.

Although there is always a certain amount of turnover among critics, the types seem to remain pretty uniform. We still get the oblique, quasi-academic burbling scribe who concentrates more on a play's implications than on the concrete constituents of its mise-en-scène; the narky, yawn-suppressing, I've-seen-it-all disdain of the critic for whom reviewing is the equivalent of cleaning out the drains; the slightly confused, plodding "regular fellow" who, in trying to be fair to all sides, produces a balanced committee report instead of an unwinnowed expression of personal taste; the crypto-sentimentalist who is a sucker for pathos and tries unemotionally to convey his endorsement of a work that has actually moved him to tears; the critic whose egoistic goal is the dissemination of his own brittle wit and who sees every play simply as an invitation for him to outshine the murk he is obliged to evaluate.

Criticism, more than playwriting, is a mirror that reflects the congenital flaws of individual personality and, that being the case, you'd think most writers would try to avoid such exposure. But like acting or whoring, it becomes an addiction that it is impossible to kick and, after a while, the critic placidly accepts himself, warts and all, on the dubious assumption that his public has done so as well.

It used to be that drama critics "led" the theater. Pundits like G. Bernard Shaw, Jacques Copeau, Harold Clurman, Eric Bentley, and Kenneth Tynan had a clear-cut predilection for a certain kind of play, and in all their writing one constantly got comparisons between the quotidian and the ideal. It often made them tendentious, but at least it revealed a genuine attachment to the art form in which they labored. Yet as anyone who has hacked away at it season after season knows full well, journalism spells the death of criticism. The obligation to convey information in order to inform consumers which shows to patronize snuffs out the waywardness and idiosyncrasy upon which great criticism depends. Both England and America are replete with "consumer guides," and theater criticism has become a culturally burnished version of "Which," but in both countries, criticism suffers from an impoverishment of personality that, I believe, ultimately affects the caliber of the published product. Diversity of opinion is a great boon in drama criticism, but when none of the notices exude an intellectual authority upon which either artists or the public can depend, it suggests the entire art form is in the grips of a creeping sclerosis.

In Los Angeles, the overriding problem is that there is no one you can trust. Raves in publications like the *L.A. Weekly* frequently express bouts of jejune enthusiasm for delicacies that more cultivated palates wincingly reject. In the *L.A. Times,* there is a reverse abuse, and provocative and unconventional works instinctively get short shrift because it is felt that the mainstream public would be turned off, and so critics, who view themselves as representatives of that public, indulge in a kind of mealy-mouthedness that brings them down on neither one side nor the other. The other major failing is that they tend to rubber-stamp successes from New York and London and reveal a morbid fear of reversing the judgments of their more prestigious Eastern counterparts.

But the bane of criticism on both sides of the Atlantic is the built-in reluctance on the part of artists to dispute the critics' findings when they are misconceived or, on the part of the general public, to "see for themselves" no matter which direction the critics' thumbs happen to be pointing. So long as artists feel intimidated and audiences refuse to think for themselves, criticism will always be self-indulgent and its practitioners somewhat despised.

72

ACTORS AND STARS

One cannot help noticing that, in recent months, several stars have forsaken their electronic firmament and wandered into the terrestrial realms of the stage. The apartheid that once separated working pros from televisusal and cinematic celebrities appears to be crumbling.

For many actors, the lure of the legitimate stage is precisely that: legitimization. A success on stage means that they're not just a pretty face or the pawn of an omnipotent film director; it means they possess artistic clout and are to be reckoned with when the annals of "great acting" are opened and savored.

Notoriety on stage is of a very different caste than cinematic or televisual stardom. It confers an unmistakable kind of seriousness, a throwback perhaps to the 1930s when Hollywood was thought of as a place East Coast artists went to in order to sell out. That myth no longer applies and wasn't particularly valid even then. A comparison of the finest films between, say, 1929 and 1942, and the prize-winning plays of the same period would rapidly reveal a much higher degree of artistry in Hollywood. Broadway never had a post–Mercury Theater Orson Welles, an Ernst Lubitsch, a Preston Sturgis, an Alfred Hitchcock, or a Fritz Lang. Until the advent of writers such as Arthur Miller, Tennessee Williams, and Edward Albee, Broadway tended to lionize nakedly commercial talents such as Kaufman and Hart, S. N. Behrman, and Garson Kanin or posthumously overrated drudges like Elmer Rice, Clifford Odets, John van Druten, and William Inge.

The distinction that's usually drawn is between the "celebrity" and the "actor"—itself a bogus distinction, because performers such as Richard Dreyfuss, Kevin Kline, Kevin Spacey, Al Pacino, Matthew Broderick, and Holly Hunter clearly inhabit both categories. But, certainly, there are those rapidly rotating TV "sensations" who, frustrated with the biodegradable nature of their sitcoms, long for the challenges of quality roles in substantial plays. The problem here is that after years of essaying schlock, it isn't the easiest thing in the world to spring from first gear into high. As any stage actor will tell you, quality in the theater is often the result of quantity—in other words, endless tours, slogging regional engagements, gradual graduation from supporting roles to parts that one can actually get one's teeth into. The more highly exposed stars are the ones who can most readily segue from TV to the stage, but the irony is that the transition often highlights the paucity of a talent that, while sufficient for television success, clearly falls short in the theater.

Then, of course, there are the avaricious playwrights who perceive attachment to a "star" as an insurance policy for stage success. Much of that thinking was revealed when, from all the first-class actresses available in New York, David Mamet and Gregory Mosher chose Madonna for the female lead in *Speed the Plow.* Perhaps the supreme version of dramaturgical opportunism was *The Blue Room,* David Hare's retread of Arthur Schnitzler's *La Ronde*—a manic grab for the brass ring that simultaneously managed to demean a classic European comedy and, with a subliminal flash of nudity, escalate a fairly competent film actress to dazzling heights of notoriety.

When an actor like Dustin Hoffman opts to appear on Broadway, whether to play a victimized Willy Loman or an equally victimized Shylock, it is hard to disentangle acting ambition from hubris. But gratuities of that kind inevitably enhance the season and sell tickets, and there is one school of thought that holds that anything that reglamorizes Broadway is worth the effort. Yet when performers such as Pacino, Dreyfuss, Hunter, or Brian Dennehy deign to grace the boards, the motivation is in no way suspect. One senses that they are there because the lure of the role and the challenge of the project are irresistible, and their being "stars" is, in some odd way, incidental.

If anything is certain—and it's a truth that haunts many film actors moving on to the boards—it is that stardom is in no way transferable. (It is interesting that outsize stars such as the Barrymores, Olivier, and Redgrave retained their aura mainly from their stage performances, even after making the transition to movies. Even today, one can't help feeling that there is almost nothing someone like Frank Langella or Nathan Lane can do in movies or television that will equal what they have already achieved on the stage.)

The number of Broadway "stars" who can ensure attendance, no matter what the quality of their vehicles, has become smaller and smaller. Seventy years ago, one could reel off the names of dozens of actors, singers, dancers, and "personalities" that the public followed slavishly: Lunt and Fontanne, Katherine Cornell, Bert Lahr, Mary Martin, Ethel Merman. If the stars were there, so was their public. That number has been badly decimated in the past half-decade and, given the monopolization of movies, TV, and video, it is unlikely ever to be restored. The temptation to poach "names" from the electronic media is a commercially justified ploy. The problem is that some of the most charismatic film and TV names simply haven't got the staying power to meet the demands of eight performances a week before a live public. Although names may initially bring in audiences, a lack of technical resourcefulness may just as readily turn them off. Or what's almost worse, stars' glittering public personae may never fully integrate themselves into the fictional grain of their roles (e.g., Burton and Taylor in *Private Lives*).

Before genuflecting in front of charismatic celebrities, it might behoove producers to examine the chemistry of recent stage successes such as *Rent, The Lion King, The Beauty Queen of Leenane, Ragtime,* and even *Art,* where the tribute paid to those triumphs owed almost nothing to stars but was founded on the kind of flair and imagination that ultimately *makes* stars out of committed stage professionals.

73

STEALING THE SHOW

In recent weeks, the question of directors' rights has exercised minds and stirred tempers both at the Society of Stage Directors & Choreographers and in the public prints. It raises a thorny issue that has long been submerged in conjecture and is invariably discussed amid the sparks from grinding axes.

Any director who is honest will admit that, despite the fact that the credit reads "Directed by So-and-So," the composite work that represents production is an amalgam of many sources. Not only is the theater a collaborative art, but it is one in which the collaboration fuses so finely it is difficult to judge where the play leaves off and direction begins or where direction ends and the performance begins.

When a director casts a role, he supplies approximately 75 percent of an artistic quantity. When an actor undertakes a role, he provides the missing 25 percent. Occasionally, if he is a gifted actor and has a mind of his own, he subsumes the director's contributions and is ultimately responsible for almost all of what happens to that character on that stage in that particular production. The director always assumes that he has administered the elixir that has brought about the actor's effects, but that is often a gesture of the director's vanity and is always debatable. The character of the actor, save in exceptional circumstances, tends to be the essential determinant in what happens on stage—even when wedged into an inflexible production framework.

A writer provides the words of the scene; frequently, his stage directions describe the effects he hopes those words will achieve. Just as often, a director, filtering those words through the sieve of his own imagination, gives them a tilt or emphasis never intended by the playwright, never imagined by the actor. A new dimension comes into being. Who created it?

The director suggests moves, confers blocking, dictates action. But often the actor, finding these suggestions uncomfortable, substitutes moves of his own, gestures never requested, actions that come to him spontaneously as he reconnoiters his passage from the page to the stage. His cross down-stage may have been given by the director, but the angle of his head, the slump of his body, the quality of his attitude will be entirely his own. Who is responsible for the meaning behind that movement? The director or the actor? The playwright, whose signals the director is interpreting? Or the actor, who is correlating them to the needs of his own personality?

Any director worth his salt tries to discern the natural impulses at work in his actor and then "directs" according to those natural impulses, so as not to impose moves that are alien or inorganic. Who, then, is the true begetter of those movements? The actor who originates them? The director who appropriates them? Or the author whose work has inspired them?

Theoretically, the director's mise-en-scène, inscribed by a stage manager and then copied into a prompt book, is the property of the director: part of the director's copyright, many would argue. But could that plot have come about without the provocation of the playwright, the impulses of the actor, the spatial invitations proffered by the designer? And since every movement is determined not by its locomotion but by the subtlety of the actor's personality suffusing it, is not the actor a partner in their creation?

Yes, directors steal blocking from other directors. I have seen them do so (I have had it happen to me), and everything inside of the director rages against the theft. "All that belongs to me!" screeches the wounded ego. But does it? Can it, when every "direction" is commingled with unavoidable factors such as the chemistry of the actor and the intentionality of the playwright?

Moves and action may be liftable; may be defended by law and copyright, by transcription and videotape, but more essential than stage-business, blocking, or spatial relationship is the overriding conception that makes one production entirely distinctive from another. As Iago might have put it: "Who steals my 'moves' steals trash; 'tis something, nothing. 'Twas mine, 'tis his, and has been slave to thousands. But he that filches from me my good 'conception' . . . makes me poor indeed." If I see Hamlet as a victim of state intrigue in a totalitarian society in which everyone is conspiring against one another (as in the Cracow *Hamlet* described by Jan Kott in *Shakespeare, Our Contemporary*), that production is patented as if every word were scrawled in the director's own handwriting. A "conception" is what causes a production to have a striking resemblance to another—whether its moves and plotting are identical or not. If the ideas motivating what occurs on a stage are derived from one governing idea and that idea is filched by another, that represents the most heinous intellectual theft—because it is part of the tacit law of theater that a director is supposed to come up with his own ideas of how to stage a play.

Although the attorneys will tell you ideas are not copyrightable, they are the only "intellectual property" worth defending and it is their willful appropriation that constitutes real theft. And why shouldn't original ideas, whatever form they take, be protected by law? The writers' ideas inscribed in words are protected. Why should not the director's, made tangible in interpretation, be equally valued? A powerful insight into a classic play that casts it in a completely new light is, to my mind, on a par with a scientific invention. It is a new and original way of viewing the world of a play. Why should patents be issued for one kind of invention and not the other? Moves, gestures, stage-business, and arrangements of furniture and decor are merely the nickels and dimes of the theater and, like loose change, will rustle differently in everyone's pocket. But a concept, whether it is a director's or a writer's, a philosopher's or a scientist's, a theologian's or an analyst's, is something germane to the mind that created it. It is the very essence of intellectual property and, being so, should be protected and defended with the same vigor Americans display in protecting their homes, their land, and their most valued personal possessions.

★★★

This piece was triggered by a bitter debate that developed in the middle-'90s, in which directors felt they were getting the short end of the stick in regard to royalties, especially in standard production contracts. Since actors are strongly unionized through Equity and producers have a very firm brotherhood of their own, but directors belong to a relatively weak union that has no power to strike and very little to negotiate, the complaint withered on the vine. But it did throw up a fascinating question as to who was really responsible for what in a theatrical production. The more it was investigated, the weaker the directors' case seemed to grow and yet we know that we live in an age of Directors' Theater (in motion pictures their power is undisputed). The directors' complaints were given short shrift, but the issues have far from disappeared.

★★★

74

THE CASE FOR A NATIONAL THEATER

"What are you gassing about?" said my surly colleague, who views all new ideas as if they were cockroaches that had fallen into the blancmange. "We've got a National Theater and we've had one for about a century. It's called Broadway."

No doubt the Broadway crowd would heartily agree, as, in their eyes, the best of what happens on American stages, if it truly is the best, emanates from, or gravitates to, the Broadway stage. But the main reason for creating an American National Theater is precisely to assault the Broadway ethic, to create an alternative to the hit-or-flop syndrome and the blockbuster mentality that permeate the elitist New York theater. "There is a world elsewhere," said Coriolanus, but nobody who inhabits the square mile from 42nd Street to Lincoln Center really believes that.

What would a National Theater do that Broadway doesn't?

First of all, by reviving both qualitative and curious works of the American theater from, say, 1900 to the present, it would make us aware that we actually possess a theatrical heritage. We know we've got a musical comedy heritage, as incessant musical revivals attest—although these shows tend to be the blockbusters of the past, heavily relied upon to become the blockbusters of the present (viz. *Showboat, Carousel, Guys and Dolls, Kiss Me Kate, The King and I, Bye Bye Birdie, Grease, Cabaret*, etc.). Whereas in a National Theater context it would be both legitimate and possibly even edifying to revive works such as *Whoopee, Pal Joey, Allegro, Lost in the Stars, The Grass Harp, Lady in the Dark, Of Thee I Sing*—intriguing works that reflect their periods and have both a historic as well as artistic significance.

A National Theater would have to support a permanent company, and, in consequence, perhaps seventy or one hundred actors would have the opportunity to develop what we nostalgically call "an ensemble"—although apart from a few oddities (e.g., the Group Theater, the Mercury Theater, the Civic Repertory Theater, the Living Theater), we really have nothing to be nostalgic about. And it is just possible that an aggregation of actors might sufficiently master the complexities of classical acting to come to terms with sixteenth-, seventeenth-, and eighteenth-century masterworks. We could finally rise from our genuflections before companies such as the RSC and the Royal National Theatre and take pride in a home-grown company comparable to the best of those in France or Germany, Norway or Sweden, even (God save the mark) England.

It would also be the natural site for a theater conservatory, where the finest acting traditions from both America and abroad could converge, and once an authoritative program had been successfully launched, it would go a long way toward routing the charlatans that now preside over a mockery of theater-training programs throughout the country. The best of American traditions—the permutations of Konstantin Stanislavsky, Michael Chekhov, Vsovolod Meyerhold, Lee Strasberg, Robert Lewis, Uta Hagen, and Sandy Meisner—would all be tossed into a stewpot, along with the mime of Jacques LeCoq, the exoticism of Jerzy Grotowsky, and the academic formality of John Barton. The actor thrown into the marketplace by such a conservatory would be ready for anything.

A repertory of both American and European plays would dispel the illusion that the Great Playwrights are Odets and Miller, Williams and Inge, Simon and Mamet, McNally and Kushner. We might come to understand that there was a whole other category of greatness inhabited by writers such as Büchner and Kleist, Wedekind and Sternheim, Anouilh and Giraudoux, Pirandello and Betti. Would it widen our horizons? Probably not. We'd still prefer the wisecracking comedies of our native sons and those perennial musicals with the hummable scores. But if the work of older European writers did manage to penetrate our consciousness, we might recognize the multinationalism out of which our modern ideas on multiculturalism have been largely fashioned. Who knows? We might even find a way to play Shakespeare in a uniquely American style or do Restoration comedy without looking like a bunch of drag-queens trying to out-diss each other.

The feminists would clamor for representation, of course, and there would be plenty to choose from: Aphra Behn, Lorraine Hansberry, Clare Booth Luce, Lillian Hellman, Jane Bowles, Beth Henley, Wendy Wasserstein, Paula Vogel—to mention only the most obvious. August Wilson would probably insist on an African-American Studio where the genius of his own people could be realized and, under the aegis of a National Theater, he would have every right to do so. And just as the Moscow Arts had three studios exploring work counter to its mainstream, so the work of ethnic minorities would be part and parcel of any cultural dispensation. There would also be an experimental arm where the performance artists and theatrical mavericks would not only be encouraged to work but would be fully subsidized in their subversive efforts; a true national theater would have to be as committed to research and development as it was to preservation of the past. Such a theater would reclaim and enthrone not only what is best in American culture but what, over the years, has passed through our social metabolism, reminding us of what we were, what we thought, and the values we revered, questioned, or discarded.

The National Theater building would be a vast edifice with four or five stages smack in the shadow of Times Square, so that its commitment to quality rather than commercialism would shame the finagling entrepreneurs of the Great White Way. It would stand as an indictment against the crapshoot mentality that is its prodigal spin-off. (The abortive effort at Washington, D.C.'s Kennedy Center—the American National Theater, headed by Peter Sellars for three seasons in the '80s—apart from everything else, was geographically misplaced.)

A National Theater would also create a platform on which the finest products of the regional theater could be sampled. After New York, these productions could tour other regions and, with the imprimatur of having played at the National, would be appreciated and sought after wherever they appeared. The theater would be "national" in a sense that the Royal National Theatre has never been, in that it would provide a conspicuous showcase for the best that was produced elsewhere—a centralized seat of power committed to radiating outward toward the margins.

Such an institution, chartered by the government but freed from any governmental control, established by legislation that would protect it from partisan abuse and financed by a 1-percent tax on every major corporation in the country, would define the American character through a procession of American works that, at present, exist only as footnotes, Ph.D. theses, or trivia titles flung out by theater-buffs.

To avoid corruption, of course, our National Theater would have to ban any artists already tainted by the debased values of Broadway, since a genuine and viable alternative would have to be manned (and womaned) by people who cherished a very different aesthetic vision. A bevy of our most lauded American artists would be prevented from having any contact with it. Later on, once its integrity was secure, these more established artists could be invited to exhibit their talents, but, more likely than not, because they would have so disparaged the new theater in its formative stages, they would decline such invitations, citing irreconcilable differences.

That, more than anything else, would guarantee its success.

★★★

75

DROUGHT OF THE IMAGINATION

As the century lagged to a close, the theater, nefariously influenced by television, began, yet again, to be seduced by Actuality. "Real people in real situations," based on the thoroughly fabricated premises of highly rated TV series such as Survivor *and* Big Brother, *seemed to be following the herd instincts of those who seemed to believe that so long as one could cook up reasonable facsimiles of contemporary life, there was no need for inventing artistic parallels. It gripped me in a real terror and brought about the* New York Times *piece with which I conclude this book. If this was to be the face of the new century, it would be more frightening and grotesque than anything Orwell had ever imagined.*

★★★

Not too long ago, an entertainment opened Off Broadway called *Lifegame,* created by Keith Johnstone and performed by the Improbable Theater, in which "real people" (portrayed by actors) present their life stories directly to the audience.

In the recently acclaimed *Boxing 2000,* the author and director Richard Maxwell admitted that his aim was to use the natural attributes of "non-actors" in recreating a more real world than is usually obtained in conventional play productions. "For me," Mr. Maxwell was quoted as saying, "it's a process of removing the things that are encouraging the person to be a performer as opposed to a person. . . ."

In the separate and burgeoning category of solo shows, increasingly the contents are painful or farcical excavations into the terror and turmoils of the performers' personal biographies.

Neo-naturalism has returned to our stages with a vengeance.

The fact is the theater, suffering from a drought of the imagination and the kind of mental energy that should be going into innovation and originality, is being squandered in a mistaken quest for facsimiles.

The playwrights we tend to admire—Ibsen, Chekhov, Shakespeare, Molière, Wilde—dissimilar as they are, all had one thing in common: they converted their perceptions of life and society into imaginative artifacts. It would never occur to them simply to "diarize" their experience or fastidiously reproduce facsimiles of the life around them. All the great "naturalists" took it as an article of faith that a drama, no matter how explicit its roots in everyday experience, had to be concocted in the mind of the artist and turned into a potent metaphor if it was to qualify as art.

But today, the irresistible temptation is to take a wodge of untreated actuality and pass it off as something "truer" simply because it has come directly from that undifferentiated dump site, "real life."

By appropriating real-life people into real-life circumstances, artists have turned themselves into poachers and the public into voyeurs. What insights or telling observations may emerge do so willy nilly, the fortuitous spin-offs of natural behavior. The "art" consists of selecting not truths about the human condition, but examples of lived experience that are then sold to the public on the basis of their authenticity—as if unvarnished truth was in some way superior to organized fiction.

It has never been Life—with a capitol L—that has been fascinating, elevating, or instructive, but the artist's perceptions of that streaming ambiguity, which occasionally put the chaos into some kind of meaningful perspective. The notion that life itself already contains the equilibrium one finds in the greatest art is a delusion of indolent artists. It takes an artist's imagination to reconstruct experience imaginatively. To parcel it out as neatly sliced entertainment commodities is to place the creative artist on a par with the supermarket wrapper.

Manufactured authenticity—whether it takes the form of asinine programs such as *Survivor* and *Big Brother* or the rationalized use of nonactors to create the legitimacy of "real people"—is, by no stretch of the lexicon, *authenticity* nor has the latter ever been a virtue in art. Authenticity's realm has always been journalism and documentary, and wherever it has surfaced (turn-of-the century Naturalism, '50s-styled Method acting, reprises of topical tabloid sensations—Charles and Di, Amy Fisher, Elian Gonzales), it has proved to be perishable and unnutritious.

Some of the dreariest experiences we have recently had, both on stage and in films, have been "based on true events." "Actuality" is no guarantor of artistic truth, and very often, ingeniously assembled falsehoods (like Michael Frayn's *Copenhagen* or Terry Johnson's *Hysteria*) come closer to capturing that elusive quality that artists doggedly chase down in the name of "truth."

Another feature of the current drought of the imagination can be found in the theater's choice of subject matter—its slavish reliance on recycling motion pictures into musicals and routinely reviving commercial plays from the past, rather than taking a risk on nonformulaic new ones. When in doubt, reheat a chestnut from the safest part of the repertory. These may be old complaints, but they are exacerbated by newer developments.

The highly prized work of a David Mamet is a good case in point. Here is a writer who expends a great deal of creativity in plausibly recreating the speech patterns of everyday life in characters whose social identities are as recognizable as the emblems on soup cans. Because he is so focused on the verisimilitude of language, he gets mired in the social clichés that language reflects.

In plays like *Oleanna* and *Glengarry Glen Ross,* there was a true marriage of orchestrated diction and relevant subject matter, but in the later plays, he appears to be parodying the work of a playwright called David Mamet. And although we recognize a tone of voice, it is not saying very much that is pertinent to our needs. His allegiance to naturalism is leading him from the hurly burly of street life into vacant back alleys.

But more troubling than Mamet himself is "Mametism": the view of art that holds that the meticulous reconstruction of external appearances somehow grapples with the larger abstractions that blanket our lives in mystery and occasionally fill us with wonder.

Voyeurism has long been the prevailing fashion of films and television and is fast becoming the formula of preference in the theater. Theater has always foraged from private lives in order to fashion public statements, but in much of its contemporary work, the processing plants have been shut down and the raw material loosed onto our stages as the thing itself. The inescapable fact is that it is harder, and ultimately more rewarding, to sift and shape human experience to a fine finish rather than indiscriminately forking out life and calling it art.

ABOUT THE AUTHOR

Charles Marowitz is the author of over two dozen books, mostly works of criticism relating to the theatre; his most recent being *The Other Way: An Alternative Approach to Acting & Directing* and *Roar of the Canon: Kott & Marowitz on Shakespeare,* due to be published by Applause Books in the fall of 2001. He is also an accomplished stage-director and playwright whose comedy *Sherlock's Last Case* was presented on Broadway after winning the Louis B. Mayer Playwriting Award and whose free-styled adaptations of Shakespeare have been performed world-wide, most recently at Tygres Heart Shakespeare in Portland, Oregon which premiered his *Variations on Measure for Measure.* Marowitz is currently Artistic Director of the Malibu Stage Company and a regular contributor to the *American Book Review* and a score of British publications. He is married to Jane Windsor, a former TV actress and now an accomplished haute cuisine cook in California.

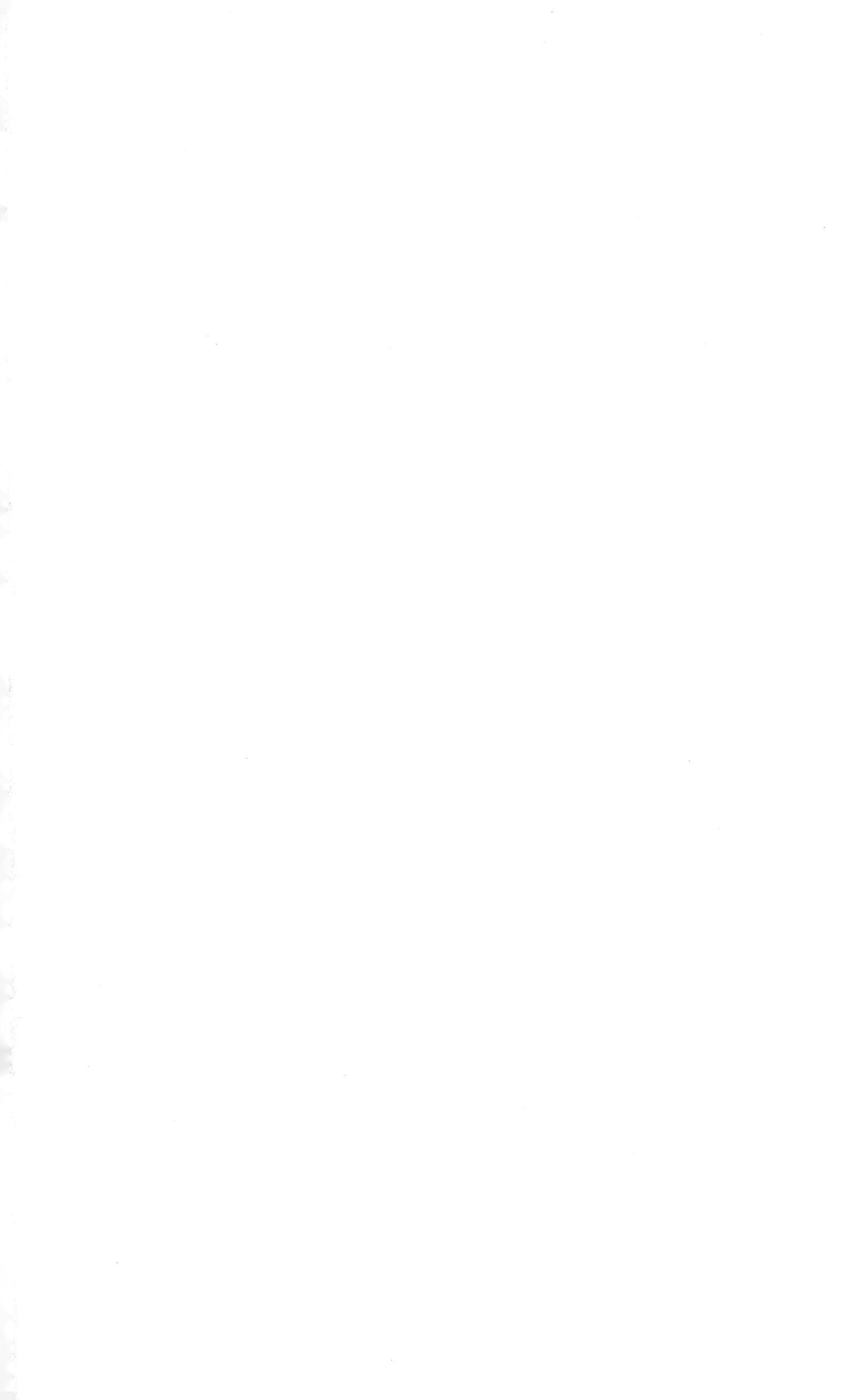